DEBATING NORTHEAST INDIA

DEBATING NORTHEAST INDIA
Mapping Ethnic Identity Formation

R. K. Bijeta
and
Vulli Dhanaraju

KALPAZ

First Published, 2017

Published by

Kalpaz Publications
C-30, Satyawati Nagar,
Delhi – 110052
E-mail: kalpaz@hotmail.com
Ph.: 9212142040

Printed at: G. Print Process, Delhi

Cataloging in Publication Data—DK
Courtesy: D.K. Agencies (P) Ltd. <docinfo@dkagencies.com>

Debating Northeast India : mapping ethnic identity formation / Vulli Dhanaraju and R.K. Bijeta [eds].
pages cm
Contributed articles.
ISBN 9789351282921 (hardback)

1. Ethnicity—India, Northeastern. 2. Identity politics—India, Northeastern. 3. India, Northeastern—Ethnic relations. I. Dhanaraju, Vulli, editor. II. Bijeta, R. K., editor.

GN635.I4D43 2017 DDC 305.8009541 23

Contents

III. Literature

IV. Politics

V. Economy

Foreword

Identity has been problematized in several ways in postcolonial discourse. Whereas sociologists conceptualize identity on the basis of an individual's inevitable relationship with society and social institutions, anthropologists tend to construct one's identity in terms of one's ethnic root. The essentialists however nourish the traditional concept of identity as' fixed' which is grounded upon eternal notion, conventional stereotype, family lineage and the personal attributes of the 'self'. The colonial discourse not only applied the policy of divide and rule to facilitate fissures among different groups of people, but also imposed their language and culture on the colonized to strangulate their identity. The post colonial critics and also exponents of cultural studies like Edward Said, Frantz Fanon, Homi K. Bhabha and Stuart Hall tend to interrogate the essentialist notion of identity as fixed and rather prefer to argue that identity is constructed on the basis of several factors such as power, politics, patriarchy, gender discrimination, and cultural hegemony, the inerasable stamp of which can be found in elitist historiography.

The French philosopher Michel Foucault (1990), in course of his analysis of psychiatry, prison and sexuality, forwards his theory of power as 'omnipresent'—a theory based on complex arrangement of multiplicity of force relations in society(remaining everywhere and coming from everywhere). On the other hand, Stuart Hall in his essay "Cultural Identity and Diaspora" (1997) emphatically observes that identity is a 'production', and by production he means that identity is 'always in process'. Hall further holds that culture always plays an important role in formation of one's identity and as such cultural identity, according to him, can be formed on the basis of one shared culture- a kind of collective self of people with a 'shared history' and 'ancestry hold in common'. Obviously then, cultural identity is determined in terms of common historical experience and shared cultural codes which facilitate to form one people with some kind of stability despite the shifting divisions and vicissitudes of their actual history. Viewed in a larger perspective, 'politics of identity' necessitates 'politics of difference' rather than homogeneity, because identity formation takes place in different socio-political and cultural conditions. Therefore, nothing is fixed, as identity of an individual is constructed on the basis of his/her relation/ connection with others in the society.

Viewed from the perspective of 'politics of identity' and 'politics of difference', the edited book, *Debating Northeast India: Mapping Ethnic Identity Formation* is a significant contribution to post- modern discourse particularly on mapping the ethnic identity in Northeast India. At a time when the recent writers on this region sincerely realize that the region has been subjected to the politics of exclusion as well as misrepresentation by the others, the book conceptualizes complex issues pertaining to ethnic identities and their diverse identity formations. While tenaciously subscribing to the postcolonial theory of the 'other' and the subaltern historiography of writing from the margin by articulating the anxiety and angst of the voiceless, this book argues how the ethnic groups are, of late, marching from the margin to write their own history, and construct their own identity through their experience of marginalization. The objective of the book is to deconstruct the elitist notions and debate the politics, culture and identity of ethnic communities from northeast perspective. While so doing, this book has meticulously acted upon the historical method in order to study the contemporary ethnic politics and identity formation.

In the book under discussion, the editors capitalized Paul Thompson's argument that in the absence of sufficient written records, a researcher has to rely on memory, myth and metaphor to reconstruct a fairly true ethnic history from oral tradition. Since colonial historiography and recent elitist scholarship otherize the history and culture of the ethnic groups by virtue of its lop-sided representation, myths and memory and rituals have been accepted as reliable sources of/ for authentic representation of history precisely because they provide reliable link between the past and the present. There is no denying the fact that myths and rituals of the ethnic communities of Northeast India go a long way to facilitate the construction of their identity.

Keeping in mind Foucault's conceptualization of power as omnipresent, the editors have problematized how the 'politics of power' was imposed upon various ethnic groups by the colonial rule and the post independent state. These two hegemonic institutions bifurcated the northeast into different territorial segments which obviously led to the emergence of new structures of identities and consequently there were major shifts in the sites of political power with the creation of separate territorial space for Nagas, Kukis, Mizos, Bodos, Karbis etc,. These groups later on claimed independent state corresponding to their separate ethnic identity. What is worth-mentioning here is that in order to secure separate political sites of power together with persistent fight for vindication of their ethnic identity, the people of different ethnic groups of the northeast launched different movements with an objective of realizing ' nation from below',' or ethnic nationalism'. While situating the ethno-political consciousness of the people of the northeast in the backdrop of the above discussion on ethnic nationalism, it is observed that ethnic identities have been shaped by socio-political and cultural movements that harp on the issues of language, script, customs, separate territorial space and culture.

Thus, this book has convincingly shown how identity as a complex concept always demands a contesting site in academic discourse, and more predominantly, how formation of ethnic identity in Northeast India in the light of dynamics of power, politics of identity and ethnic nationalism remains a complex process of being and becoming. I sincerely appreciate their engaging interest in the subaltern historiography. The deep critical insight with which they have handled the complex issues of ethnic identity and identity formation with the help of historical method deserves academic appreciation for the readers.

Dr. Bishnu Charan Dash
Department of English
Assam University, Diphu Campus, Assam

Preface

The term, 'Northeast India' refers to the eight states- Assam, Nagaland, Manipur, Arunachal Pradesh, Mizoram, Tripura, Sikkim and Meghalaya situated in the northeastern part of India. In fact, Northeast India as a single region has the largest number of the ethnic population in the country. Almost all the regions of northeast have witnessed one or the other forms of ethnic identity formation. The history of the region is viewed by different scholars from different perspectives. The ethnic communities are very complex in nature because of their unexplored ethnic identities and diverse social formations. Scholars argue that there are conflicting situations in northeast because these ethnic groups are trying to explore and construct their own history, culture and identity that they termed as 'nation from below' or 'ethnic nationalism' or 'ethnic identity politics'. However, the history, culture, identity and politics of the ethnic communities of the region are debatable in the academic discourse.

This book mainly argues that ethnic identity has become one of the pertinent issues in the political discourse of Northeast India. Identity formation is a complex process among the various ethnic communities. They are struggling for constructing their own identity through the politics of identity. Politics of identity can be defined as a phenomenon that arises out of shared experiences of injustice and marginalisation of certain sections of the society. It occurs when some ethnic groups find themselves as oppressed, marginalised and feel that their uniqueness and distinctiveness are under threat from the majority group. In such situation, there is collective mobilisation within the group with a view to secure their distinct identity.

Indeed, identity politics tends to portray differences and grievances rather than similarities and bonds among groups and individuals. It refers to a process of self construction and self presentation of group behaviours like race, culture, religion and ethnicity with a view to secure political recognition. Rosalind Brunt (1989) identified it as the politics of 'recognition' and Iris Young Marion (1990) used the term the politics of 'differences'. These conceptual ideas are very much relevant in understanding nature of the ethnic identity formation among the various communities in Northeast India. The ethnic communities in this region are always subject to the dominance of the 'other', even when they rebel and rise up. According to them, their politics has always been dominated by 'others'. In this context, Stuart Hall (1996) argues that "Far from the still small point of truth inside us, identities actually come from outside, they are the way in which we are recognised and then come to step into the place of the recognitions which others give us. Without the others there is no 'self'. There is no self-recognition". In other words, identities take shape over a period of time for varied ends and through varied means. They are historically arrived at, sociologically presented and discursively constituted. This necessitates a reading of the contexts located across cultural, social, political and economic spaces to comprehend what identities are and how they are constituted.

This book is divided into five thematic sections covering 20 chapters by scholars and researchers and other experts from Northeast India. In each section, four papers are included, each touching upon the main theme of the book. Thus, readers will find this book dealing with debates in the study of History, Culture, Literature, Politics and Economy in Northeast India. This book represents the plural voices of the ethnic groups of the region. The existing dominant discourses neglected the ideological and mass political character of the people who are constructing their identity through their politics of difference, politics of recognition and experience of marginalisation. These three ideas could be considered as their political ideology that always sustained for mapping identity formation among the ethnic communities of Northeast India.

R.K. Bijeta
Vulli Dhanaraju

Acknowledgments

Like any other works this edited book is a collective endeavour. This book is an outcome of International Conference on *"Contesting Self and Other: Identities of Caste, Tribe and Gender"* organized by the Department of History and Department of Anthropology, Assam University (Central University), Diphu Campus, Assam, India during 27-28, March, 2015 in collaboration with Maulana Abul Kalam Azad Institute of Asian Studies (MAKAIAS), Kolkata, India and Indian Council of Social Science Research (ICSSR), New Delhi, India. At the very onset we would therefore like to express thankfulness to all the chapter contributors. Without their contribution and support this book would not have become a reality in this form.

We wish to admit our gratitude to the Maulana Abul Kalam Azad Institute of Asian Studies (MAKAIAS), Kolkata, India and Indian Council of Social Science Research (ICSSR), New Delhi, India for collaboration and financial assistance in organising of the international Conference at the Department of History and Department of Anthropology, Assam University (Central University), Diphu Campus, Assam, India. We extend our gratitude to the Assam University (Central University), Diphu Campus, Assam, India for giving us an opportunity to organising the International Conference at the Diphu Campus.

We are very grateful to Dr B.C. Dash, Department of English, Assam University, Diphu Campus for accepting our request to write foreword to this book. Interacting and engaging with him in various occasions has been a great learning experience and source of intellectual enrichment. We wish to express our deep sense of gratitude to ideal couple,

Professor Y A. Sudhakar Reddy and Prof. Kanaka Durga, Centre for Folk Culture Studies, University of Hyderabad, India who have helped us even to overcome hurdles in personal life and supported us to sustain in the difficult times of life. We are deeply indebted for all the help of the loving family and the support they gave us. Their erudition and characteristic unassuming style provided inspiration and encouragement for us. Without their contribution and support this book would not have become a reality in this form. Our indebtedness to them could not be expressed in words.

We owe an intellectual debt to Mr Dharamsingh Teron, Director, Centre for Karbi Studies, Diphu, Karbi Anglong. He has always gone out of his way to help us what he is known for unfailing support without reservations or conditions throughout, and without a shred of tiredness. We also extend our gratitude to Dr Kh Narendra Singh, Associate Professor, Department of Anthropology, Assam University, Diphu Campus and also co-coordinator of the conference for his cooperation and support.

We also thank the entire faculty and staff of the Department of History, Assam University, Diphu Campus, Assam for all the academic and administrative support. We also extend thanks to the Research Scholars in the Department of History, Assam University, Diphu Campus particularly, Ms Junmoini Hansepi, Ms Nukshirenla, Ms Rupali Rongpipi, Ms Rashmi Engtipi, Ms Momoko Katharpi and Ms Steffi Rongangpipi for their assistance in proof reading of this book. This endeavour would not have come to fruition but for the support that we have received from family members.

No words are left to express our gratitude to the Kalpaz Publications, Delhi for their keen interest in the publication of this book.

-R.K. Bijeta
-Vulli Dhanaraju

List of Contributors

1. **R.K. Bijeta,** Institutional Post Doctoral Fellow, Department of Humanities and Social Sciences, IIT-Guwahati, Assam
2. **Namita Devi,** Assistant Professor, Department of History, Barbhag College, Nalbari, Assam
3. **Nakaulang Nriame,** Assistant Professor, Rangia College, Rangia, Kamrup, Assam
4. **Rahul Pegu**, Research Scholar, Department of History, North Eastern Hill University (NEHU) Shillong, Meghalaya
5. **Himasnata Dutta Sarkar**, Research Scholar, Department of Sociology, Tezpur University, Tezpur, Assam
6. **Junmoni Hansepi,** Research Scholar, Department of History, Assam University, Diphu Campus, Diphu, Assam
7. **Vulli Dhanaraju**, Assistant Professor, Department of History, Assam University, Diphu Campus, Diphu, Assam
8. **Kiryi Potom,** Research Scholar, Department of Geography, Rajiv Gandhi University, Arunachal Pradesh
9. **Bandita Teronpi,** Research Scholar, Department of Political Science, Assam University, Diphu Campus, Diphu, Assam
10. **Monalisha Khakhlari,** Research Scholar, Department of History, University of Hyderabad, Hyderabad, Telangana

11. **Bhaskar Jyoti Gogoi,** Research Scholar, Department of English, EFL University, Shillong Campus, Meghalaya

12. **Narayan Ch. Gahatraj**, Research Scholar, Department of English, EFL University, Shillong Campus, Meghalaya

13. **Tanushree Kulshreshtha,** Research Scholar, Dayalbagh Educational Institute, Agra, Uttar Pradesh

14. **Biplob Gogoi,** Assistant Professor, Department of Political Science, D.R. College, Golaghat, Assam

15. **Hasib Md Iqbal,** Assistant Professor, Department of Economics, P.B. College, Gauripur, Assam

16. **Diganta Biswas,** Assistant Professor, Department of Accountancy, P.B. College, Gauripur, Assam

17. **Sumit Kr. Sarma,** Research Scholar, Department of Political Science, University of Hyderabad, Hyderabad, Telangana

18. **Thagendra Chutia,** Assistant Professor, Department of Philosophy, Harhi College, Lakhimpur, Assam

19. **Anup Deka,** Research Scholar, Department of Philosophy, North Bengal University, Siliguri, West Bengal

20. **Jagritee Ghosh,** Research Scholar, Department of Sociology, Tezpur University, Assam

21. **Tarun Gogai**, Assistant Professor, Department of Political Science, Debraj Roy College, Golaghat, Assam

22. **Shashwati Nath,** Assistant Professor, Department of Geography, Saraighat College, Changsari, Kamrup, Assam

23. **Garima Kalita**, Associate Professor, Department of English, Cotton College, Guwahati, Assam

24. **Tamsin Aftab**, Research Scholar, Department of Sociology, Jamia Millia Islamia, New Delhi

Introduction

R.K. Bijeta and Vulli Dhanaraju

"Power is everywhere not because it embraces everything, but because it comes from everywhere"- **Michel Foucault, 1976**

The exclusion of the history of the Northeast India by the mainstream 'elitist discourse' is one of the foremost condemnations from the ethnic groups of this region. The history of the Northeast is viewed by different scholars from different perspectives. The ethnic communities are very complex in nature because of their unexplored ethnic identities and diverse social formations. Scholars argue that there are conflicting situations in the Northeast because these ethnic groups are trying to explore and construct their own history, culture and identity that they termed as 'nation from below' or 'ethnic nationalism' or 'ethnic identity politics'. However, the history, culture, identity and politics of the ethnic communities of Northeast are debatable in the academic discourse. This book deconstructs the elitist notions and views and brings forth the debate over the politics, culture and identity of ethnic communities from Northeast perspective.

I

The construction of ethnic politics is not an accidental affair in Northeast. It has evolved through several forces in the past. Therefore, an understanding of present history and politics of Northeast will certainly lead to the study of their past. However, reconstruction of their history is a very difficult task; accurately because there are few sources available which they have contributed by themselves. And the available sources are mostly written by 'others' such as colonial ethnographers, elite Assamese and Bengali writers with different interests and compulsions. However, these are mostly divorced from the objective and subjective conditions of the ethnic people. Due to this reason memory, metaphor and folklore has become vital source of information. It can be true that "tribal history can be reconstructed from oral tradition and in the absence of any written history, the numerous myths, legends and tales, as well as, other aspects of the tradition have been the only link between the historic past and the present". The same views are also reflected in Paul Thomson's *The Voice of the Past: Oral History* (1978). He argues that "the discovery of oral history by historian... is not only a discovery but recovery. It gives a future no longer tied to the cultural significance of paper documents..." Thus, memory and metaphor are not a passive depository of facts, but an active process of creation and attribution of political meanings to the ethnic identities. In Northeast, each of this tribe has its own history, tradition, culture, custom and belief systems.

This belief system has been reflected in the form of protecting their rituals practices. These beliefs are always linked with the way of life of people with its natural environment. Their beliefs and practices consist of cultural attitude of the people towards the supernatural. The most widespread manifestation of this attitude is in the shape of ritual and rites. These ritual and rites are socio-cultural phenomena, which gives the people an identity of its own in the form of religion. Hence, religion being socio-cultural phenomena includes men's endeavour to link natural and supernatural world for realisation of his own interest, as he perceives. Kevin Carrico's (2011) idea of rituals suits to understand the importance of rituals among various communities in Northeast India. Kevin stated that 'ritual is arguably a universal feature of human social existence: just as one cannot envision a society without language or exchange, one would be equally hard-pressed to imagine a society without ritual. Ritual is in fact an inevitable component of culture, extending from the largest-scale social and political processes to the most intimate aspects of our self-experience. Yet, within this universality, the inherent multiplicity of ritual practices, both between and within cultures, also reflects the full diversity of the human experience. It was then neither pure coincidence nor primitive's eroticisation that placed ritual at the centre of the development of cultural thought: it was instead ritual's rich potential in construction of tribal identity. Thus, the idea of ritual gets reflected through the various communities in Northeast in the form of collective memory. It is understood as a representation of the past shared by a group or community. It also reflects the collective politics of the community which negate the other cultural politics as James. C Scott (2011) has emphasised in his work, *The Art of Not being Governed* that the politics of the ethnic communities is an art for not being governed and live in their own cultural world.

II

The term, 'Northeast India' refers to the eight states- Assam, Nagaland, Manipur, Arunachal Pradesh, Mizoram, Sikkim, Tripura and Meghalaya situated in the Northeastern part of India. The very use of the term 'Northeast India' incites resentment from the intellectuals and the people of the area alike (Bhanwari Sharma, 2012). It is contested on the ground that it is a colonial legacy. Udayan Misra (2000) calls the term, 'Northeast' an 'illusive construct'. Sanjib Baruah (1999) argues that such generic location place names have been purposely used as a tool of political engineering because they induce no historical memory or collective consciousness. However, recent article of Thongkholal Haokip (2011) argues that there is a tendency by scholars and policymakers to club the whole northeastern states together as 'Northeast' and use the term as an analytical category for the whole region. However, the practical relevance of clubbing all the eight states together and calling it the 'Northeast' is always contested. In fact, Northeast India as a single region has the largest number of the ethnic population in the country. Almost all the regions of Northeast have witnessed one or the other forms of ethnic or sub-nationalist movements.

It is important to argue that ethnic issues of Northeast are related to the geopolitics of the region. Though there are differences among different communities in terms of their cultural experiences, they share common experience of marginalisation. A large amount of literature exists on the

Northeast which seeks to explain the ethnic problems of the region. But there are wide differences in the discourse on explaining the ethnic issues of the region. And the divide in the discourse also gets reflected on the basis of the formation ofethnic identities and the movements in the region.

The population of the Northeast consists of the original and indigenous inhabitants together with various ethnic groups. Although there are migrants of long standing that have got integrated into the local population in the historical past. Fascinatingly, each ethnic community of the region not only claims to be unique but also asserts having a long historical past of its ethnicity. However, a closer look reveals that most of the communities as they assert themselves with strong exclusive claims are much more recent than, as early as the British colonial rule in the region. Bhagat Oinam (2008) has briefed the nature of identity formation in Northeast. He argues that "colonial rule has brought major shifts in the sites of political power and emergence of new structures of identities based on these shifts. The import of modernism is one of the packages that came with the colonial power. This has led to a shift in the identity structures in the region. With the bifurcation of the proposed crown colony (India's Northeast as one half and the other half into then Burma) by the colonial powers, and in the subsequent history of dissent, new identities have been formed with new areas as one territory and many different communities as one people. Interestingly, this amorphous also had old identities and territories (in the form of kingdoms) weakened, broken down or reintegrated with the shift in power (such as the Ahoms, Tripuris and Manipuris), and new identities have emerged with claims of politico-administrative legacies (Nagas, Mizos, Kukis etc)". He also stated very interesting argument by analyzing political formation in the history of Assam. "Assam has been both the beneficiary as well as victim of these shifts in power. Ahom kingdom got consolidated during the process of 'Aryanisation' and its encounters with the Mughals and later with the British. The word, 'Aryanisation' suggests that the Aryan people in the course of their peaceful colonisation of practically the whole of India met with and overcame opposition from pre-Aryan cultural groups and that the cultural identity of the latter was nearly destroyed and at least a thick surface layer of Aryanism in all its aspects came to prevail. Assam as a modern political entity emerged and consolidated during the British rule in the region. But the state also lost several of its territories in the post independent India. The creation of Nagaland, Meghalaya and Mizoram, carving out of corresponding territories for each of these new political entities (states) out of Assam, led to shrinking, of the state's boundary. Manipur, too, experienced the same. Manipur not only lost many parts of its territory under the treaty of Yandaboo in 1826, but also gained several parts in and around the present Tamenglong district. During the span of a century, the territory of Manipur fluctuated to a considerable degree". He also stated that: "Naga and Mizo political identities have been nurtured and promoted by the colonial powers leading towards conception of Naga, Mizo, Kuki national identities. The trend has led to several corresponding claims to establishing a national character of people, a land, a territory, a political site of power (state), a world view, and a collective memory through respective histories". In the contemporary days this trend is not only confined to the Nagas, Mizos and Kukis, but all of them recast their identities with their respective nationhood and corresponding character of a national life". It is argued that even small identities are searching for their original nationhood in the name of self determined movements in the contemporary days. Thus, the nature of identity formation in Northeast is always intricate which shapes the cultural behaviour of the people.

In the context of colonialism and its administrative impact Kyoko Inoue (2005) stated that during the colonial period and even after independence, the Northeast, adjoining China, has been a difficult frontier region. Throughout the period of colonialism, the Northeast India was treated separately and differently from other regions of British India. In the early colonial period, the region formed part of Bengal Province and it was governed as though it were an adjacent subordinate area of Bengal Province even after it became the separate province of Assam in 1874. The colonialism passed the regulation called the Chin Hill Regulation in 1896 for the Lushai Hills which authorised the Superintendent or Deputy Commissioner to order an undesirable outsider to leave the area and to tax the residents, permanent or temporary, clans and villages. The Inner Line Policy was introduced in the year 1873 to certain areas of Northeast, especially in the hill areas. In 1928, the Simon Commission came to northeast and under its advice, the categories of excluded areas and partially excluded areas were created. This was enacted in Government of India Act, 1935. Subsequently, the separation and isolation policy of the colonial period created a problem for the national integration of India. As a result a sense of incongruity grew into one of resentment against being made a part of India, and an anti-India sentiment emerged among the ethnic groups of the Northeast. However, after independence the issues of sub-nationalist insurgency and self autonomy movements have been debated by various scholars by highlighting the impact of colonialism. The debatable issues of Northeast can be studied on two major view points:

The first viewpoint is 'Nation-State Building and second 'Federation Building'. The main advocates of this perspective are S.K. Chaube (1969), B. P. Singh (1997), B. G. Verghese (1996) and Myron Wienor (1978). Most of these writers do not hail from the region. The first view point argued that the problems of the Northeast are related to the issues of "nation state building"; conflict between the new middle classes, especially among the tribal of the region, which has emerged as a result of modernisation/development/transition democratisation) with the traditional leadership; inability of the system to meet the rising aspiration of this group. The second perspective is actually the critique of the first one and is available in the writings of the scholars who hail from the region. The principal adherents of this perspective are Sanjib Baruah (1999, 2004, 2005), Udayan Misra (1981, 1988, 2000, 2002), Sanjay Hazarika (1994) etc. They argue that problems of the Northeast India arose because the national leadership overlooked the perspective of the people of the region in their quest for 'nation-building'. In order to build 'nation-state' the central government adopted "step motherly" treatment towards the Northeast; ignored the "periphery" and the smaller nationalities; shown arrogant attitude towards them; have been indifferent to the human rights violation in the region. They argue for a "Federation-Building" perspective in place on the 'Nation-State Building' perspective (Jagpal Singh, 2005). The need for a "Federation-building" perspective has been most prominently emphasise by Sanjib Baruah (1999, 2005).

Indeed mobilisation of the people on the basis of markers, real or imagined, which they share-language, religion, culture, customs, race, etc. into collective is called ethnic mobilisation. Ethnic communities in such situation relate and compare themselves to other ethnic communities and have grievances which they want to get resolved. Ethnic mobilisation finds expression in the form of self-determination movements – autonomy movements, insurgency or ethnic conflicts. The tribals of India have been involved in ethnic mobilisation for different purposes both before and after independence. They have taken recourse to both the violent and non-violent means. Success or failure of ethnic movements depends on political factors. Once one set of demands in ethnic mobilization is accepted, in due course of time ethnic movements start on other demands. Thus, ethnic mobilisation is a continuous political process.

It is argued that ethnic Identity has become one of the pertinent issues in the political discourse of Northeast India. Identity formation is a complex process among the various ethnic communities in Northeast India. They are struggling for constructing their own identity through the politics of identity. Politics of Identity can be defined as a phenomenon that arises out of shared experiences of injustice and marginalisation of certain sections of the society. It occurs when some ethnic groups find themselves as oppressed, marginalised and feel that their uniqueness and distinctiveness are under threat from the majority group. In such situation, there is collective mobilisation within the group with a view to secure their distinct identity. Identity politics tends to portray differences and grievances rather than similarities and bonds among groups and individuals. It refers to a process of self-construction and self presentation of group traits like race, culture, religion and ethnicity with a view to secure political recognition. Rosalind Brunt (1989) identified it as the politics of 'recognition' and Iris Young Marion (1990) used the term the politics of 'differences'. These two conceptual ideas can be used in understanding nature of the ethnic identity formation among the various communities in Northeast India.

The ethnic communities in Northeast are always subject to the dominance of the 'other', even when they rebel and rise up. According to them, their politics has always been dominated by 'others'. In this context, Stuart Hall (1996) argues that "Far from the still small point of truth inside us, identities actually come from outside, they are the way in which we are recognised and then come to step into the place of the recognitions which others give us. Without the others there is no 'self'. There is no self-recognition". In other words, identities take shape over a period of time for varied ends and through varied means. They are historically arrived at, sociologically presented and discursively constituted. This necessitates a reading of the contexts located across cultural, social, political and economic spaces to comprehend what identities are and how they are constituted. However, what is fundamental to all identities is, as Ernesto Laclau and Mouffe (2001) argue, a process of struggle for recognition from the other. The 'other' could be other individuals, contesting communities and social groups or the State. Politics of recognition bring together identities into a process of mutual reciprocity. In India, identities have been constituted around caste (dalits/Brahmins), gender (men/women); ethnicity or nationality (Assamese/Bodos), language (Hindi/Non-Hindi speaking peoples), class and sexuality (Heterosexuals/ Homosexuals and Lesbians).

The following section briefly deals with the paradigm shifts while studying the political developments in the post-independent India. This will help us to identify the Indian state approach towards Northeast in dealing with the geo-politics of the region. Thongkholal Haokip (2011) has divided Northeast India into five phases that can be understood in form of paradigm shifts while the study of Indian state attitude towards northeast after independence. He argues that "since independence the Indian government has adopted several policies towards the region. Many of these policies have changed in the past decades. Such policies were measures to solve the complex problems of alienation, insurgency, ethnicity/cultural identity and to bring about economic development in the North Eastern region." Let us briefly discuss the five paradigm shifts in order to understanding the Indian state attitude towards Northeast.

Firstly, after India's independence India's policy towards the northeastern region can be described as 'Nehru Elwin Policy' where quick administrative expansion associated with the revivalist protectionist approach towards tribal development in the hill areas was followed. It was broadly within the framework of the colonial Inner Line Regulation policy framework, which ensures non-interference from the people of the plains and also carve out an area of unimpeded self-development for the tribes of the region. Secondly, during 1960s there was drastic change in India's policy towards the northeast due to Chinese aggression in 1962. It was the first setback in India's foreign policy and changed the course of India's security and even foreign policy. This brought back the colonial approach considering the region as a "frontier" that needs to be protected and defended militarily. But this policy also failed to address the people in this region. Thirdly, a new paradigm shift took place during 1970-1980 in the name of political representation and autonomous movements for the creation of homeland. Subsequently, the new states were created in the region during this period to fulfill certain ethnic, cultural and political aspirations for self-government among various tribal groups on the idea that they require representation in the democratic process and that once they have voice and representation in the parliamentary democracy, many of their problems would be minimised. Thongkholal Haokip (2011) argues that despite the creation of several new states, the basic problem of integration, insurgency and balanced economic development still remains. Instead of solving problems, it has a cascading affect leading to new demands from other smaller ethnic group for different levels of autonomy. The reorganisation of Northeast India has undoubtedly given the tribal a sense of pride in their separate political status, and the local elite and dominant sections of the middle class have greatly benefited in economic and political terms. Fourthly, during 1980s the central government adopted a new policy for this region and it can be termed as the 'Development Paradigm'. This policy assumes that if institutions of development were created and money poured into this region, the problems of politics, of society, of ethnic strife, and of integration will be abated. But it also failed to implement this policy. One problem that arises is that the developmental packages being left largely unimplemented neutralised the intended impact. This occurs because of poor monitoring, lack of accountability and non-adherence to the situated time frame for project implementation. Fifthly, after 1990s the globalisation created a tremendous impact on the region. Due to the impact of globalisation it created de-territorialisation and a borderless world which is often associated with economic integration. With 98 per cent of its borders with China, Myanmar, Bhutan, Bangladesh and Nepal, Northeast India has better scope for development in the era of globalisation. As a result, a new policy was created i.e. the Look East policy. The main objective of this policy is that in one direction the Northeastern region must be looking at a new way of development that lies with political integration with the rest of India and economic integration with the rest of Asia, with East and Southeast Asia. Sanjib Baruah (2004), a staunch proponent of a continental Look East Policy, advocated that 'India should take more advantage of Northeast India's history and culture as a soft power resource.' This involves reviving the shared historical and cultural ties between the people of northeast India and Southeast Asia.

Indeed, since the BJP government came into power in 2014 they have adopted a new policy towards northeast called, *'Act East Policy'* which has replaced the Look East Policy of previous UPA government. As India's Foreign Minister Sushma Swaraj on her visit to Hanoi, Vietnam stressed on the need for an Act East Policy replacing India's over two decade old Look East Policy emphasizing a more proactive role for India in this Region. It seems that they have taken the idea of 'Act East Policy' while focusing on the development of the region to help them in the assimilation of present northeast into the 'Hindu fold'. Generally, the state uses the tool of development in order to pacify the self-determination of the smaller ethnic groups of the region. We can call it as 'ideological assimilation of Hindu Fold' rather than development of the region. However, it seems as a replica of the Look East Policy of UPA government. Without the study of the historical, cultural and complex identity formations of the region any policy may not fulfill the political autonomy of the region. It has been proved since independence. Yet it has to be debated to resolve the issue of political representation of the smaller communities. These communities have been exploring their identities and expressing their resistance in different forms in order to contest the 'dominant other' interventions in the region.

III

This section deals with the theoretical issues by studying several concepts that provide an understanding of the reflexive relationships between ethnicity and identity in construction of ethnic politics in northeast India. There are two fundamental concepts in the study of ethnic nationalism. They are primordialists character of ethnicity and biological character of ethnicity (Josep R. Llobera, 1999). Primordialists believe that ethnic identity is deeply rooted in the historical experience of human beings to the point of being practically a given. Socio-biologists take this perspective a step further and assert the biological character of ethnicity. Let us review some of the important works for the conceptual understanding of the concept of nationalism and ethnic nationalism. For the purposes of this book, we would take up the concept of ethnic politics as defined by Ernest Gellner (1983), Anthony Smith (1986, 1999), Paul Brass (1991), Benedict Anderson (1983), Eric Hobsbawm (1990), Karl Deutsch (1953), John Hutchinson (1987) etc.

Paul Brass (1991) insists that ethnicity and nationalism are the products of modernity. In addition, he emphasises its constructed character. Cultures are fabricated by elites who use raw materials from different groups to create ethnies and nations. By using these representations, elites aim at ensuring their economic or political advantages for themselves. Brass's theory states that ethnic identity and modern nationalism arise out of specific types of interactions between the leadership of centralising states and the elites from non-dominant ethnic groups. Anthony D. Smith's book, The Ethnic Origins of Nations (1986), challenged the idea of a link between nationalism and modernization by highlighting the continuity between modern nations and pre-modern ethnic communities, which he called 'ethnies'. In this view, nations are historically embedded: they are rooted in a common cultural heritage and language that may long predate the achievement of statehood or even the quest for national independence. Smith nevertheless acknowledged that, although ethnicity is the precursor of nationalism, modern nations only came into existence when established ethnies were linked to the emerging doctrine of political sovereignty. This conjunction occurred in Europe in the late eighteenth century and early nineteenth century and in Asia and Africa in the twentieth century. He argues that the nationalism existing in Central Asia is based on 'ethnic and genealogical nationalism, as opposed to civic and territorial nationalism. However, the ethnic nationalism among the various communities in Northeast India can be considered as politics of identities while understanding various theoretical concepts.

However, the idea that nations are political and not ethnic communities has been supported by a number of theories of nationalism. Eric Hobsbawm (1990), for instance, highlighted the degree to which nations are 'invented traditions'. He calls nationalism as an 'invented tradition'. These definitions point out the social construction of nationalism as opposed to some sort of naturally-occurring national collective identity. Rather than accepting that modern nations have developed out of long-established ethnic communities, Hobsbawm argued that a belief in historical continuity and cultural purity was invariably a myth, and, what is more, a myth created by nationalism itself. In this view, nationalism creates nations, not the other way round. A widespread consciousness of nationhood (sometimes called popular nationalism) did not for example develop until the late nineteenth century, perhaps fashioned by the invention of national anthems and national flags, and the extension of primary education. Certainly, the idea of a 'mother tongue' passed down from generation to generation and embodying a national culture is highly questionable. In reality, languages live and grow as each generation adapts the language to its own distinctive needs and circumstances.

Benedict Anderson's book, *Imagined Communities Reflections on the Origin and Spread of Nationalism,* (1983) is another recent major contribution to the study of the evolution of nationalism. He defines 'nation as an imagined political community' and imagined as both inherently limited and sovereign. He considers it imagined because the members of even the smallest nation will never know most of their fellow-members, meet them, or even hear of them, yet in the minds of each lives the image of their communion. Unlike Ernest Gellner (1983), Anderson (1983) is concerned with exploring the psychological appeal of nationalism: 'What makes people love and die for nations as well as hate and kill in their name?' Obviously, a purely functional approach such as Gellner's will not explain the emotions engendered by nationalism, yet Anderson does not go to the other extreme of a socio-biological or primordial interpretation. He takes a historical, rather than a timeless, universalist approach, so that nationalism is seen as emerging at a specific period in European history. Anderson's originality lies in his explanation of how and why people in certain circumstances 'imagine' themselves as part of a nation, and why such an 'imagined community' has a powerful attraction for them.

Anderson's theory of nationalism has been criticised by post-colonial theorists. They contend that using the prism of nationalism to study the history of colonised countries is to conflate the experience of the elite or bourgeoisie with that of the people as a whole. Partha Chatterjee (1993) attempts a critique of *Imagined Communities* in the first chapter of his book, *The Nation and Its Fragments* which he has given title, 'Whose Imagined Community?' Here he challenges the idea of nation as being imagined from certain modular forms. He argues that nationalism is not rooted "on an identity but rather on a difference of the modular forms of the nationalist society propagated by the modern west." There was the creation of another form which is indigenous and 'original' to every nation. This 'original' form is what Chatterjee terms as a sovereign nation in the post-colonial world. Therefore, the meaning of the term 'imagined community' is not a universal one. If at all a nation is imagined, it is imagined differently by different nations.

So far we have engaged with probing into the various dimensions of the viability of political nationalism in the general discourses on nationalism, keeping aside the equally important segment of nationalism, namely, 'cultural nationalism'. John Hutchinson (1987) happens to be one of those few notable apologists of cultural-nationalism who dared to challenge its leading critics in the era of rationality and secularism. Hutchinson demonstrates that the two competing conceptions of the nation - cultural and political - must never be conflated as they form their own distinctive organisations and have sharply diverging political strategies in spite of sharing many things in common. Hutchinson argues that their common ideal is a civic polity of educated citizens united by common laws and mores like the polis of classical antiquity. Besides they also reject, in common, existing political and traditionalist allegiances that block the realisation of this ideal, and theirs is a cosmopolitan rationalist conception of the nation that looks forward ultimately to a common humanity transcending cultural differences. Hutchinson emphasises that in order to mobilise a political community on behalf of this goal, political nationalists may be driven to adopt ethnic-historical identities and in the process may become ethicised and 're-traditionalised'. Their objectives are, however, essentially modernist: to secure a representative state for their community so that it might participate as an equal in the developing cosmopolitan rationalist civilisation. By contrast, Hutchinson makes a point; the cultural nationalist perceives the state as an accidental, for the essence of a nation is its distinctive civilisation, which is the product of its unique history, culture and geographical profile.

Karl Deutsch 's (1953), Nationalism and Social Communication: An Inquiry into the Foundations of Nationality is a classic as far as the study of nationalism is concerned. In the words of Karl Deutsch, a people or nation is "community of social communication" based on a common culture. Deutsch was unusual in seeking to quantify and measure the elements of nationality, looking particularly at 'social communication' (common language and interpersonal communication of all kinds). A people or nation is defined by the 'complementarily or relative efficiency of communication among individuals'.

Antonio Gramsci's (1971) theory of cultural hegemony also helps us in order to reiterate how a dominant discourse is used to subvert other, less powerful or mainstream ideas, beliefs, and identities. Nationalism prevails as the hegemonic whereas excluded groups are subverted. Yet, if these subversive, excluded groups gain recognition and support they may quickly get appropriated into the hegemonic. This is why they may be successful at altering nationalism. Gramsci highlights a vital aspect of the social interactions in construction of ethnic ideas. A central concern for social movements is a battle not only over ideology, politics and culture, but the power to effectively enforce or change the status quo. Power can be enacted through forceful rule as Max Weber believes or through the subtle acts of hegemony.

Thus, the theories that have been discussed above are important for the understanding of nationalism in the context of this book. These theories contextualised the idea of nationalism while taking into consideration of the people's perception towards hegemonic institutions. It is always problematic in dealing with the ethnic communities and their nationalisms. In this context, the politics of ethnic identity in northeast assumed greater political importance. The region has become very sensitive and conflict affected areas due to the growing consciousness and assertion of separate ethno political identity of peoples. It is found that the process of identity formation becomes very active in those areas where multi-ethnic groups exist in a political boundary. Northeast India is culminating point of numerous ethnic tribes living in the plains as well as in the hills. Each ethnic tribe has its own culture, history, and identity. The identity assertion of various groups has been articulated through language, culture, and it has been marked that there are variation in the degree of assertion among them. Some of them have been struggling for special treatment such as recognition of Schedule Tribe status and some other have been stressing for Autonomous Council under the Sixth Scheduled of Indian Constitution for preserving their respective identities and all round development. As a means of maintaining their ethnic identity some of them have even demanded separate state on the basis of their respective ethno-cultural identity within the Indian Union.

Recent article of Bhanwari Sharma (2012) explicates the unique nature of the identity formation and complexity among the smaller ethnic communities in northeast India. He argues that smaller tribes have identified with a larger tribal identity for self-protection during combats amongst hostile identities. In Manipur, Anals have identified with the larger Naga identity; over arching *upajati* identity was contrived by some tribes of Tripura to fortify them against Bengali domination. The reverse process has happened as well. The Lais and Maras started asserting their identity distinct from Mizo to avoid Lushai domination. Paites are projecting themselves as Zomis and have even supported the Nagas against the Kukis (of which Zomis were a part). Matak, Rabha and Lalung which were quite content with them being a part of the Assamese identity are now striving to establish a distinct identity. The Koch- Rajbongshis of northern Bengal, the Ahom, Karbis of Assam are similarly poised. Social endeavours are either channelised directly into political behaviour and if that is not feasible, political ramifications are attributed to such endeavors. Most of the tribes in Northeast India are involved in consolidating their numbers and in strengthening their political followers both from within their respective groups and outside, from smaller groups who by themselves cannot launch such a process. Ethnic identities have been articulated through socio-cultural as well as political movements. The socio-cultural movements harp on the issues of religion, language and script, customs and culture, revivalism and reformation. All Assam Ahọm Association, Assam Sahitya Sabha, Naga Club, etc. have all delved on the socio-cultural aspects of ethnicity. However, accompanying the socio-cultural concerns is the political overtone of every movement. Almost all tribes have associations which voice the need for territorial reorganisation and political control. Almost all of them aim at the ultimate – ethnic homelands - such is the propensity of this lure, that if not all, most of the tribal groups have militias to back this homeland demand. Indeed, the names of the militias proclaim the names of the ethnic groups they profess to defend, e.g. National Socialist Council of Nagalim, Kamtapur Liberation Army, People's Revolutionary Party of Kangleipak, Tiwa National Revolutionary Force, Kuki National Front, Zomi Revolutionary Volunteers etc. The state response to these insurgent ethnic movements revolves around counter-insurgency operations, negotiations and peace talks, economic packages and concessions of homelands through territorial reorganisation. But the modern state failed to address the issue of ethnic politics and rather created ethnic turmoil among the smaller communities in northeast India.

K.S. Singh (1982) also explained the nature of identity formation in northeast India. He stated that: Political processes in the northeastern hills picked up on the eve of transfer of power and gathered strength later as the secular and democratic system was consolidated. Old tribes assumed new names, small tribes merged with larger tribes, tribes combined to form new ethnic-cum-territorial identity. Beyond the territorial identity states were created to accommodate tribal aspiration for autonomy. Bhagat Oinam (2008) has identified the three types of identity formation in the Northeast. Assertion of nationalism can be witnessed starting from larger communities like the Asomiya and the Bengali to the smaller communities like the Bodos, Kukis, Mizos, Nagas, and Chakmas. He also identified another identity formation among the Muslim communities. But the emergence of Muslim insurgency has been on safeguarding religious identity and interest rather than on ethnicity. Inception of PULF (Peoples United Liberation Front) in Manipur, Muslim United Liberation Tigers of Assam (MULTA), The Harkat-ul-Mujahideen, the Muslim United Liberation Front of Assam (MULFA) etc. are clearly based on safeguarding, and asserting Islamic identity. Sanjay K. Roy (2005) has explained the nature of identity formation from the nation from below perspective. He stated that "'Nations from below' in the northeast are formed on ethnic lines (mostly a tribe in a geographical area, with one name, common heritage, common language, common culture and therefore one identity); an identity formed in countering other identities and expressed in democratic movements, in anti-state armed struggle, in ethnic cleansing and similar actions. The expression that a nation from below does not make a claim for state hood cannot be substantiated by the nature of ethnic movements in the northeast, since the central demand of most of the movements is either to acquire constitutional power over a territory or to create a sovereign state outside India". But in the case of Nagaland it is different. They demanded Greater Nagaland on the lines of ethnic territory.

IV

Recently many scholars argue that colonial cartography introduced the physical boundary with the interest of colonising the northeast India. Sanjib Baruah (1999) argues that how colonial political geography reflected the ethnic politics of Assam in the post-independence period (Udayon Misra, 2000). After the British take-over, the boundaries of the Assam of the Ahom age were continuously changed to meet British administrative convenience and, as the experimentation went on; new areas were either added or deleted from the map of Assam. Baruah points out two major effects of this colonial geography and refers to the segregation of the hills from Assam and the colonial assumption that Assam was in actuality an extension of Bengal. Questions of historical or cultural continuity were never considered when the British restructured the boundaries of Assam, and one of the major casualties of this was the Naga raids in pre-colonial period on Ahom. Assam had interaction with the British East India Company as early as 1792. The persisting internal conflict led the Burmese to occupy the plains of Assam from 1817 to 1826 and Manipur from 1819 to 1826. At the request of the king of Assam the British defeated the Burmese who were forced to surrender their suzerainty over Assam and Manipur by the Treaty of Yandaboo in 1826. Eventually the British rulers annexed the whole region in the subsequent years, the Cachar plains in 1830, Khasi Hills (1833), Jaintia Hills (1835), Karbi Anglong or Mikir Hills (1838), North Cachar Hills (1854), Naga Hills (1866-1904), Garo Hills (1872-73) and Mizo Hills (1890). Thongkholal Haokip (2011) argues that these annexations brought about drastic changes in the polity as well as in the economy of the region, with the gradual decay of feudal institutions and the rise of capitalist economic entities (Thongkholal Haokip, 2011).

Thus, the historical past throw significant light on the overall discontent and grievances of the people towards the Indian state in the post-independent period. The most urgent task for the Indian government after independence was the consolidation of a new nation state. As national integration was the most pressing of the issues confronting the new sovereign state, any movement that might disrupt the process of integration had to be dealt with stringently, and in some cases oppressively. Moreover, after the India-China border conflicts in 1962, the Northeast became a strategic region as regards the national security of India. Any indigenous ethnic movement was considered as "anti-national" and became a "security trouble". As such, it had to be suppressed. Suppression invited resistance and resistance was countered with more oppressive measures from the state, creating an antipathy among the people, and providing the groundwork for armed confrontation and, furthermore, a growing aspiration for an independent homeland (Kyoko Inoue, 2005). In tracing the causes, it is important to keep in mind how closely the past and present are interwoven and linked together. The deep seated grievances and dissatisfaction of the people over the years, coupled with other factors of localised importance has given rise to the innumerable problems today. Sajal Nag's (2002) work, *Contesting Marginality* reflected the historical roots of sub-nationalism in northeastern India and predominantly focused the political meaning of sub-nationalism during colonial period. Thus, unless we understand the historical roots that played an important role in mapping the identities it is intricate to see the nature of plural voices of the ethnic identities in northeast.

V

The following section deals with nature of Indian state towards the ethnic communities in northeast. In response to this how the ethnic communities retorted the state by expressing their voice that reflected sub-nationalism in various parts of the region. However, this sub-nationalism has plural character which has been arising out of the different treatment done by the state.

During the time of Indian independence, with the recommendation of Cabinet Mission, the constituent Assembly hurriedly formed a committee named as Fundamental Rights of the Minority and Tribal and Excluded Area. Vallabbhai Patel was the chairman of this committee. It formed the sub-committee for Northeast Frontier (Assam), and appointed Gopinath Bordoloi as the chairman of the sub-committee. This sub-committee is popularly known as Bordoloi Committee. Nichols Roy, Rupnath Brahma and A. V. Thakkar were the members of the committee. Almost all the recommendations of the Bordoloi Sub- Committee were considered and accepted by the Constituent Assembly. The makers of the Indian Constitution made such constitutional arrangements for the hill people of the Northeast India that neither their autonomies were affected nor the integrity of the nation was put in stake. The provisions under the Sixth Schedule of the Indian Constitutions were made on the expectation that the creation of the District Council and Regional Council would not only satisfy the hill tribes of Northeast India but also create a sense of participation in the mainstream of politics and administration among the hill people. The Bordoloi Sub-Committee proposed that the Hill Districts should be classified into autonomous and non-autonomous areas and also autonomous districts in the case there are many diverse schedule tribes in the areas (V.R. Trivedi, 1995). One of the important functions of Autonomous District Council (ADC) is clearly stated that the ADC is empowered to make laws on subjects ranging from land use and economic development policy to social customs including succession of traditional leaders, marriage, divorce, and inheritance. But all the powers lie with the Governor of the state. But, the state legislative control the governor's role in the implementation of the ADC.

However, the Sixth Schedule failed to inspire the expected process of democratisation and decentralisation in northeast India. This was the basic core of the implementation of Autonomous District Council (ADC) through the constitutional mechanism. Despite the promises in the initial years, the Sixth Schedule in its operation for almost sixty five decades did not succeed in bringing about any noticeable change among the hill tribes in northeast. J.K. Sarmah stated that the provisions of the Sixth Schedule of the constitution was no doubt important in granting autonomy to the tribal to develop themselves, but from the very beginning the District Councils in the Sixth Schedule areas became a bone of contention between the State Government and the Council's authorities. Many limitations have come to light in the process of implementation of the Sixth Schedule which fails to satisfy the growing political consciousness of the tribal people. For instance, according to ADC, the Mikir Hills District (Transfer of Land) Act 1959 provides the land under the jurisdiction of the District Council Authority shall sell, mortgage, lease, barter, gift or otherwise transfer of non-tribal or by a non-tribal to another non-tribal except with the previous permission of the Executive Committee of the District Council. But this Act has not been implemented properly due to state government involvement. Taking advantage of the loopholes in the Mikir Hills District (Transfer of Land) Act 1959, the non-tribal has become the virtual owners of the land under permanent cultivation. The District Councils also since its inception formulated same attempts to control the land holding system of the Karbi acting as an agent of the state. They are unable to play any significant role in strengthening the planning process at the micro level. As a consequence, the councils have neither been able to do anything of standard in the interest of hill masses nor to involve the poor tribes in development activities.

After independence the central government decided to form the new states such as Arunachal Pradesh, Manipur, Meghalaya, Mizoram, Nagaland and Tripura according to the State Reorganisation Act, 1971. But the formation of state did not solve the problem of ethnic nationalism. Demands for autonomy still continued in the North Cachar Hills, Karbi Anglong and Bodoland Territorial Autonomous District of Assam, because the expectations of the people were not fulfilled. J.K. Sarmah argues that "Reorganisation was done as a hurried attempt to curb the trouble situations before it was in full bloom. Granting of state to one community lead to the demand by others and this become a never ending situation. Their demands for autonomy intensified in course of time". The ADCs serve only as a temporary solution for solving the problems of the Northeast region. An autonomy movement for separate states still continues. Thus, ADCs of Sixth Schedule are acting as an agency of the Indian state for pacifying the sub-nationalist political aspirations and also failed to uplift the ethnic communities as well.

The Assam Movement or Assamese Nationalism played an important role during 1979-1985 in Assam. According to them it was a movement primarily for the deportation of the illegal Bangladeshi migrants from Assam. Though the various ethnic community leaders of Assam participated in the movement and sacrificed their lives for the cause of the purging of outsiders. The question of outsider is a debatable issue in northeast in the context of identity formation. But this movement has created the feeling of hatredness among the ethnic groups against the Muslim communities. Many scholars argue that this movement could be branded as 'bigoted nationalism of the Assamese dominant communities'. Various ethnic communities were used for the interest of the dominant Assamese communities. During this period the tribal and non-tribal also raised their voice against the language policy of the Assamese government. They resisted against the Assamese language which sought to make the Assamese as a medium of instruction in schools and also an official language. This was seen as an imposition of the Assamese on the non-Assamese including the tribal and the non-tribals. For instance, Bengalis discontent against imposition of Assamese language in Bark Valley and Bodo's agitation in the present Bodoland. Thus, several ethnic communities felt deceived during the Assam movement and resented language policy of the Assam government. As a result the ethnic communities reacted against the hegemonic attitude of the Assamese nationalists. Subsequently, the Autonomous State movements were started in order to demand the separate statehood. These movements could be studied under the banner of sub-nationalist movement against domination of Assam state.

VI

It is very important to discuss the issue of the Armed Forces (Special Powers) Act because it has been playing a key role in order to suppress the voice of ethnic communities and acting as a hegemonic institution of the state. The Armed Forces (Special Powers) Act was enacted in 1958 in order to control the so-called 'disturbed areas' the state usually use the term, 'disturbed areas'. Governor of the State and Central Government are empowered to declare any part or full of any state as 'disturbed area' if it is in their opinion that it is necessary to prevent terrorist activity or any such activity that might disrupt the sovereignty of India or cause insult to the national flag, anthem or India's Constitution. The act has been justified by the security forces by citing the need for armed forces to have extraordinary powers to deal with militancy. However it has been a subject of intense criticism by the civil society, intellectuals and human rights organisations. The government (either the state or centre) considers those areas to be 'disturbed' "by reason of differences or disputes between members of different religious, racial, language or regional groups or castes or communities" (M. Ramakrshnanan' 2015). But the term 'disturbed' is contested by the people of the region. The state always justified their position by portraying some regions, communities and cultures as disturbed or problematic etc. in order to justify their position in northeast as colonialism did in India. James C. Scott (2011) argues in the context of primitiveness among the ethnic communities or tribal that the 'Hill Peoples' backwardness is a political choice. Conventional narratives treat these people as backward, barbarous, primitive vestiges of a pre-civilised era. Scott argues this narrative is wrong and instead insists that "Hill peoples" are, and have always been 'barbarians' by design. Hill peoples sought to position themselves outside the scope of state power. To avoid the state 'hill peoples' practice both state evasion and state prevention, which involve the adoption of a distinct set of economic, political, social and cultural practices. State evading characteristics are traits 'that make it difficult for a state to capture or incorporate a group or appropriate its material production'. State preventing traits are 'those that make it unlikely that a group will develop internally durable, hierarchical, state-like structures'. Ranajit Guha's work (1983), *Elementary Aspects of Peasant Insurgency in Colonial India* also contested the elitist writings that did not see the differences between 'Crime' and 'Insurgency'. He argues that the main objective of elitist agenda/ state is to demoralise the politics of the subalterns by using such derogative language. To Guha, crime tends to be an individualistic or small group-oriented, but secretive or conspiratorial, action. In contrast, insurgency has a mass character which manifests publicly. The two acts derive from two different codes of violence, but since in the overt form the acted violence may be similar, there is an ambiguity in violence as an internal or integral part of insurgency. In the same way the Indian state has been perusing the northeastern issues from the perspective of crime and failed to look into the ideological conscious of the people who are struggling for construction of their identity. They also failed to address the issues while considering the historicity of the region. Thus, the region is always subject to the dominance of the other, even when they rebel and rise up for the reclaiming of their land.

VII

This book is divided into five thematic sections covering 20 chapters by scholars and researchers and other experts from northeast India. In each section, four papers are included, each touching upon the main theme of the book. Thus, readers will find this book dealing with debates in the study of History, Culture, Literature, Politics and Economy in northeast India.

Section-I

History

R.K. Bijeta's chapter, 'Discourse of the Naga Raids and Resistance: Study from Historical Perspective' deals with the nature of Naga raids in pre-colonial and colonial period. This paper deconstructs the notion of the 'other' on the Naga raids while exploring the politics of Naga raids. It is argued that raids were integral part of the Naga society and economy. It was as much an economic practice as it was a cultural practice. It was also a mode of demonstrating the political power and sovereignty of the Naga. Namita Devi's chapter, 'Fostering Ethnicity: the Congress Rule in Assam (1980 -1990)' examines the role of Congress party towards ethnic communities of Assam. After independence, the Congress party was the ruling party in Assam for a long period that played a determinant role in shaping the ethnic issues in Assam. The historical scrutiny also brought forefront some important issues that are closely connected with the ethnic issues of the region and the role of the Congress led government is important for its aftermath and it played the key factor for fostering ethnicity in Assam. Nakaulang Nriame's chapter, 'Gaidinliu Movement, Sangh Parivar and the Naga: A Quest for Identity and Survival' discusses the role played by the Gaidinliu Movement among the Nagas. Gaidinliu was one such figure who fought the British in the confine of Hills in Northeast India. The Government of India did recognise her by awarding her with Tamrapatra and Padmabhushan. Apart from her political agenda, one more agenda of her movement was her attempt to preserve Naga traditions from the influx of Christianity for which she found Heraka movement. These measures however alienated many Naga who already adopted Christianity. The followers of Gaidinliu in Northeast today are at the mercy of some Hindu missionaries in their attempt to preserve the Naga culture which was one of the visions of Gaidinliu. However this brotherhood alliance between Hindu Missionaries and Gaidinliu followers invited severe criticism from the Naga Christian and separatist leaders very often. Thus, the conflict between Gaidinliu movement, Christian Naga and alliance between Sangh Parivar and Heraka presents current debates in this chapter. Rahul Pegu's chapter, 'The Question of Identity: Nature of the Autonomy Movement among the Mising Tribe of Assam' discusses the origin and causes of the autonomy movements and the question of identity of the Mising community in Assam. This chapter argues that the identities derived from various processes of assimilation and religious transformations influenced the identity struggle of the Mising Community to a large extent. This chapter seeks to illustrate the various conceptions of Mising identity and changes that has undergone; thereby explaining the role it has played in the Mising autonomy struggle. The autonomy movement of the Mising has a long historical background and it culminated in an organised movement during the 1960s and 1970s.

Section-II

Culture

Himasnata Dutta Sarkar's chapter, 'Tracing the Rabhas of Goalpara through the Perspectives of Customs and Rituals' attempts to understand and analyse the layout of the Rabha tribe and how the oral history of the tribe explains its origin and identity. This chapter argues that one has to keep in mind that a social group cannot be placed as a tribe only through the given norms. There are other elements of a group which can be taken into account for its identity. The Rabhas are one such tribe whose customs and rituals, social practices, language etc makes it unique from the rest. But such distinctiveness of every tribe is ignored at a larger level. It is therefore important to understand that every tribe or indigenous populations dwelling in various regions differ from one another and thus, they have different issues which need attention. Junmoni Hansepi and Vulli Dhanaraju's chapter, 'Culture and Identity: A Study of the Ritual Practices among the Karbis' discusses the role played by the rituals among the Karbi. Rituals are inalienable component of Karbi culture and history. Rituals are considered as an important source for the Karbi in sustaining their identity. This chapter argues that the ritual practices symbolised how the Karbi uphold and negotiate with time representing their diversity from past to present. Rituals that they perform have their connection from past to present and historical importance in understanding of the past. Kiryi Potom's chapter, 'Divination through Chicken-Liver among the Galo Tribe of Arunachal Pradesh' examines about the practice of chicken-liver omen by Galo Tribes of Arunachal Pradesh with special focus on *Roksin-Kogek* (Preliminary). This chapter has made detailed discussion about the historical background of the different purposes and types of chicken-liver omen. Bandita Teronpi's chapter, 'The Politics of Identity and Culture: Tracing the Origin and Growth of Karbi Youth Festival' discusses the origin and growth of Karbi Youth Festival which represent the Karbi culture and customs. The Karbi Youth Festival has its own historical background which started with the 'Roman Script Movement' from 1972. It was during the movement that the idea to create and organise a 'National Festival' of the Karbi was adopted. As a result, Karbi Youth Festival became a significant symbol of identity of the Karbis and a very unique way to preserve, promote and showcase the rich Karbi heritage.

Section-III

Literature

Monalisha Khakhlari's chapter, 'Medieval Assam: A Re-interpretation of European Travel Writing' examines the motives and purposes of the travellers and the generalisation that they made based on certain assumptions. It seeks to analyse the devices of representations and the dominant ideologies that led to the sheer depictions of the travellers' imaginations and perceptions. This chapter argues that the European traveller to Assam had 'some' preconceived idea through which they tried to locate their journey in their notions. The travellers to Assam, with diverse intentions, outline the character of its own identity. This clearly shows that the travel accounts cannot be taken singularly, it has to be corroborated with other sources. Travel accounts should be studied with a dose of precaution and it should be verified with other sources. Travel writing focus on some preconceived notion, as Levis Strauss rightly commented, "Travel books have preserved the illusion of something which no longer exists". Bhaskar Jyoti Gogoi and Narayan Ch. Gahatraj's chapter, 'Off the Beaten Path: Critical Ethnography of Selected Narratives on Northeast India' argues that unlike the meta-narrative of official documents, these ethnographic narratives (like travel writing, biographies, autobiographies, diaries etc.) offer a new mode of exploring textual resources and have contributed immensely in the construction of post-colonial discourses. These narratives provide a kind of alternative form of knowledge acquirement in the understanding of people and their customs and cultures. They have become a new kind of source which has brought the discourses of the marginal to the centre by deconstructing the colonists' attempts to give a voice to the natives. As such, an examination of many of the colonised texts from the post-colonialist point of view attempts to understand how the natives and the colonised were constructed in these narratives. In this context, this chapter proposes that Sir Joseph Dalton Hooker's '*Himalayan Journals*', a botanical document and Verrier Elwin's extensive works on the tribes of the Northeast will be introspected to see how these narratives highlight many aspects on the history of Northeast.

This chapter focuses on the dual role played by these narratives, first being a vivid commentator of the lives of the tribal people of the Northeast and second, being a kind of alternative history to the meta-narratives about the Northeast. In the postcolonial context, the study on colonial ethnography is in a way transforming into a diverse and interesting topic as it constructs as well as deconstructs diverse colonised identities. These identities by becoming a kind of references, produces diversified understanding of communities and ethnic groups, their ways of life and also brings forth various contestations. Tanushree Kulshreshtha's chapter, 'Identity Crisis as Reflected in the Novels of Siddhartha Deb' proposes that literature is the mirror to the society and its various forms like poetry, fiction, drama and prose have been reflecting the facts to bring a wave of revolution. Indian English writers from Northeast region through their works have presented the true picture of their homeland mostly through their poems, fictions, and prose. In this context this chapter attempts to unveil the facts and follies related to this particular theme of identity crisis suffered and faced by the people in their own country with reference to the Indian English Writers from Northeast region, especially in the context of Novels by Siddhartha Deb, exposing the hardships and turmoil to set the feet of identity in one's own country. Biplob Gogoi's chapter, 'Linguistic Bases of Identity Politics: With Special Reference to Ethnic Assertions in Assam' examines that politics of Identity formation and Nation Building is a generic phenomenon and this largely accrues to desire for survival, greater material benefits and sometimes, psychological satisfaction of the different nationalities or its organisations. There is a great variety of identity assertion and loyalty aspirations of different groups organised on ethnic lines in the Northeastern part of India, particularly the state of Assam. The existing tribal groups here represent respective ethnic communities with distinct linguistic and cultural traits and they were organised by the elites of different ethnic groups across different phases of history in the state. In this context this chapter mainly argues that in various decades before and after independence of the country, linguistic dimension of tribal identity politics has found a constituent role in the politics of identity formation and nation-building in Assam. This chapter is an understatement of the need to analyse the linguistic bases of such politics of tribal identity and find out the linkage between linguistic chauvinism and politics of tribal identity against the larger backdrop of politics of nation-building process in Assam.

Section-IV

Politics

Hasib Md Iqbal and Diganta Biswas's chapter, 'Challenges and Identity Crisis of Indigenous Bodo Community in Non BTAD Area' proposes that since India's independence Northeastern states of India has been witnessing episodes of secessionist and insurgency related violence and conflict among tribal people. These people are now fighting for the same geographical space to protect and preserve their identity and culture. Assam, the land of blue hills, green forestry and mighty river Brahmaputra is one of the tribal living states of India. Keeping in view this background, this chapter focuses on the challenges and identity crisis of the Bodo people living in the non BTAD area especially in the district of Dhubri and Bongaigaon of Assam. This chapter argues that the middle class has indeed played an important role in the consolidation of Bodo national identity as distinct from Assamese identity. However, it appears that the Bodo middle class will actually seek to protect its own interests in the proposed homeland instead of safeguarding the rights and interests of the masses. An attempt is made to explore the role of the educated middle class as a catalyst in the process of transformation and consolidation of Bodo national identity. Sumit Kr. Sarma's chapter, 'Ethnic Boundary- Making: Towards a Comparative Analytic Understanding' brings out a comparative study of the *Bodoland* and the *Gorkhaland* movement as two distinct movements of constructing ethnicity. The former takes an exclusive approach to construct a distinct ethnic group (Bodo as being distinct from other Mongoloid tribes of Assam); while the latter tries to construct an umbrella identity (Gorkha) of various distinct ethnic groups. This chapter takes into account physical, social as well as emotional boundaries when it comes to boundary making in the construction of an ethnic identity.

Taking a constructivist/instrumentalist position of the formation of ethnic identity, the work is informed by the social, cultural and geo-political compulsions of the groups in defining and asserting their self-identity. Thagendra Chutia and Anup Deka's chapter, 'Ethnic Movements of Mising Tribe of Assam: An Analysis' examines that Assam is the home land of different ethnic groups like Chutia, Ahom, Koch Rajbanshi, Bodo, Sonowal Kachari, Mising, Deori, Tiwa, Rabha, etc. with a veriety of culture speaking different languages and dialects. They have different and separate languages, customs, cultures etc. Among them the Mising tribe of Assam plays a vital role in all-round development of Assam. Ethnic movement is a worldwide phenomenon. Mising movement is one of the major movements in Assam. It started mainly due to the developmental strategies adopted by the Assam Government. The strategy failed to solve the problems of poverty, illiteracy and health insecurities. The tribe faces the problem of encroachment of their lands by money lender including acquisition of forest land. In this chapter focal objective is to identify the factors behind Mising movement by examining their socio-economic status drawn from primary sources. This chapter argues that the identity movement of the Misings started as a socio-cultural and economic movement but later it turns to the field of politics through which they wanted to develop their own community. Jagritee Ghosh's chapter, 'Negotiating Source of Power and Identity among the Konyak Angs of Nagaland' proposes that the Angs are the hereditary chiefs of the Konyak Nagas of Nagaland. The Angs are considered sacred and all powerful by its subjects. However the rituals and the power associated with the Angs have changed in the present times. The shift from traditional religion to Christianity has also changed the way and philosophical life of the Konyaks. This gets all the more complicated when we place it in the context of state and the local power head, Ang. In this context this chapter will highlight the interactions between the state and the local power structures in order to deal with the various subjects that led to contestation between the state and the local chief, Ang. This chapter therefore tries to show the Angs as the local power head and his negotiation with the state and how he maintains his authority in order to sustain his identity.

Section-V

Economy

Tarun Gogai' chapter, 'Underdevelopment and Ethnic Identity Crisis: A Linkage Analysis with Special Reference to Assam' argues that colonialism was the root cause of identity crisis that deepened the divisive roots and dimensions of multifarious identities in India. The legacy of a colonial economy was naturally adorned by the newly independent but centralised Indian state and this aggravated the already existing cultural and economic hiatus between different communities of different regions in the same country. Being trapped in the transitional phases of a decolonised economy, the Northeastern region and particularly Assam remained at the periphery of capitalist development; the crisis was profound in polity and socio-cultural life as well. The developmental fruits of an emerging economy have been poorly distributed, thus creating a sense and feeling of alienation amidst people of the peripheral region of the country. The region has always been at the receiving end of the modernisation process taking place in the entire country. The objective of this chapter is to find out the specific roots and causes of underdevelopment which may provide panacea to the long standing ethnic identity crisis and movements in the state. Shashwati Nath's chapter, 'Economic Stabilisation of Women: A Case Study with Reverine Population of Five Mouzas along the Dhansiri (South) River, Assam' proposes that women occupy the most strategic and important role in ensuring the development of the society. But the status of women in Indian society, at large, gives way to issues of lower access to resources, discrimination, exploitation and violence. Women in India are socially, economically and politically backward compared to other countries. Women's identity in the northeastern part of India becomes a relevant issue in the field of economy. It is argued that the specific situation and conditions of women in society must be analysed in order to assess the differentiated impacts of stabilisation and adjustment programmes on them in various spheres of activity, such as various occupational patterns of women and percentages of women workers to total workers and production for their community. Such an approach requires captivating the women participation in economic adjustment policies in different ways for their livelihood. Garima Kalita's chapter, 'Ethnicity and Identity: A Post Modernist Challenge from the Media and the Market' proposes that the notion of identity can never be a fixed state of egotistical expression and compulsive promotional strategy. But at the same time, it too claims admission that on a collective plane, ethnicity and cultural mode are definitive and specific identity markers. How does a cultural community within the rapid changes and historical dynamics tend to identify itself and how does this attempt still make ways for further diversification need to be understood with close scrutiny on the growth and overwhelming dominance of the growing market, media and the reducing power of myth and legend. In this context this chapter argues that the overt and covert part played by the forces of globalisation does indeed help increase and disseminate confusion regarding concepts like growth, welfare, social rootedness and cultural homogenisation. The cultural communities in the northeast are faced with two strong contradictory but contemporary crossroads which demand a reading of local history and finding resolution from the emerging social and political scene. These junctures tend to emerge from the strong sense of separateness that is historical and also politically inclining towards a federal existence. With it is fused now the globalising tendencies that apparently talks of a double bind in assimilation and coordination but which also give rise to resistance and 'othering' that identity. Tamsin Aftab's chapter, 'Witch Hunting and the Bodos in Kokrajhar District of Assam' proposes that development has reached its peak in the present day. The world is talking of the latest technological developments but on the other hand one also witnesses a picture where one is captured in the shackles of darkness and superstition. Witch hunting is one such dreadful and horrifying type of practice still prevalent amongst some inhabitants of the country, significantly the tribal community. Witch-hunting is a social practice, which has been in existence for years in Assam. Its continued existence is a matter of deep sociological importance. Killing and torturing of women in the name of witches is not a new phenomena and it has its relevance even today. This chapter mainly highlights the questions such as; why is it mostly women who are suspected of witchcraft? Why women outnumber men? Why such a practice is mostly found amongst the tribal community and not in the mainstream population? Even after the various tribal development schemes and initiatives by the local body still such a practice is rampant in such part of the state. In such a state of affairs where the tribal identity follows and how the identity of Bodo community is placed is a significant aspect in the study of development of Bodos in Kokrajhar District of Assam.

Thus, this edited book proposes that identity formation among the ethnic communities in northeast locates in the form of self-determination movements and autonomy movements. The people of this region have been involved in ethnic mobilisation for the politics of recognition. This is the slogan of the identity politics after 1980s. That is why ethnic identity construction has become a debatable issue in the political discourse of Northeast. The issue of ethnic identity is a very complex process. It is argued that the sharing of a common culture on the one hand, and harps on separateness from others, on the other. As a result, the assertion of ethnic identity led to emergence of ethnic nationalism in contemporary days. But it also created a rift not only between the different ethnic groups but also between ethnic groups themselves causing uncertainty and tension in Northeast. As a result, this book represents the plural voices of the ethnic groups of the region. The existing dominant discourses neglected the ideological and mass political character of the people who are constructing their identity through their politics of difference, politics of recognition and experience of marginalisation. These three ideas could be considered as their political ideology that always sustained for mapping identity formation among the ethnic people of northeast.

References

1. Anthony, D. Smith, *Myths and Memories of the Nation*, Oxford University Press, Oxford, 1999.
2. Anthony, D. Smith, *The Ethnic Origin of Nations*, Blackwell, Oxford, 1986.
3. Antonio Gramsci, *Selections from the Prison Notebooks of Antonio Gramsci*, International Publishers, New York, 1971.
4. B.P. Singh, *The Problem of Change: A Study of North Eastern India*, Oxford University Press, New Delhi, 1997.

5. B.G. Verghese, *India's Northeast Resurgent: Ethnicity, Insurgency, Governance, and Development*, Konark Publishers, New Delhi, 2004 (1969).
6. Benedict Anderson, *Imagined Communities: Reflections on the Origin and Spread of Nationalism*, New Left Books, London, 2006 (1982).
7. Bhagat Oinam, 'State of the state 'Mapping *India's Northeast*, No.12, East-West Centre, Washington, November, 2008.
8. Bhanwari Sharma, 'Homelands, Ethnic Conflicts, Democracy in Northeast India' (Paper presented in XXII *World Congress of Political Science)*, Madrid, Spain, Jul, 8 -12, 2012.
9. Eric Hobsbawm and Terence Ranger (Eds), *The Invention of Tradition,* Cambridge University Press, Cambridge, 1992.
10. Eric Hobsbawm, *Nations and Nationalisms since 1780: Program, Myth Reality*, Cambridge University Press, Cambridge, 1990.
11. Ernest Gellner, *Nationalism*, New York University Press, New York, 1997.
12. Ernest Gellner, *Nations and Nationalism*, Basil Blackwell, Oxford, 1983.
13. Ernesto Laclau and C. Mouffe, *Hegemony and Socialist Strategy: Towards A Radical Democratic Politics*, Verso, London, 2001.
14. Iris Marion Young, *Justice and the Politics of the Difference*, Princeton University Press, New Jersey, 1990.
15. Jagpal Singh, 'Challenge of Ethnicity to Federalism: Discourse on the Northeast India', in Akhtar Majeed (Ed), *Federal India: A Design for Good Governance*, Manak Publications, New Delhi, 2005.
16. James, C Scott, *The Art of Not being Governed: An Anarchist History of Upland South East Asia*, Yale University Press, New Haven and London, 2011.
17. John Hutchinson, *The Dynamics of Cultural Nationalism. The Gaelic Revival and the Creation of the Irish Nation State*, Allen and Unwin, London, 1987.
18. Josep R. Llobera, 'Recent Theories of Nationalism', WP núm, 164 Institut de Ciències Polítiquesi Socials, Barcelona, 1999.
19. K.S. Singh, 'Transformation of Tribal Society: Integration vs. Assimilation', *Economic and Political Weekly*, Vol. 17, No. 34, Aug 21, 1982, pp.1376-1384.
20. Karl Deutsch, *Nationalism and Social Communication: An Inquiry into the Foundations of Nationality,* MIT Press, 1996 (1953).
21. Kyoko Inoue, 'Integration of the Northeast: The State formation Process,' in Mayumi Murayama, Kyoko Inoue and Sanjoy Hazarika (Eds), *Sub-Regional Relations in the Eastern South Asia: With*

Special Focus on India's North Eastern Region, Joint Research Programmed, Series No.133, IDE-JETRO, 2005.

22. Michel Foucault, *The History of Sexuality Volume 1: An Introduction*, Allen Lane, London, 1976.
23. Myron Wienor, *Sons of the Soil: Migration and Ethnic Conflict in India*, Princeton University Press, Princeton, 2015 (1978).
24. Partha Chatterjee, *The Nation and Its Fragments,* Princeton University Press, Princeton, 1993.
25. Paul Brass, *Ethnicity and Nationalism*, Sage, New Delhi, 1991.
26. Ranajit Guha, *Elementary Aspects of Peasant Insurgency in Colonial India*, Oxford University Press, New Delhi, 1983.
27. Rosalind Brunt, 'The Politics of Identity', in Stuart Hall and M. Jacques (Ed), *New Times*, Lawrence and Wishart, London, 1989.
28. S K Chaube, *Hill Politics in Northeast India*, Orient Blackswan, New Delhi, 2012 (1969).
29. Sajal Nag, *Contesting Marginality-Ethnicity, Insurgency and Sub-nationalism in North-East India,* Manohar, New Delhi, 2002.
30. Sanjay K. Roy, 'Conflicting Nations in Northeast India', *Economic and Political Weekly*, Vol. 40, No. 21 May 21-27, 2005, pp. 2176-2182.
31. Sanjib Baruah, *Durable Disorder: Understanding the Politics of Northeast India*, Oxford University Press, Delhi, 2005.
32. Sanjib Baruah, 'Between South and Southeast Asia: Northeast India and the Look East Policy', CENISEAS, Paper No. 4, *Omeo Kumar Das* Institute of Social Change and Development (OKDISCD), Guwahati, 2004.
33. Sanjib Baruah, *Durable Disorder: Understanding the Politics of Northeast India,* Oxford University Press, New Delhi, 2005.
34. Sanjib Baruah, *India against Itself: Assam and the Politics of Nationality,* Oxford University Press, New Delhi, 1999.
35. Sanjoy Hazarika, *Strangers of the Mist: Tales of War and Peace from India's Northeast*, the Penguin Books India, New Delhi, 1994.
36. Stuart Hall and Paul Du Gay (Eds), *Questions of Cultural Identity*, Sage Publications, London, 1996.
37. Thongkholal Haokip, 'Conceptualising Northeast India: A Discursive Analysis on Diversity', *Bangladesh e-Journal of Sociology*. Volume 8, Number 2. July, 2011.
38. Thongkholal Haokip, 'Conceptualising Northeast India: A Discursive Analysis on Diversity', *Bangladesh e-Journal of Sociology,* Volume 8, Number 2, July 2011.

39. Thongkholal Haokip, 'India's Northeast Policy: Continuity and Change', *Man and Society: a Journal of Northeast Studies,* Vol. VII, Winter, 2010, pp. 86-99.
40. Udayan Misra, *Northeast India: Quest for Identity,* Omsons Publications, Guwahati, 1988.
41. Udayan Misra, 'Assam: Roll-call of the Dead', *Economic and Political Weekly,* September 14, XXXVII(37), 2002, pp. 3781-3785.
42. Udayan Misra, 'Little Nationalism Turned Chauvinist', *Economic and Political Weekly,* February 21, XVI(8), 1981, pp. 290-92.
43. Udayan Misra, *The Periphery Strikes Back: Challenges to the Nation State in Assam and Nagaland*, Indian Institute of Advance Studies, Shimla, 2000.
44. Udayon Misra, Book Review on Sanjib Baruah's *Sub-National Challenges to Indian State: An Assamese Perspective India against Itself: Assam and the Politics of Nationality, Economic and Political Weekly*, Vol. 35, No. 20, May 13-19, 2000, pp. 1727-1730.
45. V.R Trivedi, *Documents on Assam,* Part-B, Omsons Publication, New Delhi, 1995.

Internet Sources:

1. http://www.gktoday.in/blog/armed-forces-special-powers-act-afspa/ (Accessed on 20th July, 2016).
2. http://www.preservearticles.com/2011092013674/here-are-your-brief-notes-on-aryanisation.html (Accessed on 12th March, 2016).
3. Jayanta Krishna Sarmah, 'Democracy Compromised: Troubled Northeast in Post Independent India, *paperroom.ipsa.org / papers / paper_14802.pdf (Accessed on 12th March, 2016).*
4. Kevin Carrico, *Ritual, https: / / culanth.org / curated_collections / 4-ritual*, 2011 (Accessed on 5th March, 2016).
5. M. Ramakrshnanan, *LIVE MINT*, E-Paper, Thu, May 28 2015 (Accessed on 15th July, 2016).

I

History

1

Discourse of the Naga Raids and Resistance: Study from Historical Perspective

R.K. Bijeta

Introduction

Of late, modern historiography defines the raid not from the perspective of the 'subject' or 'self' and is rather done from the perspective of the 'other'. It has been critically contested by the recent historians who also defined it in terms of the political, cultural and economic essential (James C. Scott, 2011, Jangkhomang Guite, 2011, David Zou, 2005, Sajal Nag, 2002, Ajay Skaria, 2001). In contrast, raid has been described as 'savage', 'barbaric', and 'primitive' and 'uncivilised' in the discourse of colonial historiography. Since the colonisers had encountered fierce resistance from the tribals in the form of raids leading to violence and huge bloodshed they termed the raids as 'inhuman' and 'uncivilised'. In this context this chapter deconstructs the notion of the other on the Naga raid while exploring the discourse of Naga raids and their politics in Northeast India.

I. Discourse of Raids and Social Formation

Politics is about power. It is about invention and maintenance of state craft from which power emanated. Man has evolved society and there is no society which is free of politics. Certain societies are typified by social anthropologist as tribal and it is often believed that such societies are apolitical. Absence of political consciousness among the tribal society is however a myth. Politics is an integral part of social formation and thus even though it is nuanced; tribal societies too have their own politics. State is a political organisation evolved by men which are necessary for making decisions, regulating human behaviour and social control as well as resolution of conflicts. A political system is a cultural universe. Political organisation refers to the way power is distributed within the society to regulate behaviour and maintain order. It differs in from society to society in the extent to which political institutions are distinct from other aspects of social structure like kinship, religion, economy. The size of the group under organisation varies accordingly. Authority is concentrated into specific political roles which too vary in different types of society.

Tribal societies like the Naga society were independent political units but unlike 'bands' it could be integrated into larger units for collective action when there occurred threats of attacks or opportunity of attack. The integrating forces of pan tribal mechanisms are clans, segmented lineage system (kin based), ages, grades and secret societies but these forces are not permanent. They dissolve when the threat is eliminated. In these societies there are informal ways of controlling deviant behaviour. In bands and tribes local groups are economically and politically autonomous, authority is non-centralised and population tends to be small and egalitarian where roles are unspecialised. In contrast state systems which rose in the post tribal stage are complex political structure with a wide range of permanent institutions having legislative, executive and judicial functions and a large bureaucracy. There are large numbers of political roles, well established boundaries, where people enjoy rights and citizenship. It extends its territories by encroaching on boundaries of neighbouring bands, tries, chiefdoms and less powerful states. There are three different theories of state formation, Voluntaristic theory of state formation formulated by V Gordon Childe (19561), Hydraulic Theory of State formation enunciated by Karl Wittfogal (1957) and Coercive theory of rise of state given by Robert Carneiro (1970). The state system therefore is the most formal and complex form of political units which includes many communities and large population. It first appeared 5500 years ago with civilisations. It is found in societies with complex socio-economic characteristics and supported by intensive agriculture and labour specialisations. It is a highly centralised government where power and authority was invoked to draft men for work or war. It collects taxes and makes as well as enforces elaborated and regulatory laws.

The community is the unit of the politics in tribal societies and it is around the polity that it has evolved. Each of the Naga tribe occupied its own territory in which they were grouped into several villages. Each village however was an independent and sovereign unit which ran its own administration. Village Assembly alone rather than any other body developed as the apex organisation among the Nagas. The Ethnographer, J.P. Mills noted that 'as with all Nagas, the real political unit of the tribe is the village' (J.P. Mills,1929, 176). Here village represented the community. A village was a group of houses each containing a family. Hence there were a cluster of families in the village who were related through kinship ties. The villages were thus an organisation representing social, political and economic bonds of a community. The Naga village was headed by a chief whether hereditary or elected was always the head of the administration. Theoretically the institution of chiefdom arose with growing surpluses and larger populations leading to societies becoming ranked and stratified into chiefs, nobles, commoners and such different level of prestige and power. Chieftainship is generally hereditary or developed into hereditary institution after initially selected through consensus or democratic procedures. The functions of the chief were collection, storage, and distribution of goods, supervise religious festival, plan and direct use of public labour and regulation of behaviour and conflict resolution. Hence the village administration was carried out by the chief assisted by his Councilors. Chieftainship therefore was an important element of the polity. Chieftainship was an institution which was much revered, aspired, feared, awed and submitted to. Therefore whoever was the chief; he was the most powerful person in the community. Power of course emanated from his ability to lead in all spheres of life be it war, be it rivalry, be it hunting and fishing, be it security, be it in agricultural pursuits, be in prediction of weather or the fertility of a land, be it in intellectual inputs or wisdom or dealing with external forces. Such ability had to be proven. For example, if the paddy seeds sown by a chief did not sprout or grow well, it was considered that he could not claim the right to be the chief. In other words even the spirits had to favour him. Thus, an assumption of chieftainship by a person was a long and arduous process involving physical as well as intellectual abilities.

Since the Chief was higher to the people, he also had responsibilities and duties towards his subjects. The common people expected him to perform them as he was a leader and capable of succeeding in most difficult of tasks. These tasks were protecting of subject from external attacks and internal strife, guidance during natural calamities, organisation of public works, distribution and redistribution of land resources, locating water facilities and thus ensure that community was economically self-sufficient. The chiefs carried out these works through his expert knowledge of seasonal cycles governing agricultural production, organisation of stores, utilisation of the manpower available at his disposal in finding a suitable location for village settlement, construction of houses, roads and supply of scarce goods to the people. In return the subjects paid him tribute in the form of taxes or services. Thus, the chief's professed duty was to always work for the good of the people. He would organise a militia of able bodied young men. This militia was employed to carry out public works. Other than the construction of roads, tanks, embankments, bridges and canals the militia was also employed to reclaim cultivable land from forests, search water bodies and raiding of the neighbouring tribes or plains to procure scarce goods or demonstrate power. In the selection of chiefs outstanding personal qualities such as good physique, leadership and fighting skills and wealth were also taken into consideration.

The Angami Nagas in northeast India maintain that they never had a strict system of chieftainship. Only in times of war or aggression a commander-in-chief was selected to lead them. For normal times a council of elders would perform the role of leaders. Among the Sema Nagas chieftainship was hereditary and chief (Kukami) was very powerful. No doubt there for chief was the most important political institution in the Naga polity.

He was of course aided by a council of advisors called *Chochomi*. The power of the chiefs could be democratic, semi-democratic and autocratic (N. Venuh , 2005, 21). The Konyak Chief known as *Angh* were highly autocratic. He was assisted by a council of advisors. Such a council is called *Sese* in Chakesang, *Senden* in Ao, *Ho-Ho* in Lotha and *Chochomi* in Sema. They combined the functions of executive, administrative and judicial. The council was responsible for the construction and maintenance of village water supply, foot-paths, construction of new paths and bridges over water bodies. Such being the nature of Naga polity where politics mostly around the internal organisation and regulation of the community, raids played an important part of political practice.

However, fascinatingly 'raids' were always seen from the perspective of the raided. Either it is the border folks, or the Ahom State or the colonial state of the later times. The raid itself is a colonial concept seeing from the point of view of the Europeans trying to build a colonial state in South Asia. The versions of the tribals have not been known or understood. In fact, the available literature on raids, the Naga, Kuki and Lushai word for the practice of what is known as raid is not known. The oral history of the tribes perpetuating the raids has also not been recorded. Hence the view of the raiders as to why they committed raids or what was the objective of raids is completely ignored. It provided the colonial officials as well as European anthropologists to view a particular practice of the tribe who occasionally swoop down on the hills or plains people and indulge in plunder and arson were constructed as raids. Raids are not always necessarily murderous. But in the colonial construction raids were associated with violence, bloodshed, head-hunting, killing and kidnapping. These theories then were made a part of the 'civilisational discourse'. In this discourse raids were seen as features of savagery and barbarism and hence the people who committed such acts were also seen as savage and barbaric. A simple economic practice was thus given a civilisational colour and also a rationalisation for the suppression, conquest and subordination of the tribe itself.

II. Ahom Kingdom and the Idea of Naga Raids

The Nagas have always perpetrated raids into the plains or the foothills from the time of recorded history. These raids were basically economic in nature. The hills of the Nagas where they lived did not have any source of salt which was one of the most important consumer items. As against this the Brahmaputra valley had a number of salt springs under the control of the different powers that ruled the area. The Nagas often attacked and raided the plains only to take control of these Salt springs. Kachari state had a number of salt springs in its frontier with the Nagas. To take control of these springs the Nagas had driven them out of Mohong long before the advent of the Ahoms and took possession of the Salt springs.

The same struggle over salt springs continued in the Ahom period too. As seen above, the Naga raids were not just to declare their sovereignty or take revenge. Often they were to procure consumable items which were not available in the Naga Hills. One such item was salt. There were several salt springs and rock salt hills in the Ahom territory. The Nagas were traditionally dependent on these sources for their salt which they obtained freely. But the rise of Ahom state and establishment of border posts had curbed their natural movement to obtain these precious items. Some of the salt springs were earlier in the Naga territories which were forcibly taken away by the Ahoms. Hence these had now to be obtained through raids in the form of booties. This was because even the Ahom territory was deficient in Salt. The Assamese mostly collected salt from the salt springs which were not sufficient for the entire population. Hence the common Ahom subjects evolved a technology by which they produced a substance called *Khar* which they used as a substituted for salt. A series of Ahom Naga conflict during the entire pre-colonial period was over these salt springs.

According to some Buranjis, in the years (1458 saka -1536 A.D.) the Ahoms obtained possession of one salt well in Mohong by defeating the Nagas which the Nagas had wrested from the Kacharis earlier (Laxmi Devi, 1968). The Borduarias and Paniduarias were Nagas living at the eastern extremity of the Sibsagar district who were also called Mohongias (G.A. Grierson, 2005). The Mohongs was one of the most important salt producing places of the land of the Nocte Nagas. Thus, economic interest of the Ahoms also compelled them to fight against the Nagas living between Borhat and Jaipur. The Ahoms in course of time obtained exclusive possession of several salt wells and they had to send several expeditions against the Nagas to retain their rights in the salt wells intact.

Another reason of Naga raids on the plains were head hunting. The colonial historians proposed that the Nagas perpetrated raids on the plains to hunt for human heads. Although the British were talking about their own colonial times where they showed that the Nagas perpetually raided their territory and killed British subjects because the Nagas were traditionally a head hunting tribe and such raids were made to kill plainsmen and collected human heads as their trophies which were required for various reasons like proof of masculinity, tribal ritual of fertility, mortuaries rites of dead chiefs and so on. Naga raids were thus seen by the colonial historians as a continuation of Naga history of raids from the pre-colonial period.

During the reign of Jayadhvaj Singha, (1648-1663 A.D.) for the first time there were reports of the Lakma Nagas, one of the Konyak Naga tribes living between the Mooloongs and the Changnois. Konyak of both India and Burma were known to be head hunters. In 1650, they raided the Ahom dominion, killed a number of Ahom subjects and cut off the heads of two men and four children (Laxmi Devi, 1968). In other words, they practiced head-hunting. However, there was no record to show that they carried the heads. If a raid and murder had been committed for human heads, the human heads would certainly be collected and carried. It was also not known whether there was a death of any major chiefs when this raid had taken place for whose mortuaries rites human head might have been necessary. For fertility rites which is a regular annual occurrence if heads were needed than why there were no earlier records of beheading and collection of heads before this raid.

While the above mentioned raids were basically economic and cultural in nature, a number of raids were also committed for political purposes. As was seen in the pre-colonial period both the Dimasa and Ahom states were subjected to Naga raids frequently. A number of such raids were on the frontier where the plains met the hills. These were natural boundary between the Naga and Ahom/Dimasa territory. These raids were reactions to either the Ahom expansionism or to pre-empt the Dimasa expansion into Naga Hills.

The Ahoms right from their initial migration into the Brahmaputra valley had confronted the Naga resistance. It is interesting that though the Ahoms devastated the Nagas on their way to the plains of Brahmaputra valley, they did not occupy the Naga territory. This was perhaps because they were looking for river basin plains land where they could practice wet rice cultivation. But once they settled in the plains and developed a state of their own, they did try to contain the Nagas. The Nagas wanted to continue their economic raids on which their survival depended but the Ahoms countered it strongly. The result was fierce confrontation between the two. The Ahom expeditions were met with fierce Naga raids on the frontier. These were raids of political nature. The other political raids perpetrated by the Nagas were to demonstrate their sovereignty and political power.

The Nagas often committed raids on the Ahom territory to show their political strength and to pre-empt any Ahom invasion of their land. The idea was to demonstrate that the Nagas themselves were as sovereign as the Ahoms were. Hence the Nagas raided the Ahom territory to demand equal rights as two sovereign neighbours often with profitable result and sometimes with devastations. What is however true the Ahoms was in the seven hundred years of rule had hundreds of confrontation with the Nagas and Nagas committed hundreds of raids but the Ahoms did not venture to occupy the Naga habitat.

III. Colonialism and Naga Raids

When the power was transferred from the Ahoms to the British not only the raids by the Nagas were viewed differently by the new government, the nature of the raids itself changed. The annexation of the Brahmaputra valley (1826) brought the British into direct confrontation with the Nagas who lived in the adjacent hills. The repeated raids, plunder, loot, headhunting practices and murders were seen by the British as features of savagery and barbarism and were decided to be dealt with accordingly. With the transfer of power to the British, the nature and frequency of the Naga raids too increased manifold which bewildered the British. They tried to counter it by sending punitive expeditions one after the other which devastated the tribal habitat in Naga Hills, blocked their outlet to the plains and restricted their movement within the hills. There was a virtual declared war on the Nagas.

The raids, expedition, establishment of outpost pattern of British policy continued from 1826 to 1878 when a British outpost was established in Kohima which thenceforth became the fort from which the colonialists dealt with the Nagas. For the Nagas however the pattern of raids had changed from essential part of their living to a frequent fight to resist the colonial power. The advent of the British coincided with the discovery of tea in Assam (1823). By 1832 tea was emerging to be the most lucrative industry of East Indian Company. The closure of Chinese tea had necessitated an alternative source of supply. Assam bestowed them with that opening. Since tea plantation required hill slopes, the British gradually started to colonise the hill lands.

Although the British did not initially really want to go into the hills to expand their empire, the advent of tea and growth of tea industry changed all that. Tea was discovered in Assam in 1823. An experimental tea garden was set up in 1836 and by December 1837 first Assam tea was successfully manufactured. In 1840, two-thirds of official experimental gardens were transferred to the Assam Company set up in rent free terms for three years. The British colonial power sought to 'rid Assam of its wilderness' by 'bringing wastelands of Assam under colonial culture and productivity' and subject it to the 'civilisation of the tea garden.' Tea would give 'Assam a culture which was worthy of being linked to the Empire.' To facilitate private investment in the tea industry and grant cheap land to the tea planters, new waste land settlement policy was formulated in 1838 which was revised in 1854. Riding on the back of colonial policies, tea planters now attempted to grab more land than they required or could manage. In the process they came into conflict with the tribal. The quick advance of the tea planters into the hilly region was a threat to the tribal land, their ancestral habitat and their sovereignty. Their livelihoods were in danger too. It was not just tea gardens that were coming up in their land. Their forests were being depleted for timber and wild animals. As early as 1860, the Assam company had taken land in the Naga Hills for tea cultivation and by the turn of the century there were more than 40 tea gardens on the land claimed by the Nagas. All these tea gardens accounted for hundreds of acres of land encroached and occupied by the tea gardens owned by White Planters. Such extensive land mass had belonged to the Nagas as per their claims. Indeed these tea gardens were the land and forests where the Nagas had their hunting and collection of their forest products; they would come down for their raids and claimed suzerainty over them. Some of the tea gardens like Wokha T E, Jamguri T E, Mukharan T E, Kheriema T E, Nagajunka T E, Naginijan T E, Singloo T E, Tiphooknamti T E were tea garden where actually the Naga habitat. The rise tea gardens in these lands actually displaced a number of Naga villages. The government endeavour to grant lands- A claimed by the Nagas as their own- to the planters resulted in a crisis situation.

Although the government claimed the whole country up to Manipur and Burma as British territory, it had hitherto treated Naga tracts as outside Assam for all civil purposes. The tea planters had long since in many places both in Lakhimpur and Sibsagar taken up lands south of the revenue line, in some instances paying revenue to the British and in others to the Naga chiefs. The earlier settlers found it to their interest to conciliate the Nagas and did not seek government protection. But now they sought police protection at all times.

IV. From Raid to Resistance

The Nagas took it not only as an encroachment but also an invasion into their territory. When their appeal and arguments were ignored, the helpless Nagas resorted to their own primitive means of registering objection and thwarting such invasions. To obstruct British plans the Nagas led perpetual raids on the plantations and killed people. In 1869, the Changno Nagas carried off three labourers from a tea garden. Similar reports of disturbances were coming from other plantations too.

Naga habitat did not mean only the Naga villages which were the only defined Naga area. The forests, rivers, streams which lie around the Naga habitat were also considered as Naga areas by the Nagas. In fact, more than a matter of cartography, it was a matter of perceived geography. The Naga territory was in the Naga mind. Thus, the foothill areas where they committed their raids were also considered by the Nagas as their territory and the people on whom they perpetrated the raids were seen as their subjects.

The Naga perception of sovereignty was therefore entirely a matter of perception. It was a Naga construct. There was no material proof of it. Hence it could not be questioned or challenged. Any attempt at trespassing even these foothills which legally was a British territory was also seen by the Nagas as a trespass and violation of their sovereignty. The British did not understand this and hence failed to act accordingly. It was also a matter of prestige for the British government. Every Naga raid was reported in the London newspapers and the loot and plunder in the frontier was seen as a utter failure of the mighty British empire. The helplessness of the British Empire against a horde of raiding Nagas was ridiculed by the newspapers and British society. They wanted the British forces to crush the raiding Nagas and proved their might. But it was not easy on the ground. The British were indeed helpless against raids of the Nagas as they did not know what caused them and how to tackle them. They tried non-interference in the Naga areas as a policy. But even their policy of non-intervention was bound to fail as they had already intervened in the Naga sovereignty and the Nagas were aware that it was a matter of time when the British entered their land and reclaim their sovereignty. This was the last struggle of the Nagas. They too had realised that if they lost this last struggle against the British they would not only lost their habitat but also lose their sovereignty which they dearly protected for last so many centuries.

But it was not an easy fight. The Nagas had also realised that the British were a mighty force. They were technologically much superior against the defence of the Nagas. The British gun power could easily demolish the Naga arms strength.

The need therefore was to acquire gun power and strengthen their defence against the mighty colonial power. Once the Nagas became convinced of the necessity of fire arms, they were determined to acquire these at any costs. Before long they learned the use of guns and muskets but at the beginning they had depend on the neighbours like the Cacharis and Manipuris for arms and ammunitions. It appears that the Nagas not only learnt the use of firearms from the Kacharis and Manipuris but also received supplies of fire arms from them. The Nagas actually purchased them from these tribes by paying them money and goods which they captured through raids. The bulk of their supplies came through their agents in Manipur, Cachar and plains of Assam. They also acquired guns by raiding the British outposts, guards on frontier duty and by surprising parties of traders and elephant hunters. Some Naga youths joined the British army only to get hold of the fire arms, get the training and then desert and disappear with the firearms. The powerful villages of Mozoma, Khenoma, Jotsoma and Kohima were reported to have collected arms from different sources with the object of driving the British out of their hills. In reality Khenoma had acquired sufficient quantity of fire arms and was waiting for an opportunity to revolt. It was believed some 6000 Nagas representing all the Angami clans were armed with at least 500 firearms.

Thus, empowered, the Naga started a series of raids on the British. Unable to withstand the frequency and ferocity of Naga raids, the British contemplated a change in policy. It was decided to conquer the Naga land and bring the Nagas under the 'civilised' influence of British administration. It was felt that once under the civilised influence of a benevolent British administration, the Nagas would give up their savage ways and stop raid the British territory. The endeavour was thus for an outright takeover of Naga territory. Even though raids continued and Naga wars of resistance were all around, British began to think of taking over Naga Hills beginning with Kohima. It was only a matter of time before the rest of Naga Hills were captured by the British.

Conclusion

Thus, this paper argues that Raids were integral part of the Naga society and economy. It was as much an economic practice as it was a cultural practice. It was also a mode of demonstrating the political power and sovereignty of the Nagas. It remained so for centuries till the time of the Dimasas and Ahoms who built strong states in the vicinity of the Nagas. But once a modern military colonial power like the British succeeded the Ahoms, the nature of raid as a practice underwent momentary changes. The British did not understand the economic nature of the raids and why raids were such an important part of Naga mode of production. They ruthlessly countered it and tried to stop it on the pretext of it being a trespass on their sovereignty and violence on their subjects living on the frontier.

Secondly, the British did not understand the cultural practices of raid rather they termed it head hunting and therefore a trait of savagery and barbarity. They again opposed such practices on the ground of civilisation, rationalism and humanism. A series of counter-raids were unleashed to stop such 'atrocities' on the plains. The opposition to raids was seen by the Nagas as a clever ploy to blockade their economic necessity, commercial transaction and a threat to their sovereign practices. They initially continued despite the opposition of the British as a reassertion of their sovereign practices. But once the tea planters in collaboration with the white rulers started to climb up the hills and occupy their ancestral land without even taking permission from them they saw it as outright invasion. The economic nature of raids therefore was transformed. It was begun to be used as a political weapon against colonial invasion and expansionism. Raids thus transformed its character to resistance. Raids were no more an economic imperative. It was a political weapon of resistance against colonial expansionism.

It finally argues that raid into the plains has been an integral part of the Naga's survival strategy in the history of northeast. Raids essentially meant a violent attack on a people or areas through which a terror was created in the minds of the victim. The purpose of which was manifold: to reinforce their authority over the area, vanquish an identified enemy, pre-emptive counter, extraction of surplus, plunder and loot, procurement of essential items that are scarce in the hills as well as kidnapping of people who would subsequently be converted into slaves to replenish the manpower short tribal economy.

References

1. Ahoms Buranjis (1340-1826).
2. Ajay Skaria, *Hybrid Histories: Forests, Frontiers and Wildness in Western India,* Oxford University Press, New Delhi, 2001.
3. David Zou, 'Raiding the Dreaded Past: Representation of Headhunting and Human Sacrifice in North East India', *Contribution of Indian Sociology*, No. 39, 1, 2005.
4. G.A. Grierson, *Linguistic Survey of India*, Vol. 1. Low Price Publication, Delhi, 2005.
5. G.H. Damant, *Report on the Administration of the Naga Hills for the Year 1878-79,* Shillong, 1879.
6. Golap Chandra Barua (Ed), *Ahom Buranji: from the Earliest Time to the End of Ahom Rule,* Spectrum Publications, Guwahati, (Reprint) 1985.
7. H.K. Barpujari, *Problem of the Hill Tribes: North East Frontier*, Vol. II, NEHU Publications, Shillong, 1998.
8. J. P. Mills, *The Ao Nagas*, Macmillan, London, 1929.
9. J.H. Hutton, 'Head-Hunting', *Encyclopedia Britannica,* Vol. XI, 1929.
10. James C. Scott, *The Art of Not being Governed: An Anarchist History of Upland South East Asia*, Yale University Press, London, 2011.
11. Janet Hoskins (Ed), *Headhunting and the Social Imagination in Southeast Asia*, Stanford University Press, Stanford, 1996.
12. Jangkhomang Guite 'Civilization and its Malcontents: The Politics of Kuki Raid in Nineteenth Century Northeast India', *Indian Economic Social History Review,* Vol. 4, July/September, 2011, pp. 3339-376.
13. Karl Wittfogel, *Oriental Despotism: A Comparative Study of Total Power*, Yale University Press, New Haven, 1957.
14. L.W. Shakespear, *History of Upper Assam, Upper Burmah and North-Eastern Frontier*, London, 1914.
15. Laxmi Devi, *Ahom Tribal Relations: A Political Study*, Lawyers Book Stall, Guwahati, 1968.
16. N. Venuh, *British Colonization and Restructuring of Naga Polity*, Mittal, Delhi, 2005.
17. R. Reid, *History of the Frontier Areas Bordering on Assam, from 1883-1941,* Shillong, 1948.
18. Robert Carniero, 'A Theory of the Origin of the State', *Science*, 21st August 1970.
19. S.E. Peale, 'The Nagas and Neighbouring Tribes', *Journal of the Anthropological Institute,* Vol. Ill, 1874.

20. Sajal Nag, *Contesting Marginality: Ethnicity, Insurgency and Sub-nationalism in North East India,* Delhi, Manohar, 2002.
21. Tajenyabu Ao, *A History of Anglo-Naga Affairs*, Author Publications, Mokokchung, 1958.
22. Tajenyabu Ao, *British Occupation of Naga Country*, Naga Literature Society, Mokokchung, 1993.
23. V. Gordon Childe, *Man Makes Himself*, New American Library, New York, 1951.

2

Fostering Ethnicity: The Congress Rule in Assam (1980 -1990)

Namita Devi

Introduction

Ethnicity and ethnic consciousness is a nineteenth century phenomenon. The Oxford dictionary defined the term as "relating to a group of people having a common national or cultural tradition". The term is derived from the Greek word 'ethos' which generally means 'nation'. It currently refers to people who thought to have common ancestry and shared a distinctive culture. Again, members of an ethnic group are conscious of belonging to an ethnic group may be termed as ethnicity or ethnic identity which is further marked by the recognition from others.

In modern times, ethnicity emerged as a counter effect of the encounter and conflict with external groups such as immigrants and the indigenous people. From this point ethnicity comes to stand in opposition to 'national' to refer people with distinct cultural identities who, through migrations or conquest had become subject to a nation or state with a different culture from the mainstream which can be termed as sub-nationalism (Sanjib Barua, 1999). The western notion of nation states where language, religion and political sovereignty are the basic boundary and are the balance ball for nation state.

The main aim of the paper is to scrutinise the role of Congress led government in both centre and state concerning the ethnic issues. The study is purely historical and analytical. For that, the paper looks at the laws and policies of Congress government of the proposed period and its impact on the issue. The data is based on some selected version of the Assam legislative debates, the Constitution of India and the laws and acts of the central and state government of India. The study is confined within the ruling period of Congress-I in between 1980 to 1990.

As per the meaning of the term, Northeast in general and Assam in particular, is a bunch of ethnic group and by the time becomes one of the most conflict prone zones. It is not a new concept in the context of Northeast society and polity. This geographical area of Indian continent is an admixture of divergent population with varied language, culture, races, caste, creed , who are termed as different 'tribes' and become hotspots for the growth of ethnicity.

However, the ethnic consciousness, which is a living issue in Northeast politics, has a different entity. The geographical location of the area and demography is different from the mainstream India. It is naturally situated between the two 'great traditions'; traditions of Indic-Asia and the traditions of Mongoloid-Asia so that this region stand between the 'racial-cultural definition and politico-administrative definition of their identity'.

It is interesting to note that in India, politically the term 'ethnic' is not used to denote the ethnic groups of northeast and Assam. Dilip Hazarika says that "tribalism is artificial; it is done for the convenience of administrative system that is thoroughly influenced by caste stratification mindset and politically controlled by the caste Hindu society but whatever the motive behind this termination, the term tribe was labeled on the ethnic group of northeast by the post-independent Congress government". Article 342 of the Indian constitution simply says that 'the President of India can specify tribes and tribal community ...to Schedule Tribes' and he has the power to include and exclude. The Indian government does not make several criteria to justify the enlistment. It enlisted the criteria such as 'tribal language, animism, primitiveness, hunting and gathering, carnivorous in food habits, naked and semi-naked, fond of drinking and dance'. Not all these criteria are the basic norms of tribalism from the anthropological point of view. Again the ST and SC also appear with similar description and privilege bestowed by the constitution of India. The northeast and Assam's tribes neither are in primitive stage rather they are rich with their unique socio-political culture.

I. Ethnic Issues and Assam Politics-Historical Background

From the colonial period, two basic issues are confronting Assam politics and ethnicity with far-reaching effects. One is the immigration or foreign influx from the neighbouring countries and the other is linguistic sub-nationalism. However, the governing policy of the British has indirectly enhanced the issues furthermore. To study the role of a ruling party and government in some particular issues, the historical sequential factor cannot be ignored and history always linked up the situation to its consequential events.

A historical overview of the history reveals that all these issues played a determinant role in shaping the ethnic issues and ethnicities in Assam and Northeast during the colonial period. Indeed, two basic issues are confronting Assam politics. The Indian National Congress mainly dominates the Administrative responsibility of the post-independent India and Assam. Henceforth the ethnic issues or conflict of Assam politics is the issue of Congress politics as well. So the point is that, what are the policies of the Congress government about this issue and with what impact? It is significant to know the issue better.

The governing policy of the British Indian government towards the Northeast was quite different from that of the other part of India. Above all, the area comes under the British jurisdiction quite lately. Due to its geographical location, demography and culture, the British had followed a policy of segregation because their main concentration was on economic benefit and they thought that the underdeveloped tract of Northeast would be an administrative burden. Therefore, they decided not to interfere in their way of life. Nevertheless, the British were dared not to interfere as they often attacked upon the foreign officers. Their resistance are called as 'raids' or 'uprising' (N.K. Das, 2009). There is long chronology of tribal resistance. In 1828-30, the Khasis resisted against the British policy of holding in 'duars' (custom post) areas. The British at that time took interest in those tribal areas for economic benefit and strategically importance of the area. On the basis of the Bengal Eastern Frontier Regulations of 1873, British authority introduced the Inner Line policy to protect Crown interest in tea, oil, and elephant prohibiting British subjects entering to this area in the name of protection of tribal identity and culture. The 'citizens of India' replaced the word 'British subject' in 1950. So the policy of the colonial government was only meant for segregation, and left the ethnic tribes on their own fate. The colonial policy only emphasised on Protection and not on the development or upliftment of the tribal life. The following events of ethnic conflict and resistance show that the issue is concentrated on both protection of their entity and identity development.

Ethnic issue shook Assam politics since 1930. At that time, the focus in controversy was on the Line system that sought to restrict immigrant settlement. The Assamese politician wanted the tightening of the Line System; while some immigrant politician like Maulana Basani advocated unrestricted immigration (Sanjib Barua, 1999) between 1937 to 1947 the issue of migration is the major cause of the political instability in Assam. In 1937, the Assam government appointed a committee to enquire into the operation of the Line System. The committee recommended both the continuation of immigration and the tightening of the line system. In the midst of Congress-Muslim League rivalry the views of the ethnic Assamese was subdued. Three of the nine members stood for the Assamese cause. But the success of this policy in its aim was a big question, as it failed to project them in the following years. Based on this policy, the Scheduled District Act 1874 was enacted, by which further, some hilly areas were termed as excluded areas. This act became a stepping-stone for further policies of segregation. I prefer the word segregate because from this time onwards, the hill tribes got the point to think that they are different and extra from the mainstream of India. Later based on this Act and with the initiative of Bordoloi Ministry of Congress I, provision of sixth Schedule was created in the constitution of India. In 1919, the Montague- Chelmsford Reforms recommended that the typically backward tract should exclude from the jurisdictions of Reform Council. Thus, this policy of British government tried to keep away the tribal or ethnic tract from the mainstream administrative structure. Therefore, the policy only keep the tract aloof from the mainstream administration, for not be an additional programmed for the upliftment of those backward tract. The Government of India Act 1919 again stated that Governor-General in council reserves power to declare only territory to be a backward area under Section 52 (A) of the Act. On January 1921, the council declared all the hill districts as backward tracts. The Assam Frontier Tract Regulation Act 1880 also empowered the Governor to direct the withdrawal of any enactment in force in those areas. The Simon Commission also recommended the exclusion of typically backward tract have to be administered through the Agency of the Governor. Later on, the Cabinet Mission Plan of the British raised another issue that was responsible to enhance the ethnic issues later on, that is the grouping system.

After partition, Assam and the Northeast fell in a crisis of Hindu and Muslim refugee. In this matter, the role of Indian Congress government was hostile towards the complexity of the issue and its aftermath in Assam politics. Rather, the Congress Governor under the leadership of Jawaharlal Nehru advocated for sheltering refugee in Assam. Bordoloi urged that 'Assam could not accommodate very many refugees'. However, Nehru writes that 'if land is not available in Assam it is still less in the rest of India.' Besides, he threatened that 'if Assam adopted an attitude of incapacity to help to solve the problem; the claims for Assam for financial help will obviously suffer' (Nirod Barooah, 1990). This attitude of the central government towards immigrant was responsible to create a fear among the ethnic Assamese at a latter. Immigration reinforced the Assamese desire for cultural entity (Sanjib Barua, 1999).

Thus, the fear thwarted the ethnic issue to another direction that is to linguistic and cultural identity. The language is also another focal point in the question of ethnicity in Assam and the role of Congress led government played an important role in thwarting the issue in that direction. The language issue came into forefront in the Assam politics from the policy taken by the Independent Indian government for the reorganisation of state in the Independent Indian dominion. The state reorganisation committee recommended to reorganise state based on language. It concluded 'Linguistic homogeneity in the formation of new province, is certainly attainable, but at the cost of creating a fresh minority problem' (Sanjib Barua, 1999). But as a member of Linguistic Commission, Nehru confidently and emphatically stated that this country stood for and represented culture, race, history, individuality and finally the sub-nation' and by the seventh amendment of the Indian constitution, many of Indian provinces where reorganised on the basis of language.

Assam was also enthusiastic to have a national identity and therefore lean towards linguistic identity. However, the enthusiasms overshadowed the reality of Assam's demography.

Table-1

	Language	*1951*	*%*
1.	Assamese	4971229	56.29
2.	Bengali	1717381	19.45
3.	Hindi	334879	3.79
4.	Khasi	292876	3.32
5.	Garo	234752	2.67
6.	Bodo/Boro	166427	1.88
7.	Lushai/Mizo	162301	1.84
8.	Nepali	122823	1.39
9.	Karbi	129305	1.46
10.	Oriya	114033	1.29
11.	Manipuri/ Maitei	89144	1.01
12.	Santali	92638	1.05
13.	Miri	57615	0.65
14.	Munda	2415	-

The census report of 1951 reflects the (Table-1) picture that layer upon layer language minority existed in Assam and the majority language speakers were hardly more than 50 per cent.

The state reorganisation commission of 1955 recognised the linguistic basis for two other states of present day India viz. Manipur and Tripura, which had not been a part of colonial Assam, also got merged with Assam. The result was that soon after demand for autonomy from the various ethnic groups began to emerge.

To compensate the ongoing linguistic nationalism the Congress government passed the Assam Official Language Act 1960, which further polarised the society and politics of Assam. Thus, the Congress Government moved forward the wrong done by the previous government.

By this time, the autonomous statehood to the Khashi-Jayantiya Hill was almost finalised in 1969, but the Congress Government and Assam Pradesh Congress Committee tried to appease them by the promise of creating a separate district in N.C. Hills. Again, the language policy of 1972 of imposing Assamese as the sole medium of instruction frustrated the hill ethic groups from 1973 to 1980 followed three memorandum were submitted for the political autonomy of the Khashi and N.C. Hills.

From 1967 onwards, the plain ethnic groups also raised their voice for autonomy. The Plain Tribal Council of Assam (PTCA) submitted memorandum to the President of India on May 20, 1967 with a demand for the protection of their land, effective check on economic exploitation, to conserve their language, culture and custom and to prevent political domination (Dutta, 1993). In 1973, they upgraded their demand for Udayachal.

Under the leadership of PTCA, a mass movement was organised against the Assam Government's order for the by-election of Kokrazar constituency (Talukdar, 2014). The government labeled this activity as secessionist movement. The repressive policy taken by the Congress Government further intensified the plain tribes' issue. The legislative constituency was made in such a way that the ethnic minority population will not be able to play a dominant role in the election. In 1974, another issue arose on the agenda of script in Bodo medium school. The Assam Government imposed Assamese script while the Bodo Sahitya Sabha argued for Roman script and started agitation on this issue. The then Home Minister of Congress Government ordered to suppress this forcefully. Even the members of Bodo Sahitya Sabha had to go underground to save their lives. These repressive measures widened the rift between the ethnic Assamese and the plain ethnic tribes. They lost faith on the Congress leadership. On this political outfit after emergency, the PTCA sprung up in Assam politics with a remarkable performance in the election of 1976 and thus ethnicity got the political platform.

All these reveals that the language policy of post-independent Congress led government provoked the ethnic polarisation furthermore. The colonial legacy of segregation was not been minimised and there rather was a tendency of authoritative suserainty that was being noticed in the post-independent government policy.

II. Issues and Governance 1980-1990

Some intricate historical facts and phenomenon of 1980 to 1990 brought the ethnic issue to another direction; the Congress party also played a critical role in this matter. The period witnessed the famous anti-foreigner Assam movement, which further perverted the ethnic issues and make it more intricate. At this critical juncture, the Congress lead government had to deal with the problem in caution.

(a). Immigration Issue

During the whole period of movement, the immigration issue came into forefront and become the basis of ethnicity. In the different phase or intensity of the movement, the anti-foreigner issue turned to different parameters. It was sometimes anti-foreigners, both Indian and outsiders. At the early stage, the attitude of the Congress government was anti-movement. The contemporary media accused Congress I for its pro-immigrant attitude and the government tried to suppress it forcefully.

After independence, the Congress government under the leadership of Gopinath Bordoloi and Bishnuram Medhi, followed nationalist attitude and even sometimes stood against the policy of the central government concerning the issue of immigration and refugee question. However, the Indian government showed a sympathetic attitude in case of the rehabilitation of refugees. For that, the task of identification and deportation of immigrants under the scheme of Prevention and Identification of Pakistani (PIP) ceased to work in an effective manner. At the time of the by-election of Mongoldoi in 1979, the simmering grievance on the immigrant issue burst out. Another important point is that at the initial stage, the ethnic organisations like Purbanchaliya Loka Parisad, Plain Tribal Council (Brahma), Karbi Parisad, All Assam Tribal League offered their support to the movement. The movement was one of the causes for the failure of Janata Government and consequently the Congress led coalition government came into power. The new Chief Minister Jogen Hazarika agreed to rectify the voter list, but another Congress leader Sarat Singha on the other hand emphased on defining the term 'foreigner' in the context of Assam. This point created a controversy and for sometime diverted the agenda of the movement to another direction. The by-election of Mongaldoi eventually got cancelled.

The decision of the central government under the leadership of Congress-I and Indira Gandhi to held election at the midst of the turmoil situation created an atmosphere of anarchy from where the misunderstanding between the ethnic Assamese and ethnic tribal started to root in the soil. Most of the tribal associations were suspicious about the movement in later phases. The Congress was well acquainted with this situation and knew that it would be beneficial for them. The Hiteswar Saikias Government took stern repressive measure against the agitators that led to creating a rift among the various social groups.

Continuing the legacy of Jawaharlal Nehru, Hiteswar Saikia government urged the central government to implement new law to handle the immigrant issue. The then law minister of Assam Abdul Muhib Majumdar raised the famous IMDT law that was applicable only in Assam. As against the Foreigner Act of 1946, this act made the provision that the prosecutor has to prove himself the charge against the accused immigrant with his own initiative. It was therefore an open secret that the IMDT Act was for the benefit of the migrants and not for the indigenous. Thus, it can inferred that this Act was responsible to keep immigrant issue alive for future, which became one of the important issues of ethnic conflict in later phase.

During the turmoil situation of the Asom movement, an antagonistic rift took root in the politics of Assam. The Congress led Saikia government played the situation for power politics. In addition, that policy had widened the rift between the ethnic Assamese and the ethnic tribes. For instance 'the Saikia government actively patronised the Bodo Sahitya Sabha and promoted it as a rival of Asom Sahitya Sabha' (Barua, 1999). The annual function of the organisation was attended by most members of Saikia cabinet and by contrast declining the share of government resources to reconsider its active involvement in Assam movement (Mishra, 1988) so can therefore be Safely infer that rather than solving the ethnic rift the Congress government tried to utilised it for power politics.

(b) Land and Policy

Land is another issue of the ethnic conflict and violence. The community proprietorship and jhoom cultivation of the ethnic groups of Assam and North East India have opened the road to the immigrants for the acquisition of land. The traditional land pattern of the tribes gives every community a well-defined boundary. However, lack of individual ownership opened it for the acquisition by the outsiders. Again, in the name of environmental preservation, the state has taken initiative to change the pattern of cultivation to permanent mode, which makes a group of tribes, as they have to sell off their land to cope-up the money economy (Partha Pratim Sarma, 2014).

Thus, the land is an important issue of ethnic conscience, which is clearly put by the plain tribal council of Assam in their memorandum submitted to President of India in 1967.

However, the land policy taken by the Government of India under Congress leadership has not been able to minimise the grievances of the tribal people. For the protection of the tribal culture, community and land, the British introduced the line system for the protection of tribal culture, community and land. It is noted that instead of protecting the tribal areas, by this system the non-tribal ruling class got the authority over the areas. The subsequent provincial Sadullah Government in 1942 opened the reserve forest for the settlement of immigrants under "grow more food campaign" (Brahmachoudhury, 1993). It is said "the government stand on land question become an open secret at the local level both officials and interested party found out ways and means to violate the line system". With the initiative and personal interest of the Bordoloi Government to retaliate the demand for the protection of tribal land, introduced the tribal belt and block by the incorporation of chapter X in the Assam Land Regulation act 1886 by an amendment. However, a scrutiny of the act reveals some loopholes. In the amendment version, the very word 'Tribal' was omitted. Again the clause 160 (2) empowered the government to take decision on which classes of people benefited from it. Thus, the decision of protection was left to the discretion of the government. The deputy commissioners were also empowered with the authority to allow transfer of land within the belt and block. The rules under section 171, subsection 5(2a) said that when the settlement has to be given to individual preference shall be given in the following order:

Settlement holder belonging to classes of people under section 162 or mentioned in section 163(2) who have been rendered landless due to flood erosion or earthquake or due to acquisition of their land by the government for public purpose. As the Muslim cultivators who have traditionally settled in Char and Chapori of Brahmaputra which frequently faced the natural calamities of erosion and flood. It becomes difficult to distinguished people of Char areas of long time settlers or new immigrants. So that "protection of tribal peoples land is still an illusion" (The Assam Tribune, 2011).

(c) Language Issue

The language policy of the previous government was not changed and policy of the Congress government of 1980 onward goes on the same footing. For instance, the Board of Secondary Education of the state imposed Assamese language as a compulsory subject in all non-Assamese secondary schools in 1982. This had wounded the injury of the tribal sentiment. Again in spite of the strong protest from the non Assamese people of the state, the Academic Councils of Gauhati University and Dibrugarh University passed a resolution in 1972 to the effect after 10 years, i.e. in 1982 only Assamese would be the soul medium of instruction in the university level. All these policy adversely effected the situation in Assam. It created an atmosphere of misunderstanding between the ethnic Assamese and the ethnic tribes.

Summary and Conclusion

The study partially analysed the situation of Assam politics and the role of Congress government in particular issues that played a determinant role in shaping the ethnic issues in Assam.

The government of independent India, from the very beginning was not able enough to maintain the socio-cultural entity and indivisibility of the region and politics as well. The Constitution of Independent India with its definition on the Tribes of India where the northeastern tribes are placed in the same footing with the tribes of the other parts of India had done the first wrong. Another pertinent mistake was to set the criteria of tribes, which is theoretically a misjudged criteria in the context of Assam and Northeast.

The historical background of the ethnic issue and the governance also reveals that the Indian Government tried to keep this region isolated for the convenience of administration and for fear of overburden. In the later phase of the colonial rule when the importance of the ethnic areas increased from the strategic point, the British government followed a policy of segregation as well as tried to keep a supervised authority on the resources of the areas through the Line System. Later on the Line System, became the key factor for promoting immigration to this soil as the Britishers advocated immigration to the waste land which provided revenues. The Congress Muslim rivalry of the pre-independent period again perverted the issue further. On the basis of the line system, the Scheduled District Act of 1874 was enacted which further made provision for some areas as excluded areas by which those areas were kept aside from the administrative policy of greater India. This attitude and policy thus infused the ethnic tribes of Assam to lean towards secessionism and a feeling of humiliation.

The post-independent political scenario reflects that there was an antagonistic relation and attitude between the central Congress leadership and the provincial Congress. The Central Congress leader Jawaharlal Nehru advocated sheltering refugees in Assam but the State Congress leadership rightfully realised that it would create problem. At this time, the role of Congress was nationalistic for this attitude of the Congress; Assam was saved from the demographic reshuffle, which would make the ethnic Assamese and the tribes a minority in their own soil.

The historical scrutiny also brought forefront some important issues that are closely connected with the ethnic issues of the region and the role of the Congress led government is important for its aftermath. The Congress led government raised those issues in the field of Assam politics, which later became the key factor for fostering ethnicity. One of it is the Language and the other is Immigration and the Land Policy.

The Congress led government's decision in reorganising the provinces of the independent India based on language opened the path for ethnic conflict in Northeast and Assam, where minority combination overshadowed the major Assamese language. Had the government realised the demographic complexity of this region and would followed a policy of recognition to the ethnic language, it was possible to minimise the rift between the ethnic Assamese and ethnic tribes. Instead of it, the Congress government failed to realise the fact and tried to establish linguistic identity forcefully by the Official Language Act of 1960. It was very difficult situation in Assam to recognise one language as an official language because the assimilation process had stopped from the colonial regime. An open-minded government and positive attitude was needed to solve the problem. However, the successive Congress government just continued the colonial legacy and their policy reveals that it only tried to satisfy the majority community. At the time of the Assam Movement, the Congress government just fostered the issue for political benefit. The passing of IMDT, creating controversy on the definition of foreigners, its patronage to the ethnic social organisation are the example of it. The loopholes of the laws and in many tribal development was not restified by the Congress government. Therefore, it reveals that the Congress wanted to keep alive the issue for political benefit.

Thus, a half-heartedness and discriminating mind of the Congress government is reflected in regard to ethnicity. There is many more example of it. From January 1980 encroachment in the tribal areas are stopped in the pretext of law and order. The various plan that were initiated for tribal development under Tribal Sub Plan, Schedule Caste component Plan etc is reported by the Planning Commission that the execution of those plans are far from satisfactory.

Based on the study it can be concluded that a heartiest eagerness and open mindedness is needed to solve the issue from the government and the social organisation. Some suggestions are forwarded in this direction:

- Instead of wasting time in the question of detecting period, strict preventive policies should be made for further influx and immigration by the government.
- As land is one of the major issues of conflict, the government should enact strict land policy for the protection of land and property of ethnic community and the indigenous.
- To solve the language controversy and to find out a common and acceptable way for all the ethnic community, the government should take initiative for an open discussion.

References

1. Brahmachaudhari and Bijaya Laxmi, *Bodos (Kachais) At a Glance,* Tribal Institute, Bongaigaon, 1999.
2. Dilip Hazarika, *Encyclopedia of Assam*, Vol. II, Anmol Publications, New Delhi, 2009.
3. H.K. Barpujari, *The Comprehensive History of Assam*, Publication Board, Assam, 1990.
4. P.S. Dutta, *Autonomy Movement in Assam* (Documents), Omson Publications, New Delhi, 1993.
5. Partha Pratim Sarma, 'Development and Marginalisation: Sociological study of Tribal Land Alianation in Assam' *Asian Journal of Multidisciplinary Studies*, Vol. 2, issue 7, July 2014.
6. Sanjib Baruah, *India against Itself: Politics of Nationality in Assam*, University of Pennsylvania Press, Philadelphia, 1999.
7. The Assam Tribune, September 24, 2011.
8. The Assembly Debates 1982, 1981.
9. The Constitution of India.
10. www.assam.portal
11. www.india.govt.in

3

Gaidinliu Movement, *Sangh Parivar* and the Nagas: A Quest for Identity and Survival

Nakaulang Nriame

Introduction

It is everybodys knowledge that geographical remoteness confined many accounts of struggle against the British by the people of Northeast India among their own people, independent of the so called elite group of nationalist historian. To cite some example, the revolt of Tikendrajit of Manipur, U.Tirot Singh of Meghalaya, Sambudhan Phonglo of Assam, Gomdhar Konwar of Assam etc. has failed to attract the mainstream historians. However, as asserted by the subaltern historians, the history of Indian national movement is completed when it included the contribution of people on their own which are independent of the elites (Ranajit Guha,[1982,3]). Irrespective of the immediate causes and aims of the movements, many such revolt of the subaltern groups including those of Northeast India are therefore a part of Indian freedom movement. Gaidinliu movement in Northeast India is one such movement of the lesser known group. However, Gaidinliu movement is unique in many respects for it was not only a political movement for freedom from the British rulers but also a movement for social upliftment and preservation of tradition and culture of the Zeliangrong, in particular and Nagas in general against the spread of Christianity.

I. Who are the Zeliangrong?

The Zeliangrong are one of the sub-groups of the greater Naga ethnic groups of Northeast India. The Zeliangrong are further sub-divided into three kindred groups, the Zeme, Liangmei and Rongmei. As such the term Zeliangrong is a recent name first coined on 15 February, 1947 by adding together the first three syllable of the Kindred group Zeme, Liangmei and Rongmei (Gangmumei Kamei, 2005, 10). According to traditions, the Zeme, Liangmei and Rongmei were the three brothers of the same parent. But due to long separation, three different but kindred dialect the Zeme, Liangmei and Rongmei emerged which later became their sub-ethnic identity. To undo this wrong and bring them together a term Zeliangrong was coined to give them a common identity. Before the coming of the British and subsequent demarcation of states boundaries, the Zeliangrong Nagas lived in compact areas. But demarcation of modern state boundaries scattered them into three different states. They are scattered in Tamenglong and part of Senapati district of Manipur, Peren, Dimapur and Kohima district of Nagaland, and Dima Hasao (N.C. Hills) and Cachar district of Assam. Even today, if we keep aside the state boundaries their inhabited area is more or less contiguous.

II. Background of Gaidinliu Movement

The root of Gaidinliu movement lies in the anti-British struggle started by Jadonang. Gaidinliu became his most trusted lieutenant and successor. Jadonang was a martyr who was born sometimes in 1905 at Puilun Village of Tamenglong, Manipur and was thus 10 years older to Gaidinliu. As per existing records, Gaidinliu was born on 26 January 1915 at Longkao Village, in remote Tamenglong district of Manipur. According to some authors, political consciousness of Jadonang arose after his return from France and Mesopotamia where he served as a labour corps during the First World War (Asoso Yonou, 1982, 41). However in the absence of any proof and considering his young age, the chance of his enlistment in labour corps is very lean. Initially Jadonang movement centred around socio-religious issues and he acquired leadership by promulgating about the needs of social reforms as he was aware of the conservative and orthodox practices of traditional Zeliangrong community

(Gangmumei Kamei, 2005,148). Using his knowledge of indigenous traditional medicines he also used to heal the sicks. From socio-religious purification and upliftment, he leaned toward political upliftment of his people when in 1928 Jadonang started proclaiming the end of the British Raj and the beginning of Naga Raj (*ibid*,153). Although there is no specific evidence about his direct connections with Indian National Congress workers it is generally believed that, he was aware of Gandhi movement. The main thrust of the public grievances against the British was imposition of new house tax and the coming of Christian missionaries. Jadonang advised his people to resist them. As the British authorities were looking for a pretext to arrest Jadonang, an unfortunate incident occurred in Jadonang's native village where a section of infuriated villagers murdered some Manipuri traders who were accused of violating the village tradition (Thunbui Zeliang, 2005). The village was observing a ritual where an entry of outsider was restricted. However, the traders allegedly not only entered the village but also burnt a fire at the guest house which was not allowed as per rituals tradition. In olden days, Nagas as a whole observed were many such rite and rituals where entries of outsider or going out of the village was not allowed on certain occasions. The breach of which they believe would invite the wrath of the village deities. Ultimately Jadonang was accused of that and was arrested and hanged at Imphal Jail. It was said that Jadonang was away when the entire episode of the murder of the Manipuri traders took place. While on trail Jadonang plea of not guilty was turned down. No proper trail was probably carried out as his people were unfamiliar to the British legal system. The British probably needed a pretext and they found their reason in the report of a surgeon who examined him during his trail. The British surgeon who examined the mental state of Jadonang reported that Jadonang turned abnormal while interpreting a dream but, he was normal while committing a 'crime' (Arkotong Longkumer, 2010, 51). He was hanged at Imphal on 29 August 1931.

III. Progress of the Gaidinliu Movement

Under the guidance of Gaidinliu the movement continued. Gaidinliu was around 17 when the responsibility of leadership was entrusted on her shoulder. Initially, the British administrators in Manipur were not aware of her presence. They came to know of her from *Lambu*– a local agent mostly Manipuri who acted as a bridge between British Officials and Hill people. British Officials records mentioned Gaidinliu movement as semi-religious, semi-martial movement of the Kacha and Kabui Nagas i.e. Zeme and Rongmei Nagas whose sole aims were to achieve 'Naga Raj' (Assam Administration Report-1932). As the movement continued no sooner it became a headache for the government. Gaidinliu asked her people to stop paying annual house taxes for which the British government used to utilise the service of *Lambu*. She also instructed the Naga to resist enlistment as coolies of the visiting or touring British officials and troops.

It needed to be mentioned that the British administrator already had bitter experiences of tackling the hill men during the Kuki rebellion in 1919 and 1920. Therefore, the administrators were put on alert once Gaidinliu activities came to their notice. They were probably taken by surprise as they anticipated the end of Zeliangrong revolt with the death of Jadonang. Therefore, the British Government in Manipur announced of Rs 200 or gun for the apprehension or any information relating to her whereabouts. Later on the amount was not only augmented to Rs 500 but a 10 years full remission of house tax on any village or state which provided information for the arrest of Gaidinliu *(ibid)*.

As the British Government continued their search, Gaidinliu movement spread to other Zeliangrong Naga inhabited area of present Dima Hasao (erstwhile N.C. Hills district) in Assam. Gaidinliu established her base at Hangrum which is the biggest and oldest Zeliangrong Village of the area. As the British government spread their intelligence wings the presence of Gaidinliu at Hangrum village came to the notice of the British troops which resulted in the battle of Hangrum in February, 1932. The oral narration of the battle goes that the first fire from the British troops turned into water as Gaidinliu magic works. This oral narration found its resemblance in the story of Angiolillo and Nikola Suhaj of Italy (E.J. Hobsbawn, 1979) and back home Birsa Munda (1872-1900) of Chotanagpur areas.

Taking this advantage Gaidinliu followers killed a couple of British troops. A reinforcement and new cartridge however killed at least eight followers (Gangmumei Kamei, 2014). After the battle Gaidinliu left the village to safe enclosure and took shelter at another village Hejaichak for six months. Meanwhile many houses were burned down by the British in Assam and Naga hills. From there she moved to the present Naga Hills accompanied by her trusted followers.

IV. Arrest on 17th October, 1932

It was on the onset of winter when Gaidinliu decided to establish her base once again at Puilwa (Polomi) village and started the construction of a wooden fortress. Unfortunately, a section of Naga under the leadership of Dr Haralu who had already converted into Christianity were against Gaidinliu and her followers and helped the British administrators in tracing out Gaidinliu from her hide-out (Asoso Yonou,1982). Dr Haralu later died of the bullet of Indian Army due to mistake identity (B.M. Kaul, 1967).

As Gaidinliu and her followers were preparing to meet the British forces, Mr J.P. Mills, the Deputy Commissioner received the intelligence report and dispatched a strong force of Assam Rifles under the command of Captain Macdonald, accompanied by Mr Hare Blah to Puilwa. Captain Macdonald made a surprise attack on Puilwa village at dawn on 17th October 1932. The rebels were completely surprised and could not offer any effective resistance. (Asoso Yonou,1982, 105) They surrendered and young Gaidinliu was arrested from a house. She was taken to Kohima and brought to Imphal for trial. This way Gaidinliu was arrested and confined to British jail till the British left India in 1947.

The apprehension of the resurgence of Gaidinliu movement however haunted the British government as they continued their enquiry regarding Gaidinliu supporters. As a precautionary measure against any possibility of resurgence of movement many punitive measures were also adopted by the British authorities. They imposed fines by raising the usual house taxes of Rs 2 to Rs 3 and also confiscated the rice of villagers as a punishment (J.H.Hutton). The movement was however continued by her followers but they maintained low profile as the threatening from the British forces still loomed large in all Naga areas.

V. Social Reform of Gaidinliu and the Birth of *Heraka* Sect:

Another dimension of Gaidinliu movement was the preservation of Zeliangrong tradition and culture from the influx of Christianity and western culture. This movement was known by various names like *Kamphai* Movement which was later christened as *Heraka* Movement. Gaidinliu and Jadonang emphasised allegiance to one Supreme God-*'Tingwang'* as opposed to the monotheism as per traditional belief. The reforms also aimed at discarding previous practices like animal sacrifices to various deities and social taboos associated with those practices (Pautanzan Newme, 2010, 4). By reforming evils in their traditions Gaidinliu attempted to thwart the activities of the Christian missionaries to convert the Nagas. The cult was the first of its kind with no comparison in its anti-Christian propaganda in Northeast India (F.S. Downs, 2014, 150).

The anti-Christian stands of Gaidinliu alienated some of the converted Nagas from her movement and ideologies. Not surprisingly, today many of the second generation Naga youth i.e. those who are born of converted parents would question Gaidinliu's identity, as Indian or Nagas especially, as a section of Nagas are still fighting a separatist movement against the union of India (The Naga Blog, 2014).

VI. Gaidinliu Political Movement in Independent India

By 1947, the momentum of Naga separatist movement under the banner of NNC was at its peak. Gaidinliu however, demand for integration of Zeliangrong Naga into a single administrative unit under the union of India. Thus, came into confrontation with the NNC. Not only that, NNC was then dominated by converted Nagas (Christianised Nagas). On the other hand, Gaidinliu was opposed to conversion. As a result of this, a conflict developed with the Naga separatist group and Gaidinliu. Therefore, she went underground in 1960 (Ramkuiwangbe Newme, 2015). She came over ground at the request of Indian government in 1966.

After her surrender, Gaidinliu continued her political movement demanding the integration of Zeliangrong people scattered across Assam, Nagaland and Manipur into a single administrative unit. A memorandum demanding a creation of Zeliangrong district was submitted to the then Prime Minister Indira Gandhi on 22nd February, 1966 (Gangmumei Kamei, 2014, 226). To give a common platform and to garner support from her people, she organised the *Seliangrong Peoples' Convention* in 1980 (*ibid*, 228). The demand for either a district, state or union territories for the Zeliangrong people lingered on till her death in 1993 but it could not be materialised.

VII. Gaidinliu's Place in History Today

In the preface to his well known book, *'The Periphery Strikes back'* Udayan Mishra (2000) mentioned the role of the Naga during the freedom struggle led by Gandhi and the Congress as 'nil'. Sometimes back an English National Daily carried a column lamenting the status of Gaidinliu in history of Indias struggle for independence as unfamiliar, fading from the memory of the masses and has become myth to her own people only (Suchitra Vijayan, 2014). This indignation is not without an element of truth. At the same time one cannot overlook the sheer size of India as a country and numbers of people, inhabited by multiple races and linguistic groups. The account of their struggle for independence from the British rule was not only prolonged in terms of duration but also involves masses from different background with varied methods of struggle. The grievances of the Indians against the British were also characterised by their respective background, region and cultures. For example, the educated Indian middle class were more concerned by the lack of opportunities in government jobs, political liberty etc. In some places, especially rural peasant society, the grievances of the masses was towards their immediate overlords like big Indian Zaminders and Bankers. In the hills the general grievances was against the coming of business people from plains, restriction on the usage of forest resources and expansion of tea gardens on the foothills and to some extent prevention of raids on the plains and imposition of house taxes. In writing the account of such gigantic history it is only obvious that accounts of people from the fringe areas are left out from the notice of historians.

But this is also the fact that great and influential Historians in India and the world over are mainly from the plains educated townsmen who obviously have little interest to understand the hills and marginalised people who are unlike themselves (E.J. Hobsbawn, 1979, 2). Back home in Northeast, the pages of freedom history are mostly covered by the activities confined in the valleys. This is more so because, the hill people in Northeast do not have the tradition of writing their own history.

On the face of such socio-political and cultural settings the omission of Gaidinliu's accounts from the knowledge of common people in the plains is no longer a shocking story. Who was Gaidinliu and why was she so particular for Nehru to crown her 'Rani' of the Nagas? In fact on learning about Gaidinliu's Nehru was so impressed by her story that his only subject of communication with the then Premier of Assam (Bordoloi) was alleged as Gaidinliu centric by some writers. Nehru even forgot to acknowledge many good works done by Bordoloi in his communication to the later (Nirode K Barooah, 2010, 57). But no wonder, many students of history today would just give a surprise stare on any questions about Gaidinliu.

VIII. Sangh Parivar and the Heraka Followers Today

As a fitting tribute to Gaidinliu movement, the Government of India on their part recognised and honours her with *Tamrapatra* in 1972 and *Padma Bhushan* in 1981. A postal stamp was issued in her honour. Unfortunately, Gaidinliu still cut a sorry figure among the Christian converted Nagas. Credit must be given to the *Sangh Parivar* for resurgence of Gaidinliu as a national hero in the recent past. The *Sangh Parivar* found good reason to support her and her people not only for her role in anti-British political movement but also for her anti-Christian stands. As the *Sangh Parivar* subscribe to Savarkar's version of 'Hindu Dharma Society' which encompasses all religion or sect originated in India or Bharat that included Vaidiks, Sanatanis, Jainism, Sikhism, Buddhism, so called animist (Shreerang Godbole, 2010) and therefore the *Heraka* as well. However, it will be interesting to see how the greater Hindu Society (the rest of Hindu society who do not subscribe to Sangh ideology) conceives their Hindu identity vis-a-vis the *Sangh Parivar* notion of 'Hindu Dharma Society'. Hindu society being caste and class ridden, where would the *Sangh Parivar* and the greater Hindu society place the section of people like the *Heraka* who are socially and culturally different, in the Hindu social scheme?

One more aspect of the *Sangh Parivar* and *Heraka* relationship is the later's dependence on the philanthropic works of the *Sangh Parivar*. Many indigenous sects especially *Heraka, Doni-polo, Seng Khasi* etc depend on the *Sangh Parivar* in the field of education. They are indigenous religious group of Arunachal Pradesh and Meghalaya. At a time when the very existing of indigenous sects like *Heraka* of Gaidinliu was threaten by the Christian missionaries, when the government scheme failed to reached the hills of Northeast India, the *Sangh Parivar* came to the rescue of these people (The Morung Express, 2014). The *Sangh Parivar* is offering service among section of hills and backward people. However, while delivering or availing social services there is a silent and slow penetration or assimilation of Hindu elements among the followers of *Heraka*; which are quite alien to original *Heraka,* which in the long run may threaten its unique and distinct identity. While the followers of *Heraka* concede to their being close to *Sangh Parivar* they however asserted their distinct identity different from Hindu and defined their relationship as a sort of mutual and brotherhood alliance. However, a close observation at the functioning of a section of *Heraka* sect gives a clear indication of Hindu influence. In a recent 'Birth Centenary Celebration of Gaidinliu' organised by Zeliangrong *Heraka* Association, NEI held at Boro Haflong, a life size image of *Bharat Mata* was placed on the one side along with Gaidinliu's image on the other side of the stage. The author had an interaction with some senior participants from the village. It was found that they were unaware of who was *Bharat Mata*. This is a clear indication on confusion engulfing the society because of the influence of *Sangh Parivar* among a section of *Heraka* leaders of which the innocent villages are unaware of.

Another interesting effect of the *Sangh Parivar* and *Heraka* alliance is the attitude of converted Nagas towards the followers of Heraka and Gaidinliu. The Christian Naga sees this alliance as anti-Naga (Arkotong Longkumer, 150). This is so because the *Sangh Parivar* also advocated '*Akhand Bharat*' as against any separatist ideology. Christianity itself is however an import faith and thus an alien to Naga traditions. However as majority of the Nagas are Christian, the second and third generation Nagas Christian sees Christianity and Nagas as two sides of the same coins. For them being Christian means being Nagas, which is again a distortion of Naga history for Christianity, was introduced in Naga society in seventeenh Century only. However, Gaidinliu and *Heraka's* close association with *Sangh Parivar* has become a dot for her critics. Some scholars of her society even blame the *Sangh Parivar* for their alleged attempt to 'hijack her (Gaidinliu) narrative into the folds of Hinduism and thus distort the history of Gaidinliu.

Conclusion

Thus Gaidinliu and her movement present a state of Quest for Identity and survival. The movement started against the British regime and the spread of Christianity in British India. After independence, as the majority of their own converted into Christianity, Gaidinliu and her followers are alienated from the mainstream Zeliangrong in particular and Naga society in general because, of their anti-Christian stand. As per recent position, a major chunk of Zeliangrong group in Manipur Hills has embraced Christianity while, those in Imphal valley and Cachar (Assam) has embraced another sect *Tingkao Raguang*, which is akin to *Heraka* (a reform sect of Gaidinliu) and *Paupai Chapriak*. The *Heraka* i.e. Gaidinliu followers are concentrated in Dima Hasao district of Assam and few pockets of Peren District in Nagaland. In Nagaland too those settled in Dimapur and Kohima district has embraced Christianity. Gaidinliu followers are now a tiny minority people who fought for the preservation of their identity and survival. These are the people whose days start with struggle for their basic daily need for survival and for identity. In their daily struggle they are left at the mercy of *Sangh Parivar* and majority Christian counterpart. The *Heraka* choose their close neighbour the *Sangh Parivar*, which in the long run could however deform the original and indigenous identity of *Heraka*. In such a case the demarcation line between Christian missionaries and *Sangh Parivar* becomes blurred.

References

1. Administrative Report of Assam,1932, Pitt River Museum Archive (Online access on 24-11-14).
2. Arkotong Longkumer, *Reform, Identity and Narratives of Belonging*, Continuum International, London, 2010.
3. Asoso Yonuo, *Naga Struggle against the British under Jadonang and Gaidinliu 1925-1947*, Leno Printing Press, Kohima, 1982.
4. B.M. Kaul, *The Untold Story*, Allied Publishers, New Delhi, 1967.
5. E.J. Hobsbawn, the *Primitive Rebels* (Reprint), University of Manchester, Manchester, 1979.
6. F.S. Down, the *Mighty Works of God*, (Reprint), Christian Literature Centre, Guwahati, 2014.
7. Gangmumei Kamei, *History of Zeliangrong Nagas from Makhel to Gaidinliu*, Spectrum Publications, Guwahati, 2005.
8. *Imphal Free Press,* November 21, 2014.
9. J.H. Hutton, *Tour Diary*, Pitt River Museum Archive, Oxford (Online access on 24-11-14).
10. Nirode K Barooah, *Gopinath Bordoloi, the Assam Problem and Nehru's Centre*, Bhabani Press, Guwahati, 2010.
11. Pautanzan Newme, *Heraka, The Primordial Religion,* ZHA, NEI, Haflong, 2010.
12. Ramkui Newme, *Rani Gaidinliu: A Pen Picture*, ZHA, NEI, Haflong. 2010.
13. Ramkuiwangbe Newme, *Rani pui Gaidinliu rasam*, Herigate Foundation, Guwahati, 2015.
14. Ranaji Guha (Ed), *Subaltern Studies I: Writings on South Asian History and Society,* Oxford University Press India, New Delhi, 1982.
15. S.K. Chaubem, *Hill Politics in North East India*, (Third Edition) Orient Blackswan, New Delhi, 2012.
16. S.M.A.W. Chisti, *Political Development in Manipur: 1919-1949*, Kalpaz Publication, New Delhi. 2005.
17. *The Hindu*, February 8, 2014.
18. *The Morung Express*, November 18, 2014.
19. *The Naga Blog,* Access on September, 19, 2014.
20. Thunbui Zeliang, *Haipou Jadonang*, Heritage Foundation, Guwahati, 2005.
21. Udayon Misra, *The Periphery Strikes Back Challenges to the Nation-State in Assam and Nagaland*, Indian Institute of Advanced Study, Simla, 2000.
22. Vijay Chauthaiwale (Ed), *Hindutva in Present Context*, Bharatiya Vichar Manch, Ahmadabad, 2010.

4

The Question of Identity: Nature of the Autonomy Movement among the Mising Tribe of Assam

Rahul Pegu

Introduction

The Misings, an Indo-Mongoloid group of people are settled in the plains of Assam and the hills of Arunachal Pradesh. They are known to the outside world as "Miri" and belonged to the family of Tani People and are close cognate of the Adis of present Arunachal Pradesh. Originally, the Misings were hill dwellers and lived along with the *Adis* in Arunachal Pradesh. They migrated from the eastern Himalayan regions in Tibetan plateau and entered in batches in to the central belt of Arunachal Pradesh. They further moved to the plains of Assam, around the thirteen century A.D. and followed the course of the Brahmaputra River, gradually spreading to other stretches of land lying on the banks of the tributaries of the Brahmaputra River. They retain their mythological, linguistic and institutional affinity with the Adis and the Nisis of Arunachal Pradesh (Tabu Ram Taid, 2013, v). After their migration to the plains, considerable changes have taken place in their ecology, pattern of adaptation, cultivation, and language, rituals, dress and house construction. At present, the Misings are scattered in eight eastern districts of Assam, namely- Dhemaji, Tinsukia, Dibrugarh, Lakhimpur, Sivsagar, Jorhat,Golaghat and Sonitpur. They are also distributed in the Subansiri and East Siang districts of Arunachal Pradesh.

From time of recorded the Mising tribe of Assam have been sharing and staying together with the *Asamiyas* (here Asamiyas means those people who had accepted Assamese language as their mother tongue) in the Brahmaputra Valley. During the colonial as well as post-period, the plains tribal including the Misings could not make any significant progress compared to the *Asamiyas.* Though some progress was made in the post-colonial period they were kept away from the economic and political benefits by the much developed *Asamiya* class. Unlike the hills tribals of Assam, the plains tribal were derived of the autonomy benefits and constitutional safeguards. The areas which were dominated by the plains tribals were created as tribal-blocks and tribal belts during the time of independence. But interestingly, these areas were not spared by the *Asamiya* ruling class and they allowed the non-tribals to purchase land and settle in the tribal blocks and belts which were meant for safeguards and protections of the plains tribals. Likewise, the dialects and languages and the cultures of the plains tribals were neglected during the colonial and post-colonial period (M. Hussain, 1993, 57). This situation did not last long and during the 1960s and 1970s the identity consciousness began to grow among the plains tribals and as a result the government has been paying some attention to develop the plains tribals economic condition, culture and dialects. But the effort of the government is limited to the unlimited problems of the exploited plains tribes.

In the process of consolidation of the ruling Assamese, the plains tribes were derived of the various economic benefits and developments that took place in Assam during the post-independence period. Therefore, the frustration and dissatisfaction of the tribals of Assam was visible in the form of ethnic and autonomy movement from the 1960s and 1970s onwards. The autonomy movement among the Misings of Assam was one of them which ultimately resulted in the creation of the *Mising Autonomous Council (MAC).*

I. Objectives

The objective of this chapter is to assess the causes of the autonomy movements of the Mising community in Assam.

The state of Assam is known for various ethno-cultural groups with their distinct cultures and identity. In the colonial period, the British Government tried to bring together different communities of India with uniform rule of law for their administrative convenience and they were not fully successful due to various religious and other problems that existed in India during that time. After Independence the situation became more acute and the nation building process in India shows state designed policies of homogenization and integration of different ethnic groups within the fold of a dominant language. Moreover, the quest for revivalism and identity were gaining ground throughout the country with more propound in the Northeast due to different geographical and cultural variation of different communities and tribes of the region. The above mentioned problems opened up discontent among many ethnic communities of Northeast which led to the initiation of autonomy movement for their cultural revivalism and establishment of identities. The autonomy movement by the Mising community of Assam to establish separate socio-cultural and political identity is significant one among them. The autonomy movement of the Misings has a long historical background and it culminated in an organized movement during the 1960s and 1970s. There are many causes that contributed to the discontentment among the Mising community which resulted in the form of autonomy movement of the Misings.

II. Data and Methodology

The study was undertaken during 2013-2014 by conducting survey in districts of upper Assam where the Mising population are scattered especially in the Dhemaji district where the Headquarter of the Mising Autonomous Council (MAC) is located. In writing this paper, both primary and secondary sources have been used. Primary sources include oral history, interviews, official records, contemporary newspaper reports etc. Secondary sources include books and journals. A descriptive content analysis of the information obtained from secondary and primary data have been taken up for a comprehensive understanding about the socio-historical background and the growth and genesis of the assertion of ethnic identity of the Misings along with the recent trends and implications of the identity assertion movement of the Misings in Assam.

III. Analysis and Discussions

In the post-colonial period the nation building process in India aimed to build culturally homogeneous states with singular identities. In Assam also similar kinds of efforts were followed by the Assam Government in order to assimilate the tribes in to the Assamese society. The Assamese people backed by the Assam Government followed the *Assamisation* policy and imposed the Assamese language and culture on the tribes against the provisions of the Indian Constitution (P.S. Datta, 1993, 225). These developments of Assam during this period have a far reaching impact on the tribes including the Misings. As a result, the small minority and ethnic groups started to feel the domination of the large group, as the large group started consolidating power and tried to justify its socio-cultural dominance over the minority ethnic groups.

The provisions of Schedule Sixth and Eighth which gives limited tribal autonomy in the form of Autonomous Councils and provisions of special language privileges respectively has influenced and shaped autonomy aspirations in Assam like other parts of the country. It is to be noted that identity consciousness among different ethnic groups in Assam is not new (Bijan Kumar Kunda, 2007, 145). The provisions of sharing political power in the Indian Constitution had definitely influenced and molded the respective aspirations of various ethnic groups demanding autonomy.

Unlike the autonomy movements in other parts of India, the autonomy movements in the Brahmaputra valley is quite different in its nature and character. The most important dimension of the autonomy movements in Assam is the difference between the autonomy movements in the Hills and Plains districts of Assam. In other words, the autonomy movements and aspiration developed first among the hill people of Assam and from the very beginning it were of political in nature and character (P.S. Dutta, 1986,17). On the other hand, the political aspirations among the plains developed later than the hills and were non-political in nature although in course of time it definitely developed its political nature and character.

The first identity consciousness and assertion of the Plains tribes in Assam was visible as early as 1929, when four Memoranda were submitted by some educated tribal leaders of Assam to the Simon Commission on January 4, 1929 and placed their grievances before the Simon Commission. Therefore, we can assume that the identity consciousness of both the Hill tribes and the Plains tribes were visible during the colonial period and the colonial government placed all the hill districts together with the North East Frontier Tract by the Government of India Act, 1935 (Bijan Kumar Kunda, 2007, 147-148). But the Act of 1935 did not benefit the plains tribals of Assam and benefited only the hills tribals of Northeast India.

After independence the issue of autonomy and question of identity became more acute and pronounced among the tribals- both hills and plains which ultimately led to the disintegration of Assam. In the subsequent years with the mounting pressure from the tribals of Assam the Congress government implemented the provision of Sixth Schedule which provided autonomous administrative areas in the hills district of Assam. But this implementation of the Sixth Schedule was only in paper and not in spirit. Moreover it was only for the hill tribals and the plains tribals were derived of this provision.

After the break up composite Assam in the 1970s, the Plains Tribal Council of Assam (PTCA) which stood for the plains tribals of Assam including the Misings held a meeting in Lakhimpur district on 18th April, 1967 and submitted a memorandum to Dr. Zakir Husain, the then President of India on May 20th. The Plains Tribal Council of Assam under the presidentship of Shri Biruchan Doley submitted the memorandum to the President of India demanding full autonomy in the predominantly plains tribal areas of Assam. The demands included:

(a) Adequately protect the tribals land

(b) Preservation of their language, culture, customs etc.

(c) Effective check to economic exploitation of tribals by non-tribals

(d) Prevent political domination by non-tribals over tribals and imposition of anything which would disrupt their traditions and customs (Memorandum to the President of India, 1967).

The impact of the assertion, in whatever magnitude and forms was obvious. It led to a cultural revivalism process in the Mising community led particularly by the educated middle class.

There are various reasons which were responsible for the ethno-autonomy movements of the Misings tribe of Assam. Main important reasons are-

Like the other tribals of Northeast, the Mising tribe also is agriculturists and their main sources of livelihood are derived from agriculture. But with the growth of Mising population in the last one hundred years and pouring of large number of Bangladeshi immigrants into the tribal areas resulted in the crises of land among the growing Mising population. Apart from the Bangladeshi immigrants, local greedy non-tribal businessmen, money-lenders and traders also have been occupying the lands belonging to the Mising tribe. Moreover, the Assam Land and Revenue Regulation Amendment Act, 1947 which constituted several tribal belts and blocks in order to restrict transfer of land by sale, mortgage, lease, agreement, exchange or otherwise, to protect the tribal land from any kind of encroachment is only in paper and not implemented in spirit. All these created serious problems in the Mising society. According to Verrier Elwin :

"... the first cause of tribal depression was the lost of their land and forests. This had the effect so enervating the tribal organism that it has no interior resistance against infection by a score of other serious evils" (Verrier Elwin, 2002).

This statement of Elwin is applicable to the Mising society because Mising inhabited land is occupied by many immigrants and local non-tribals by using unscrupulous means. This has created serious situations and question of identity and securities among the tribe.

Apart from loosing of land to other non-tribals and immigrants, the important reason for the grievances of the

Mising tribe is the failure on the part of the Assam Government to adopt and implement permanent and effective flood and erosion control machinery and measures to solve the flood problems in the Mising inhabited areas. The homeland of the Mising tribe is cursed by nature where frequent and recurring flood and erosion washed away and destroy hundreds of hectares of cultivable land and rendered thousands of Misings farmers homeless and landless in their own homeland (Memorandum to P.V. Narasimha Rao, 1993). Moreover, the great earthquake of 1950 had altered and changed the very geographical location and landscape of entire Assam including the Mising homeland and the Brahmaputra River and its tributaries changed its direction which causes flood and erosion in the agricultural lands and as a result the fertility of the soil is destroyed. Despite this no proper help and services are rendered by the Assam Government which created a feeling of alienation from the mainstream Assamese society.

Anti-tribal attitude of the government is another main reason for the ethno-autonomy movement of the Mising people of Assam. Majority of the Mising inhabited areas are underdeveloped and no development programme is done for the Mising community either by the administrators or by the government. The policies and programmes' implemented by the state government are always antagonistic to the rights and interests of the tribals including the Mising tribe (Memorandum to the President of India, 1967). Under these circumstances, no developments and progress can be expected in any fields.

The another important factor for the ethnic movements of the Mising community is the *Assamisation* policy of the Assam Government and the Assamese people has already posed a threat to the very existence of the Mising tribe in Assam. They are making vigorous attempts to forcefully impose Assamese language and culture upon the tribals including the Mising tribe of Assam. The Assamese people backed by the State Government tried to assimilate the tribals into the Assamese society violating the Indian Constitution (*ibid*). This attitude and *Assamisation* policy of the Assamese people and the State Government had created identity crisis among the Misings of Assam. As a result, ethnic movement among the Misings is inevitable.

One of the main causes which are responsible for the alienation of the Misings from the mainstream of Assamese society is/was the attitude of the Assamese people towards the tribals in general. In real sense, the Assamese people during the Ahom period and till today never accepted the tribals as a part and parcel of Assamese society, though in theory they give a motivated slogan of Greater Assamese Nationality. Their general attitude is/was always anti-tribal. The Assamese people want to dominate the Misings and they are always against the special facilities and provisions given by the Constitution of India. They always follow the expansionist policy to capture and dominate all corners of Assam including the Mising inhabited areas. Moreover, in the political field also the Assamese people never want to share the political power with the tribals because they want to dominate the tribals including the Misings for an indefinite period (Memorandum to Rajiv Gandhi, 1987). They are opposed to any kinds of democratic movements by the Misings and cannot tolerate the existence of Tribal organisations including the Plains Tribal Council of Assam (PTCA), Takam Mising Porin Kébang (TMPK), Mising Autonomous Council (MAC), etc.

Due to heavy pressure from various Mising organisations, the Government of Assam have decided to introduce the Mising language with Roman script as a subject language for Mising students in the schools of Mising dominated areas especially in the primary levels. But the half-hearted attitude and policy of the Assam government resulted in the non-implementation of this decision with zeal and sincerity (Memorandum to P.V. Narasimha Rao, 1993). This half-hearted attitude of the Assam Government created frustration and dissatisfaction among the Mising people and question of their identity.

Backwardness of the Mising dominated areas created a kind of dissatisfaction and alienation among this tribe of Assam. A part from natural calamities like flood and erosions that cause untold miseries to the Mising people, the indifference of the Assam government to develop the backward Mising inhabited areas is one of the main factors for movement among the Misings. Majority of the Mising areas are without or with no regular electricity and without proper motorable road. Till 1985, the entire Misings areas have had only one college with facilities for science education in Degree level. The backwardness of Misings areas in every field resulted in a sense of alienation.

Article 46 of the Indian Constitution states that government should strive to protect and promote the education and economic interests of the members of the scheduled castes and scheduled tribes and other backward classes and to safeguard them from exploitation (Khireswar Borah, 2013, 12). But these constitutional provisions are only in paper and the government is yet to implement it whole heartedly. This attitude of the government led to the fear and discontentment among the Mising community.

Yet another important cause which contributed much to the autonomy movement among the Misings was the attitude of the All Assam Student Union (AASU) and the Asom Gana Parishad (AGP). The All Assam Student Union is a banner for all students including the tribal students of Assam but its leaders are dominated by non-tribals and instead of uniting all the tribals and non-tribals students it took the character of anti-tribals. Likewise, the AGP instead of uniting all people of Assam irrespective of caste, creed, race etc. started acting as the guardian of Assamese speaking people only. When the Assam Scheduled Castes and Scheduled Tribes Act 1978 which was meant for the reservation of SC and ST in various posts and services was passed in the Assam Legislative Assembly there was resentment and opposition among the anti-tribal lobbies in Assam. The AASU even went further and demanded abolition of all tribal belts and blocks, reservations of jobs for ST in various posts and services, scholarships for ST students etc. in the state (Niru Hazarika, 2005, 242). This attitude of the mother student organisation alienated the Takam Mising Porin Kébang (TMPK) and the student unions of other tribals in the state and as a result Assam witnessed an uncompromising struggle of the tribals against the anti-tribal lobbies and forces.

When the AGP came to power the situation turned from bad to worse with many tribal bodies demanding autonomy due to the anti-tribal activities of the ruler. The AGP came to power as a result of the Assam Agitation where every people of Assam irrespective of caste, creed and race joined hands together in order to safeguard the interest of the every local inhabitant in Assam. But the AGP after coming to power not only betrayed the tribal people of Assam but also started discrimination in the field of education, services and posts (*ibid*, 242). This attitude and step-motherly treatment of the rulers left the tribals including the Misings of Assam with no alternatives but to demand for autonomy where they can safeguard their own interests.

Lastly, the root causes of the ethnic movement among the tribals of Assam including the Misings lies in the economic backwardness of the tribal areas in Assam and this economic and political dissatisfaction was reflected in the autonomous movement (B.C. Bhuyan, 1989, 148) among the Mising tribe in a large scale. The problem became more acute when the AGP government came to power with its inherently intransigent ideology and narrow political outlook.

Thus, the development and growth of ethnic ideology and its subsequent movement had an adverse impact on various ethnic groups in Assam. Moreover with the decline of Congress government there was no political party to present an alternative ideology and hence it was natural that the ruling party popularises the local ideology again and again among the tribes in order to gain the support of the innocent tribals of Assam. This attitude of the ruling classes towards the tribals of Assam was dominant features of politics in Assam during the 1970s. This has a deep impact on the autonomy movement of the Misings of Assam.

All these factors contributed to the ethnic and autonomy movement among the Misings and emerged as a distinct nationality parallel to the development of the Assamese speaking population. This ethnic development found strong expression in the form of aspiration for right to self-determination among the Misings. Therefore, the Government of India formed a Three Member Expert Committee on Plains Tribals of Assam (ECOPTA) headed by Bhupinder Singh in 1993. The Committee was formed in the wake of Bodoland movement with the objectives of giving legislative, administrative and financial autonomy to the plains tribes including the Misings living in the north bank of Brahmaputra (Bhupinder Singh, 2002, 100). The Three Expert Committee supported the Mising peoples demand for autonomy and thereby recommended the granting of autonomous council similar to that of Bodos.

The growing popularity of the autonomy movement among the Misings forced the Assam Government to come to the negotiation table. Hiteswar Saikia, the then Chief Minister of Assam announced the grant of Autonomy to the Misings and invited both the Takam Mising Porin Kébang (TMPK) and Mising Mimag Kébang (MMK), the two leading organisations to the negotiation table. As a result of this negotiation the government of Assam decided to create an Autonomous body named as Mising Autonomous Council (MAC). The written proposal of the government could not satisfy the Mising people. About nine rounds of talks were held between the Government of Assam and the leaders of TMPK and MMK but failed to come to any fruitful solution. The state government decided to break the movement and created overnight an organisation named Mising Autonomous Demand Committee (MADC) to divide the Mising people (Ranoj Pegu, 2012,154-155). This move of the State government created confusion and fear among the Mising people to a great extent.

Meanwhile, the Mising Bané Kébang (MBK) and MADC agreed to accept the proposal of the government including the boundaryless Mising Autonomous Council. This move of the state government as well as the MBK and MADC created resentment among the Mising people and under the banner of TMPK and MMK there was strike and protest in the Mising dominated areas which soon turned violent and resulted in the killing of two persons and injuring many others including women and school going children. The state government came into agreement with the leaders of the MBK and MADC when most of the leaders of the TMPK-MMK were in jail. The agreement between the leaders of the MBK and MADC and the state government resulted in the signing of the so called Mising

Accord on 14 July, 1995. In the following year in 1996, AGP government came to power and after two years, in 1998 entered in to another agreement with the leaders of the TMPK and MMK and promised to demarcate boundaries of the Mising Autonomous Council and to hold elections in a democratic manner. Accordingly, a High Power Committee headed by Cabinet minister Thaneswar Boro was appointed by the State Government to suggest suitable amendment in to the Mising Autonomous Council Act. However, this committee failed to come to any fruitful solution. Therefore, another Ministerial Sub Committee headed by Dr. Bhumidhar Barman was appointed in the wake of mass movement to include MAC in to the Sixth Schedule. The committee recommended certain amendment to the MAC Act, 1995 (*ibid*, 155-157). Thus, the Mising Autonomous Council was given final shape to hold election in a democratic manner as a result of the ethnic movement of the Misings.

The Mising Autonomous Council was constituted by the Government of Assam under the Mising Autonomous Council Act, 1995 on 4th October 2005 for all round development in the area of economic, educational, socio-cultural and ethnic identity of Mising People as well as all other communities residing in the council area. The Council was run on ad-hoc basis with nominated interim bodies for long fifteen years and then by an Administrator for three years, after which the first elections were held in October, 2013 and 34 Members were elected to constitute the General Council which assumed its office on 6th November, 2013. The Headquarters of the MAC is located at Gogamukh in Dhemaji district of Assam and covers compact 'Core Area' as well as 'Satellite Areas' in eight districts namely, Dhemaji, Lakhimpur, Sonitpur, Golaghat, Jorhat, Sibsagar, Dibrugarh and Tinsukia. The population figures as per 2001 Census are as follows: (Mising Autonomous Council Act, 1995).

IV. Findings and Conclusion

Thus, it is seen that the ethnic and autonomy movement among the Mising tribe of Assam is mostly due to the antagonistic policies and programms' implemented by the Assam government and the attitudes of the Assamese people towards the tribals in general and Mising tribe in particular. There are various provisions in the Constitution of India for the protections

MAC	Total Village	Total Population	SC Population	ST Population	% of ST Population
Core Area	1289	638977	30165	428207	67%
Satellite Area	392	246002	18421	160847	65%
Grand Total	1681	884979	48586	589054	66%

MAC	Total Village	Total Population	SC Population	ST Population	% of ST Population
Core Area	1289	638977	30165	428207	67%
Satellite Area	392	246002	18421	160847	65%
Grand Total	1681	884979	48586	589054	66%

and preservation of tribals belts and blocks, language, culture, etc. But these provisions were not implemented by the State Government properly and these provisions were only in name and not in spirit. Moreover, the passing of the Assam Official Act of 1960 in a conspiracy to assimilate the tribals in to the fold of Assamese society created a wave of identity quest not only among the Misings but all over North-East India. This attitude of the State Government had created dissatisfactions among the Mising tribe and in the process give birth to the ethnic and autonomy movement among the Mising tribes of Assam. With the rising ethnic movement among the Misings, the anti-tribals and anti-Misings attitude of the Assamese people is growing more and more with the passage of time which poses a threat to the very existence of united Assam. This gloomy situation will not improve as long as the anti-tribal lobbies continue to exercise political, social, economic and administrative powers in the State. Therefore, the exercise of political and administrative power by the Misings themselves alone can protect and safeguard the interest and rights of the Misings in every field.

References

1. B.C. Bhuyan, *Political Development of the North East*, Vol. I, Omsons Publications, New Delhi, 1989.
2. Bhupinder Singh, *Autonomy Movement and Federal India*, Rawat Publications, New Delhi, 2002.
3. Bijan Kumar Kunda, *Politics in the Brahmaputra Valley since the Assam Accord*, Om Publications, New Delhi, 2007.
4. Khireswar Borah, *Satellite Autonomous Councils of Assam and the Tribal Law(s), The Mising Autonomous Council (MAC)*, Vol. II, Advanced Law and Allied Publishers Group, Guwahati, 2013.
5. M. Hussain, *The Assam Movement: Class, Ideology and Identity*, Manak Publications Pvt. Ltd., New Delhi, 1993.
6. Memorandum to P.V. Narasimha Rao, Honourable Prime Minister of India, Submitted by the Mising Mimag Kebang (Mising National Action Committee) and Takam Mising Porin Kébang (All Mising Students' Union), New Delhi, 15 September 1993.
7. Memorandum to Shri Rajiv Gandhi, Honourable Prime Minister of India, by Binai Kr. Basumatari, Chairman, United Tribal Nationalists Liberation Front (UTNLF), dated 10th November, 1987, Darrang, Assam.

8. Memorandum to the President of India, submitted by Shri Biruchan Doley, Samar Brahma Choudhury, Charan Narzary on behalf of the Plains Tribal Council of Assam, Dated: May 20th, 1967, Kokrajhar, Assam.
9. Memorandum to the President of India, submitted by Shri Biruchan Doley, Samar Brahma Choudhury, Charan Narzary on behalf of The Plains Tribal Council of Assam, dated May 20, 1967, Kokrajhar, Assam.
10. *Mising Autonomous Council Act, 1995, vide Govt. Notification No. TAD/BC/358/2005/27, Government of Assam, 4th October, 2005.*
11. Niru Hazarika, *Ethnic Autonomy Question in N.E. India: Search for an Answer*, Spectrum Publications, Guwahati, 2005.
12. P.S. Datta, *Autonomy Movements in Assam (Documents)*, Omsons Publications, New Delhi, 1993.
13. P.S. Dutta (Ed.), *Electoral Politics in North East India*, Omsons, New Delhi, 1986.
14. Ranoj Pegu, Autonomy Movement of the Mising People, in J. J. Kuli (ed.) *The Misings: Their History and Culture*, Kaustubh Prakashan, Dibrugarh, 2012, pp.154-155.
15. Tabu Ram Taid, *Mising Folks Tales*, Sahitya Akademi, New Delhi, 2013.
16. Verrier Elwin, *A Philosophy for NEFA*, 1949, cited in C K Sharma, 'Tribal Land Alienation: Government's Role', *Economic and Political Weekly*, Vol 36, No. 52, 2002.

II

Culture

5

Tracing the Rabhas of Goalpara through the Perspectives of Customs and Rituals

Himasnata Dutta Sarkar

Introduction

The Indian scenario has been multi-cultural and diverse in many forms. The landmass is filled with different groups and communities which makes India unique from the rest. Variety is the hallmark of Indian society. And this variety has been an ongoing process. It is a place of various Communities co-exisence. Each group is unique in it and differs from each other in many ways. This paper is an attempt to understand and analyse the concept of 'tribe' as a whole society. It is also to be marked that the term tribe is not a homogenous group and one cannot have a uniform understanding of the term 'tribe'. This chapter focuses on the Rabha tribe of Assam and attempts to understand and analyse the ethnic identity of the tribe and interplay of various elements of the tribe such as customs and rituals in forming its identity.

The term tribe as defined by the *Oxford Dictionary of Sociology* refers to a social group bound together by kin and duty and associated with a particular territory. Members of a tribe share the social cohesion associated with the family, together with the sense of political autonomy of a nation. The term 'tribe' as a category has been described as a colonial construction (Beteille, 1995, Singh, 1999 cited in Xaxa, 1999, 1519). The colonial administrators used the term in general parlance referring to a group of people claiming descent from common ancestors and living in a primitive or barbarous condition. The early British administrators did not use to study the groups from caste/tribe perspective; rather they studied them as human groups/communities. The description of tribe has been done differently by many from time to time. In the census reports of 1881 when the first 'proper' all-India census was undertaken, the term used was not 'tribe' but 'forest tribe' under a broader category of agricultural and pastoral caste. Risley and Gait, in charge of the 1901 and 1911 censuses respectively, added 'so-called animists' in the table for caste and others. Tribes were defined as those that practised 'animism' (*ibid*). Marten at the census of 1921 followed the same practice, only changing the heading of "Animism" to "Tribal Religion". Hutton at the 1931 census went on to substitute the term "Primitive Tribes" for "Forest Tribes" (Ghurye, 1963). Ghurye went on to describe the scheduled tribes as 'Backward Hindus' while looking from the broader category of Hindu society (Xaxa, 1999). Ghurye in his book, *The Scheduled Tribes* attempted to present his conceptualisation of the term 'Backward Hindus'. He maintained that the so-called aboriginal tribes of India have migrated from somewhere else to India and so the history of internal movement of people is not known, they cannot be considered to be autochthones of their present tracts. It was also mentioned that the aboriginals have a tendency to integrate themselves into the Hindu society. Ghurye in his writing quoted Bradley-Brit who pointed out the strong tendency among "almost all the aboriginal tribes" to embrace Hinduism when they came in contact with it (Ghurye, 1963). He mentioned that "(T)he so-called Aborigines who form the bulk of the Scheduled Tribes and have been designated in the Census as Animists are best described as Backward Hindus" (*ibid*. 20).

During the colonial rule the term Scheduled Tribe was introduced which was later adopted by the Constitution of India as well. "A tribe becomes Scheduled Tribe only when it is notified as Scheduled Tribe under Article 342 of Constitution of India" (Suresh, 2014, 794). According to the 12th Five Year Plan of

India, "the Scheduled Tribes (STs), with a population of 84.33 million as per 2001 Census constituted 8.2 per cent of the country's population and have been traditionally concentrated in about 15 per cent of the country's geographical areas, mainly forests, hills, undulating inaccessible areas. Most of them live in isolated groups in relatively remote areas which made it more difficult to deliver essential services to them and has also made it much more difficult for them to benefit from the acceleration of overall growth than is the case with SCs. Out of the total ST population, 2.59 million (3.07 per cent) belong to Particularly Vulnerable Tribal Groups (PVTGs) earlier referred to as Primitive Tribal Groups (PTGs). There are 75 identified PVTGs spread across 17 States/UTs" (12th Five Year Plan, 228).

It is often seen that many ethnographic accounts do not trouble about having a general definition of tribe. They provide working definitions that apply to a particular case under examination. To have a definition of tribe that will fit all the existing communities that have been defined as tribes has been proved difficult. The nineteenth century view on the tribe was that the tribe represented not only a particular type of society but also a particular stage of evolution. There are tribes defined on the basis of criteria like isolation, self-sufficiency, primitive etc (Béteille, 1998). Morgan posited three stages of evolution based on technological inventions where society had progressed from a hunting-and-gathering stage i.e. "savagery" to a stage of settled agriculture i.e. "barbarism" and then on to an urban society possessing a more advanced agriculture i.e. "civilisation" (Britannica Encyclopaedia). Earlier tribes were being known as migratory group as they were engaged in shifting cultivation rather than settled cultivation, which required movement from one place to another. With the changing scenario, the situation in the tribal societies also changed. With the increasing population in India, the scarcity of space emerged as an important issue. "In India, the history of interaction between tribal and nontribal populations has been a long and complex one in which both population have undergone many transformations through usurpation, miscegenation, and migration. By the middle of the nineteenth century, what are called tribes today had on the whole been either subordinated or marginalised economically, politically, and socially" (Beteille, 1998, 198).

Xaxa maintained that in India, there has been ways in which tribes are being tried to be understood in relation to caste, peasantry and social differentiation. It has generally been assumed that tribe and caste represent two different forms of social organisations governed by different principles. Caste groups are being regulated by the hereditary division of labour, hierarchy, the principle of purity and pollution, civic and religious disabilities, etc, and tribes being characterised by the absence of the caste attributes. Tribal society is said to be governed by kinship bonds whereas inequality, dependency and subordination are regarded as an integral features of caste society. Caste groups are supposed to be heterogeneous in nature while tribes are supposed to be homogenous in nature. (Xaxa, 1999). While being differentiated from caste category, the tribes are depicted in certain ways that the non-tribal have engrained crystallised images of their tribal counter-part. "Anthropological writings, popular articles, and coffee-table books on tribes reinforce certain images in which they wish to project them. These writings and pictures earnestly wish to captivate the readers' attention, thereby promoting their sale. For serving this interest, it would be better if they succeeded in capturing the "bisarreness" of tribes, showing them as head-hunters, tattooed, cannibals, practising some strangest forms of marriage with their family, cooking, disposing of their dead, wearing more of jewellery than clothes, and living in compact pockets, having least communication with the outside world. These are the images in which non-tribal wish to see their tribal brethren" (Srivastav, 2008, 30). While depicting the differences between the tribe and caste, attempts have been made in the post colonial period to show the close interaction between the tribes and the larger Hindu civilisation. The conceptualisation of the process of interaction has been done differently by different scholars from time to time. Xaxa cited different scholars in his article *Transformation of Tribes in India: Terms of Discourse* having different takes on the conceptualisation of the process of interaction. For instance, Sinha (1958) viewed tribes from the dimension of little tradition which cannot be understood unless it is in relation to great tradition. Beteille (1986) views it more in terms of distance from state and civilisation in contexts where tribe and civilisation coexist. Though the distinction is maintained, the two are treated not as isolated but in interaction with each other. One of the dominant modes in which the transformation of the tribal society has been conceived is in terms of a tribe getting absorbed into a society that represents civilisation. Scholars like Kosambi (1975) has referred to tribal elements being fused into the general society while N K Bose (1941) makes a reference to tribes being absorbed into Hindu society. Tribes are said to have accepted the ethos of caste structure and to have got absorbed within it. The transformation of tribes into castes is conceived to occur through methods which have been diversely conceptualised. Sanskritisation is seen as another method through which tribes are absorbed into Hindu society. The other significant method of tribal assimilation is what Sinha (1962, 1987) calls the state formation. According to him the process of acculturation, hinduisation and social stratification within the village could not be properly understood unless the data are examined in the broader context of the formation of the principality. He adds that the formation of the state provided the decisive socio-political framework for the transformation of the tribal system into the regional caste system (Xaxa, 1999). M.N. Srinivas in his book *Social Change in Modern India* talked about the subject of social change as a vast and complex one which needs an adequate understanding of the various aspects of the society. He regards Sanskritisation to be one of the various processes which leads to the social change. He defined Sanskritisation as the process by which a "low" Hindu caste, or tribal or the other group, changes its customs, ritual, ideology, and way of life in the direction of a high, and frequently 'twice-born caste'. According to him, Sanskritisation is generally accompanied by, and often results in, upward mobility for the caste in question; but mobility may also occur without Sanskritisation and vice versa. However, the mobility associated with Sanskritisation results only in positional changes in the system and does not lead to· any structural change (Srinivas, 1966). As mentioned above, the tribes do not attain higher status in the Hindu caste fold even after getting integrated into the Hindu caste society. Xaxa puts forward some questions relating to it in his article as in "Why do tribes Hinduise themselves even though they attain no higher status? Do they want to be absorbed into the larger society? Well, this may have been the case in the past but no longer. Today acculturation means among the tribes that adopting the ideas, values and practices of the dominant community rather than being part of that society by assuming a caste status" (Xaxa, 1999, 1521).

Tribal societies are studied in India not only in relation to caste societies but also in relation to peasant societies. There are differences among the two societies mentioned above as the tribal societies are regarded as whole societies. The tribal societies are self-sufficient, having kinship bonds, having mechanical solidarity, egalitarian etc while "in contrast, peasant society is seen not as a whole society but as a part of a society with part culture. Shanin (1973) defines peasants as small agricultural producers who with the help of simple equipment and family labour produce mainly for their own consumption and for the fulfilment of their obligation to the holders of political and economic power. Tribes have been classified on the basis of the characteristic mode of livelihood. Bose (1971, 4-51), for example, divided the tribal people into: (1) hunters, fishers and gatherers; (2) shifting cultivators; (3) settled agriculturists using plough and plough cattle; (4) nomadic cattle-keepers, artisans, agricultural labourers; and (5) plantation and industrial workers. Some of these are considered no different from the non-tribal peasant population. The process of 'peasantisation' among tribes in Indian history is attributed largely to cultural contact with the non-tribal world. It has also been attributed to the development strategy of Indian state especially after independence. In support of the theory of the transformation of tribes into peasants some scholars have focused on the fact that tribes have moved away from hunting/fishing or shifting agriculture to terraced or settled agriculture. Others note that tribes have shifted to plough agriculture. In fact, more often than not tribes have been described as peasants without the criteria used for defining peasants being adequately applied. Some scholars describe them as peasants because they see little difference in the way tribes make their living from the way the larger non-tribal community does" (Xaxa, 1999, 1523).

Tribes has also been tried to be understood in terms of social differentiation as mentioned by Xaxa. It has been seen that in earlier times tribes in India are not only being analysed in relation to caste category or peasant but also with concepts like class differentiation. Xaxa pointed out that homogeneity had been an important criterion of a tribal society in earlier times but not anymore. Tribal societies have been turning into heterogeneous societies. Along with it occupational differentiations within a tribal society has been noticed, which in turn has led to the growth of economic, cultural, political, social change within the tribal society. The rise of the class factor within the circle of tribal sone is clearing visible from such situations.

The tribal population of the country is tried to be understood in terms of some fixed ideas which is carried forward from past. This chapter is an attempt to explore and analyse the Rabha tribe of Goalpara district of Assam, not merely as a Scheduled Tribe but as a tribe whose ethnic origin and identity is unique from others and whose customs, tradition, rituals etc enhances its identity as a tribe.

Ethnic Identity of the Rabhas

The ethnic individuality of the tribe as well as the origin of the tribe has been expressed in diverse views by many scholars. The origin of the Rabhas has many traditional stories linked up. One such story prevalent among the Rabhas published elsewhere (1960) was reproduced in "The Peoples of Assam by B.M. Das".

In the remote past, Dadan was a powerful King of the Rabhas. He was married to Toba Rani. He was originally believed to be the leader of a group of people at Sonitpur (Tespur) under the mythological Hindu King named Ban. Probably Dadan was the General of the then King i.e. Ban. After the death of Ban, Dadan had to fight with some of the east and of the south kings of Sonitpur. He won the first battle but being defeated in the second he had to leave the place with some of his followers and proceed to Bhutan in search of aid and shelter but they were refused entry by the King of Bhutan. From there they proceeded towards the Brahmaputra Valley and reached Dubu Hill near modern Lakhipur where he established his first kingdom and gradually started expanding his area of rule. His fort was at Tikirikilla and in the nearby area he used to train his soldiers. Dadan was a very brave warrior and he had to resist the aggression of many other kings. In his last battle he lost many of his soldiers and he along with his family fled to Tura. During that time he was hunted down by his enemy rulers and was killed by a soldier of the latter ruler. The descendants and the followers of Dadan are recognised as the Rabhas of Assam. Another such story prevalent among the Rangdani Rabhas is that a section of the tribe lived in the Garo Hills along with the Garos. And very often the two tribes came into conflict and finally the Rangdani Rabhas had to leave their habitat in hills and came down to settle in the plains. There are many other stories related to the migration of the Rabha people which is passed orally from generation to generation having some changes in the names of the persons as well as places. All this stories reveal the settlement process of the Rabhas in Goalpara (Das, 1987, 45-46).

The Rabhas are a distinct tribal community belonging to the Indo-Mongoloid racial group (Singha, 2012) and are speaker of Tibeto-Burman languages. The early settlement of the group were said to be found in different historic time in Yangtse Kiang and Hoang-ho river in south-west China. At one point of time a group of Tibeto-Burman people left their original habitat and moved towards south. One group moved towards further south to reach as far as Southeast Asia, while one group migrated westward following the foothills of the Himalayas and reached as far as Nepal, Tibet and Bhutan, and later they migrated towards south to occupy the hills and valleys of Assam. Some members of the first group moving towards Southeast Asia changed their direction and moved westwards to enter into different parts of northeast India. All these people scattered in different parts of Northeast India and came to be known by various names like Boro, Naga, Kuki, Rabha, Tiwa etc (Das, 1987).

The Rabhas are one of the plain tribes of Assam who are scattered in different parts of the area. As per the 2001 Census total Rabha population of Assam is 277517. It is 8.4 per cent of the total ST population of Assam. The Rabha tribe is distributed in the district of Goalpara, Kamrup, Darrang, Dhubri, Nalbari and Kokrajhar. Beside Assam they are also found residing in Garo Hills of Meghalaya, and in Jalpaiguri and Cooch Behar District of West Bengal (Chakrabarty, 2012).

Different writers had shown five to seven endogamous sections of the tribe. E.A. Gait had shown 5 sub-tribe of the Rabhas such as 'Rangdani', 'Pati', 'Maitory', 'Dahuri' and 'Kachari'. Rev. Endle had presented seven sub-tribes of the Rabhas which are 'Rangdaniya', 'Maitoriya', 'Pati', 'Koch', 'Bitliya', 'Dahuriya', and 'Sangha' Rabhas (Bordoloi, 1987, 120). This division of the tribe has very interesting story behind it. It was believed that the King of the Rabhas i.e. Dadan decided to celebrate 'Baikho Puja' collectively in a place named Aathiyabari in Kamrup District for the very first time. For the preparation of the entire occasion the people were divided into groups so that the works are carried on smoothly without any chaos. So the divisions were made on the basis of the works. Those people who were grouped together to bring stones from the hills for establishing the totems for the celebration were known as the Rangdania Rabha as in Rabha language 'Rang' refers to stone. Similarly other groups got their names according to the works assigned. The Pati Rabhas were provided the task of making arrangements of leaves i.e. 'Pat' to serve the food to the people. The Maitory Rabhas were handed over the task of cooking rice as 'Mai' in Rabha language means rice. The Dahuri Rabhas were allotted the task of keeping the birds away from the place where the celebration was held. The Sunga Rabhas were asked to make 'Sunga' i.e. long hollow vessel created from bamboo to serve the local liquor. The Bitliya Rabhas had to entertain the people present in the Puja with their performance and humour. The Hana Rabhas were assigned to do the killing of the animals which were used in the purpose of the puja. There are some more sub-tribes of the Rabha tribe which are very small in sise and are residing in some peripheral areas of the state. However, B.M. Das believed that the Rangdani, Pati and the Maitory Rabhas used to enjoy superior status compared to other sub-groups of the tribe (*ibid.*,120).

The Rabha language is confined only to the Rangdani and the Maitory Rabhas. The Koch or Koccha Rabhas also speak the same language but their word structure and phonetics differ slightly. Other minor groups like the Dahuris, Sunga, Bitliyas speak their own dialects and dialectical variations in them are quite considerable. The Pati, Hana, Totlas and other few groups have discarded their mother tongue and adopted Assamese as their language (*ibid*., 137-138).

The Rabha tribe is one of the important plain tribes of Assam. They are culturally very rich and unique from others. And just like any other tribe, they have their way of life, language and literature, social life and institutions, religious practices, festivals, marriage, birth and death ceremonies which makes them a whole society. The Rabhas have many customs and rituals which are distinctive. The Oxford Dictionary of Sociology defines customs as the established ways of thinking and acting in societies. They can be taken to mean the distinctive nature of a whole culture or of a cultural area (a geographical area in which the inhabitants share a common culture- which may embrace a number of subcultures). Ritual is defined by the Oxford Dictionary of Sociology as an often-repeated pattern of behaviour which is performed at appropriate times, and which may involve the use of symbols. Religion is one of the main social fields in which rituals operate but the scope of ritual extends into secular and everyday life as well.

The Rabhas have a rich socio-cultural institution. Their social life is governed by traditional customary laws which are known as 'Pandulipis'. "These 'Pandulipis' are framed by the consensus of the village people on the basis of customs, usages, traditions and religious beliefs covering such subjects as juridical power of the society, mode of inheritance, succession of office of socio-religious nature, type of marriage and principles of marital relationships and degree of prohibition, the roles of 'Khoum' and 'Barai', the liability for atonement on committing mischief and unnatural offences and the procedures governing these atonement, birth and death rites etc. etc" (Bordoloi, 1987, 124). In the districts of Goalpara and Kamrup, two sets of 'Pandulipis' are found which are 'Mespara Purbanchal Rabha Samaj Bidhi' and 'Dudhnoi Purbanchal Rabha Samaj Bidhi'. The area of operation of the former covers Dudhnoi to Lakhipur in the west and upto the foothills of Meghalaya and the latter covers eastward of Dudhnoi to the western part of Kamrup. There may be more 'Pandulipis' available in that area which were not covered in the article. The Rabhas were known to be matrilineal tribe where the descent is always traced in the female line and the children of a marriage always belong to the mother's 'barai' (*ibid*, 125). In Rabha society two types of marriage was prominent i.e. 'Marriage by Service' which means the practice of adopting the groom by the bride's family and 'Marriage by Elopement' which means to run away from the village and marry. The basis of their religious beliefs is mainly based on animism and their primary deity or Creator is known as 'Risi'. The Rabhas have different festivals which are celebrated at different time periods. And every festival is unique and holds importance for the tribe. Festivals like 'Baikho', 'Kesa-Khaiti', 'Langa Thakurani', 'Xoksi', 'Bonobaxi' etc are celebrated from earlier times and are still celebrated. A section of the Rabha i.e. the Pati-Rabhas have assimilated with the neighbouring Hindu culture and have begun to take part in all religious festivals like the Durga Puja, Ganesh Puja, Siva Puja etc. This section of the tribe maybe described as the followers of both Saktism and Saivism over their adherence to the traditional faith in animism. Also there is adoption of Christianity by a section of the tribe (*ibid*, 140). The social life of the Rabhas is rich and colourful and there is inter linkage of the various aspects of it.

Conclusion

Every tribe is different from one another in terms of language, culture, tradition, customs, attire, way of living etc. To understand a tribe one cannot rest only upon the prescribed notion of the same. One has to keep in mind that a group cannot be placed as a tribe only through the given norms. There are other elements of a group which can be taken into account for its identity. A group can be categorised as a tribe based on many criteria. The categorisation of a tribe may vary from region to region along with time. Every tribe is unique in their own way. Each has a different pattern of living based on the spatial surrounding, customary laws, food habits, dress patterns, jewellery, customs, rituals, etc. which places them in the unique sone from other tribes. The livelihood pattern of the tribes also varies from each other. The area of settlement plays a vital role in the selection of the livelihood pattern of a particular tribe, as based on the available resources one proceeds to indulge in a work. It is hard to have a uniform understanding of tribe. As for instance, the categorisation of tribes as Scheduled Tribes and its further division into ST Plains and ST Hills provides a picture of the difference that prevails among tribes based on the area of settlement. It is important to understand that tribe as a category is a whole society as a tribal society is self-sufficient in nature and it cannot be compared it with caste, peasant, or any other social category which are only a part of a larger society. The Rabhas are one such tribe whose customs and rituals, social practices, language etc makes it unique from the rest. But such distinctiveness of every tribe is ignored at a larger level and even during policy making and other such processes, tribal groups are categorised as homogenous groups which lead to submerging of the many issues indigenous people face differing from place to place. It is therefore important to understand that every tribe or indigenous population dwelling in various regions differ from one another and thus, they have different issues which need attention. Regional disparity, spatial differences, population size etc are some of the factors which are to be taken into account to look into the different issues of the indigenous population. Thus, placing tribes into one category and formulating policies for such a category will not help in eradicating tribal issues.

References

1. John Scott and Gordon Marshall, *Oxford Dictionary of Sociology*, Oxford University Press Inc., New York, (1994), 2009.
2. Virginius Xaxa, 'Transformation of Tribes in India: Terms of Discourse', *Economic and Political Weekly,* 34.24, June, 12-18, 1999, pp.1519-1524.
3. G.S. Ghurye, *The Scheduled Tribes,* Popular Prakashan, Bombay-400034, (1943), 1963.
4. *Documents of Twelfth Five Year Plan (2012-2017), Social Sector,* Volume- III, Planning Commission Government of India.
5. Devath Suresh, 'Tribal Development through Five Year Plans in India- An Overview', *The Dawn Journal*, 3.1, January-June, 2014, pp.794-816.

6. Andre Beteille, 'The Idea of Indigenous People', *Current Anthropology,* 39.2 (April 1998), pp.187-192.
7. Vinay K. Srivastava, 'Concept of 'Tribe' in the Draft National Tribal Policy', *Economic and Political Weekly*, 43.50, Dec. 13 - 19, 2008, pp. 29-35.
8. M.N. Srinivas, *Social Change in Modern India*, Orient Blackswan, New Delhi, 1966.
9. B.M. Das, *The Peoples of Assam,* Gyan Publishing House, Delhi, 1987.
10. M.G. Singha, 'Tribal Development in North-East India with Special Reference to the Rabhas', *Siri-Phak*, Nikhil Rabha Jatiyo Parisad, Chotomatia, Goalpara, Assam, 2012, pp.183-186.
11. P. Chakrabarty, 'Social Changes among the Rabhas: With Special Reference to the Religious Aspect', Editorial Board of the Reception Committee (Eds), *Troumani Chamancha* Adoroni Samiti, 2012, pp. 356-359.
12. B.N., Bordoloi, G.C.S. Thakur and M.C. Saikia, *Tribes of Assam, Part-I,* Tribal Research Institute, Assam, 1987.
13. LINK:http://www.britannica.com/EBchecked/topic/392246/Lewis-Henry-Morgan (Accessed on 9/9/2014).

6

Culture and Identity: A Study of the Ritual Practices among the Karbis

Junmoni Hansepi and Vulli Dhanaraju

Introduction

Northeast India is the most ethnically and linguistically diverse region in India. The region has a high concentration of ethnic communities. Each community has their distinctive tradition and belief systems. These beliefs are always linked with the way of life of people with its natural environment. And each of these ethnic community has its own history, tradition, culture, custom and believes system. There is no society without ritual practices. These ritual and rites are socio-cultural phenomenon. Indeed these rituals practices express the people through their memory and metaphor.

However, the ethnic community history, culture and identity look very different to one another. Every community has its own sense of identity, history and culture. One of the purposes of their rituals is to assert a sense of shared identity. That's why rituals are so important and it represents the history, culture and identity of the community. In this context, the rituals are significant component of Karbi culture, history and identity. Karbis are one of the major ethnic groups in Northeast India and particularly in the hill areas of Assam. The Karbis, belonging to the Tibeto-Burman linguistic family, are among the oldest inhabitants of Assam. They were earlier referred to as Mikirs but they call themselves *Arleng* meaning 'men' (Charles Lyall, 1908, 4). It is difficult to know the origin of Mikirs and also could not imagine where they hailed from. It is of course, as a matter of the fact due to absence of their written history of their tribe since the immemorial time (Barelong Terang, 2003). A Karbi scholar, Phukan Ch.Phancho (2003) in his book, *Karbi Anglong and North Cachar Hills* has described about the Karbi migration to the different parts of Karbi Anglong.

In Karbi society rituals are associated with festivals which are linked to their day-to-day life and for the community welfare. Rituals and festivals which are mostly performed mainly for the welfare of the society from birth to death that include rich harvest, for good health or general prospective and welfare, illness and epidemic or to eternalise behaviours, actions and occasions, have survived the test of time as an occasion of joy and entertainment held the community together and strengthened its identity. Mongol Sing Bey (2009) stated that these rituals symbolised how the Karbi uphold and negotiate with time to represent them diverse from past to present. The Karbi society is blended with folklore, folks-song and folk-tales. Therefore, most of the traditional ceremonies and festivals are done through religious mysteries of the Karbis (Mongol Sing Bey, 2009).

I. Conceptualising Rituals

Before going to discuss about the Karbi rituals it will be useful to conceptualise ritual and social behaviour of the rituals that has been debated by various scholars. The word 'ritual' has the Indo-European root, Ri, meaning 'flow' or 'rhythm'. It is upon 'Rita' that the cosmic functions of the universe are based. The performances that keep the rhythm of the universe are named therefore, rituals Paul Ricoeur (1987, 405). Ritual is a concept and the definition of ritual will depend upon how the concept is used. The exact identification and interpretation of ritual still remain debatable to the scholars. They agree in essence, that all culturally defined sets of behaviour which are communicative through memory to some extent can be termed as rituals.

Catherine Bell (1992) argues that rituals can be characterised by formalism, traditionalism, invariance, rule-governance, sacral-symbolism and performance. Ritual utilises a limited and rigidly organised set of expression which anthropologists call a restricted code. Thus, a working definition of rituals may be constructed, based on its enacted nature, symbolic content, and its discrete form. Ritual action, it is proposed, is a form of social action in which a group's values and identity are publicly demonstrated or enacted in a stylised manner, within the context of a specific occasion or event. Examples of this phenomenon might include a formal speech, a graduation ceremony, or a dinner for new employees. These examples are similar in that they are conventionalised enactments, rather than spontaneous behaviours, and contain clear-cut beginnings and ends.

Some Anthropologists like Glifford Geertz (1973) and Victor Turner (1977) who are interested in the explicit meaning of ritual symbolism. They point out that ritual act do endow culturally important cosmological conceptions and values. This symbolic meaning of rituals is stressed by Nancy Munn (1973). According to him, "I define ritual as a generalised medium of social interaction in which the vehicles for constructing messages are iconic symbols (acts, words or things) that convert the load of significance or complex socio-cultural meanings embedded in and generated by the ongoing processes of social existence into a communication currency. In other words, shared socio-cultural meanings constitute the utilities that are symbolically transacted through the medium of ritual action." Thus, ritual can be accepted as the formalised behavior patterns which are symbolic, verbal and non-verbal, necessary for the establishment of relation among members of a group or between groups.

According to Durkheim (1954), to understand the symbolic meaning in rituals, it should be re-interpreted in terms of the modern social contexts. Durkheiman theory has three components, for the study of rituals. One is how certain situations of collective effervescence generate and recreate religious beliefs and practices and evolve a functional theory of the consequences of those beliefs and practices. Durkheim attributes two aspects to his interpretation of religious beliefs and rituals. One is as a cognitive means of interpreting the social world. It is to understand the world in a metaphoric or symbolic way. By attributing some theatrical aspects to it, he calls ritual 'a flag', 'a rallying sign', 'and a set of dramatic representations'. This can be seen as analogous to games and the principal forms of art. It clearly shows that he connected rituals to aesthetics here.

II. Study of Rituals through Oral History

Like many other tribal groups of the world, the Karbis did not have a written language and hence there is no written history about their origin, spread and settlement and ritual practices too. That is the reason why we have given title as memory and metaphor which can be studied under oral tradition. Oral history tradition in this sense holds out hopes for understanding the historical evolutions of those societies without recorded history and where beginnings might have to be made with interpretation of the legends, myths and folklore. However, we should admit that there is a density in the Karbi context. Though, the Europeans were the first to write about the Karbis, their ways of life and their myths and traditions, the validity of the information given by them, especially their transcript versions of the oral traditions of the Karbis remains uncertain. This skepticism complements Samuel's arguments that the "spoken word can easily be mutilated when it is taken down in writing and transferred to the printed page". Some distortion is bound to crop up whatever the intention of the writer; simply by cutting out pauses and repetitions (Raphael Samuel, 1998, 389). The writer has his own purpose and these may be only coincidently those of his informant. Irrelevance (as it appears to the writer) may be patiently listened, but be given short shrift when he comes to single out passages to reproduce (*Ibid*). In this context, the written tradition is seen to be emerging as the stronger contender since the oral tradition being transcript becomes a static source like the transcript version. Moreover, there are opinions that the oral traditions in course of time either become too exaggerate, insignificant, or forgotten. To quote Moyer as "Trained to depend on written records, traditional historians have been known to shudder in horror at the potential problems and inherent weaknesses of oral history. What of the failings of human memory? What of the human tendency to impose a narrative structure on events that may not be closely connected? What of the self-serving motives of the story teller? What of the power relationships between interviewer and interviewee that affect what and how events are reported? What of the difference between the spoken and written word? What of the inaccuracies that creep into meaning when trying to put a conversation onto paper? (Judith Moyer, 1993).

The present paper, therefore, depended on oral sources. Since there is no particular work on Karbi ritual practices the following conceptual works will help us to understand the meaning and metaphor of the rituals in order to construct the Karbis identity.

Oral tradition therefore, is not only an important source for the construction of Karbi history of the pre-colonial and colonial periods, it is also important for a better understanding of the present days Karbi society. It can be true that "Karbi history can be reconstructed from oral tradition and it is true that in the absence of any written history, the numerous myths, legends and tales, as well as, other aspects of the tradition have been the only link between the historic past and the present" (Amongla Imsong, 2004, 1). These views go on well along with Paul Thomson's (1978, 19) opinion that 'the discovery of oral history by historian... is not only a discovery but recovery. It gives a future no longer tried to the cultural significance of paper documents...'

Thus, the Karbi society is also guided by their customary principles, which are observed and followed by the people. The customary laws show uniqueness of the Karbis from other communities. The Karbis attach great importance to established norms of human behaviour. The traditional history of the Karbi orally passed on from generation to generation in the form of ritual practices. The social behaviour of the Karbis is called rituals. Thus, the rituals played an important role in the identity construction of the Karbis.

However, some written documents also reflected the memory and metaphor of the Karbis. During the British period ethnographers like B.C. Allen, Edward Stack, Charles Lyall and the Baptist Christian missionaries like Miles Bronson, W. Ward, etc. recorded many aspects of the Karbi life after gaining personnel contact with them. These records can be treated as ethnographical writings for writing Karbi history. Some Indian scholars like K. L. Baruah, worked on some social and historical accounts of the Karbis. Apart from Baruah, S.K. Chatterjee and P.C. Choudhary also worked about the cultural history of the Karbis.

But recently the Karbi scholars also started writing about their history in the Karbi language and some works in English. Bidor Sing Kro's Souvenirs, *Jutang Amung* (2005) shows that how Karbi rituals are performed in the form of oral narratives, folk tales, folk song, folk dance, ballads and other legends. Where all kind of rituals are perform by an old grown up man who has a high position in respect to his knowledge of performing such ritual. He performs it orally like his forefathers and it will continue in the same form. Karbi rituals are considered to be so important for every Karbi household for the wellbeing of their stay in this world and after. Bidosing Rongpi's book, *Adamsa*r (2004) is an attempt to give a view of wedding ceremony of the Karbi. Two days and one night ceremony is performed in a big gathering including the old man with a high social position. This marriage ritual is very important in Karbi society because *Hemphu Mukrang* (The Karbi God) is very much needed for good wellbeing of the family without which *Chomangkan* can't be performed for that particular couple and would not attain eternal peace and wellbeing of the dead person. Bouchery Pascal's, *The Karbi House and Ritual* are recent source material to understand the cultural history of Karbis from historical perspective. Dharamsing Teron's *Karbi Studies* (Four volumes) initiated the mission in order to reconstruct the Karbi history from oral perspective. However, even these writings could not escape its own silences and selectivity and defiance of the presence of its own margin.

III. Importance of Community Based Rituals of the Karbis

There are three types of rituals among the Karbis. They are; Community Based Rituals, Family Based Rituals and Individual Based Rituals. However, this paper mainly focuses on the Community Based Rituals because these rituals are primary component of Karbi culture integrating the community on the community cultural ties. There are three type of rituals related to the community. The community as a whole performs these rituals in order to show the unity and collective social behaviour of the community. Let us discuss these three types of rituals in this section.

1. Rongker (Great Annual Village Festival)

Rongker is an annual compulsory village religious festival held at the time of the beginning of *jhum* cultivation and in some villages during the cold season. *Rongker* is not worshipped individually but the village as a whole. The Karbis are mainly hill dwellers, who believe in the hills and mountain as their savior. It is performed to seek the wellbeing and protection of all villagers, as well as their success in various fields. *Rongker* is a very open ritual among the Karbis, as even those families not having *Hem Angtar,* like that of widows families can also participate for blessing (Interview, 18th Nov 2015). Mongol Sing Bey (2009) opined that it is the combination of hundred god heads. It is an annual social religious festival of the Karbi society in combination for the wellbeing of the village people for the year. (Bidor Sing Rongpi, 2015). Goats and fowls are sacrificed during *Rongker*. The flesh of the sacrifice is eaten with rich and rice beer. But only men can take part at the sacrificial ceremony. They must sleep on the *Hong* the space of the house apart from their wines that very night. The gods are invoked in the following terms, "we live in your district, save us and help us, send no tigers or sickness, prosper our crops and keep us in good health and year we will sacrifice like this, we depend wholly upon you". There is no music and dance in the *Rongker* festival. *Rongker* are of six types in which the prayer and the purpose are different:

(a) Havar Rongker: *Havar Rongker* is known as *Than Rongker*, which means domiciling place of god head. *Havar*

Rongker is performed by the people who are staying in the hill with a view to cultivate jhum cultivation for livelihood, with whom they have to be at peace for the years to come. So they contribute everything for the successful worship of *Havar Rongker*. *Havar* literally means paddy field where the people perform jhum cultivation. It is worship for the good harvesting and to ask for blessing for good health and free them from various sicknesses (Mongol Sing Bey, 2009). The ritual is done with the collection of more than ten to twenty villages, which is performed by the *Vophong Asar*. The night before the *rongker* it is very compulsory to perform *Si-Kasadi*. During the ritual they pray to *Hemphu Mukrang Rasinja, Arnam Pharo, Chintong Arnam, Lamki, Longle-Ahii, Inglong Arlok, Thengpi-Thengso than Kibi Kethe, Sonti-Sonlon*. In this kind of ritual there may be more than thirty to forty gods. The *Kuru Sar* may belong from any of the villages but his duty while performing the ritual is to ask blessing to all of the villages who are included in the *Rongker* (Bidor Sing Rongpi, 2015).

(b) Pirda Rongker: *Pirda Rongker* is also known as *Rongkerpi* (annual great *Rongker*). It is performed the people of some villages with contribution as a whole. It is a combination name of *Hemphu, Mukreng, Rasinja* and other god of the locality where the village is situated (Mongol Sing Bey, 2009). It is performed for the well being of an area or *mauza* to live in peace and tranquility. In this particular *Rongker* they create an earthen hump or *Dovan* for the god who is known as *Aarnam Pharo, Langhe-rong Anglong* and *Sonti Sonbon*. It is very important to keep in mind that the earthen hump or *Dovan* which they create for the ritual to perform during *Pirda Rongker* will be permanent forever (Bidor Sing Rongpi, 2015).

(c) Ajo Rongker or Mavur Rongker: It is also known as *Ajo a Rongker*, as it is performing during the night. It is not performed individually but with the contribution of various villages as a whole. It is performed to protect and for precautionary measure to get rid of epidemic (Mongol Sing Bey, 2009, 35). It is mainly performed during the month of *There-Jangmi* or April because during this month it is very often to spread various sicknesses. The ritual cannot be completed without the usage of egg. They perform a ritual known as *Rongphu- Ronglin Vur-Krem Kangthin Ase* so because of this ritual the *Kuru Sar* have to visit each house in the villages using *Sobai* to find the cause of any misery in the family. After visiting each and every house the *Kuru Sar* will go to the main entrance of the village and perform a ritual which is called *Ajo Ase*. In which they pray to *Hemphu, Mukrang, Rasinja* and other like *Chong Long Recho, Pok Keso Akrong Ase Doan, Bangso Arong Arlo Hoi-Mai Lut Un-e Aphan* (Bidor Sing Rongpi, 2015, 42-43).

(d) Vophong Rongker: *Vophong Rongker* is known as *Longri Rongker* which means to say place. To perform *Vophong Rongker* people of a mouza or *Longri* contribute everything for the success of the *Vophong Rongker*. This *Rongker* is performed once in a year (Mongol Sing Bey, 2009, 35). Day before the *Vophong Rongker* it is compulsory to have *Se-Kasadi*. Early morning on day of the ritual they will proceed to the *Dovan* and pay tribute to than *Theli, Langroi-Langjeng, Inglong-Arlok, Thengpi-Thengprang*. After the completion of the ritual all the participants will have the meal together (Thekar Arnivang, 14th March, 2016).

(e) Dengja Rongker: It is also known as *Dovanso Rongker* and it is worshipped where the *Dengja or Kuru Sar* worshipper of the *Rongker* resides. It is performed just to get rid of any conflict with tiger of the *Longri* or place. It is interesting to mention here that *Bilo* scapegoat is procured by the god head himself. It is performed once in every 10 years (Mongol Sing Bey, 2009, 35). The night before the performance of the ritual the *Dengja* will perform *Se-Kasadi*. On the very day they will create an earthen hump or *Dowanso* and will perform a *Bilo Jon Pho Ase*. During this ritual everyone is not allowed to interfere, and who ever involve in the Ritual get purified by sprinkling water on them. Soon after that they pay tribute to *Hemphu, Mukrang, Rasinja* in the *Dengja* house. After that they go to the place where they build *Hamren* or the place where they decide to perform the ritual and pay tribute to *Than Theli*. At the end they will go back to the *Dengja* house and prepare for the meal (Bidor Sing Rongpi, 2015, 51).

(f) Tongprop Tongso Rongker: The name of the *Rongker* itself denote prompt and immediate. This *Rongker* is performed when there is a probability of natural calamity or conflict in the *Longri.* It is the precautionary and preventive measures of the approaching natural calamities like drought, epidemic type of disease and clash in the *Longri* (*ibid*).

2. Botor Kekur (Worship for Good Weather Conditions)

Botor Kikur (*Volo Keter*) is performed in the month of *Thang Thang* (February) once in a year. *Botor Kekur* is considered as a very important ritual but at the same time it cannot be performed individually. It is mainly performed by *Katharpo* for the Karbi community as a whole. The Karbis are an agriculturist society who depends on their environment for their livelihood. *Botor Kikur* in the Karbi society is mainly for good wellbeing in the field of agriculture or the environment and showing helping hands to each other in the field of work for the entire Karbi society. It is considered as one of the compulsory ritual to be performed by the Karbi society (Interview, 13th Feb 2015). As the Karbis depend on their environment for their livelihood they performed various rituals for the good harvesting like *Rit Anglong, Chotiki Anglong* and *Hemphu, Mukrang, Rasinja* and followed *Ronghang Rongbong* near big place where they prepared a *Dowan* or earthen hump and pray to *Hemphu, Mukrang, Rasinja*. sacrifices is made in the *Dowan* by using two red cock to *Hemphu, Mukrang* and one white fowl to *Rasinja*. After the completion of *Se-Karkli Katherpo* he pays tribute to weather queen or *Botor Kungripi* that is *Ha-I* to which he will sing *Ha-imu Alun* song. Lastly, in the finishing point the *Katharpo* sings in three different steps from *Dowan* till they reach the house. First to *Hemphu* in the *Dowan* secondly on the way to *Vokrokchur* and before reaching the village to *Chongho Korso* then after reaching the village to *Ha-i* thirdly to *Ha-imu alun* to *Ha-i* for rain (Bidor Sing Kro, 1998, 2-5).

Conclusion

Rituals are inalienable component of Karbi culture and history. Rituals are considered as an important source for Karbis in sustaining of their identity. Rituals and customs are associated with festivals which is further linked to their day-today life and for the community welfare. Rituals and festivals which are mostly performed mainly for the survival of the society from birth to death which include rich harvest, for good health or general prospective and welfare, to understand the notions of nature and wild animals, illness and epidemic or to eternalise behaviours, actions and occasions. These festivals and rituals have accumulated joy and entertainment that held the community together and strengthed its identity. These rituals and festivals symbolised how the Karbi upheld and negotiated with time to time representing their diversity from past to present. The Karbi society is blended with folk-lore, folks-song and folk-tales. Therefore, most of the traditional ceremonies and festivals are done through ritual practices. Rituals that they perform have their connection from past to present and historical importance in understanding of their past. This paper also proved that the women are given importance during the rituals. They actively participate in the ritual ceremony. When we see the rituals among the caste Hindus the women remain excluded in such rituals. This clearly shows the Karbis concern towards gender equality. Since the Karbis are forest dwellers they grew and are brought up in the midst of the nature where they live. Like other tribes, the Karbi have their own intense beliefs that reflect their social behaviour.

References

1. Amongla Imsong, *Myths and Ancient History: Case Study of Ao-Naga Myths*, (Unpublished M.Phil Dissertation) Department of History, University of Hyderabad, 2004.
2. Barelong Terang, *The History of Karbi*, Published by Kaveso Rongpipi, Narangi Tiniali, Guwahati, 2003.
3. Bidor Sing Kro, *Jutang Amung*, Karbi Lammet Amei, Monjir Press, Diphu, 1998.
4. Bidor Sing Rongpi, *Hirjume Lapen Rongker*, Malong Offset, Diphu, Karbi Anglong, 2015.
5. Catherine Bell, *Ritual Theory, Ritual Practice*, Oxford University Press, London, 1992.
6. Charles Lyall, *The Mikirs*, United Publisher, Guwahati, 1908.
7. Judith Moyer, *Step-by -Step Guide to Oral History*, 1993.
8. Mongol Sing Bey, The *Karbi Belief*, Karbi Lammet Amei, Diphu, Karbi Anglong, 2009.

9. P. Thomson, *The Voice of the Past: Oral History*, Oxford University Press, London, 1978.
10. Paul Ricoeur, *Encyclopedia of Religion*, Vol. 12, 1987.
11. Phukan Ch. Phancho, *Karbi Anglong and North Cachar Hills*, (Individual Publication) Printwell, Diphu, 2001.
12. Raphael Samuel, "Perils of the Transcript" in Robert Perks and Alistar Thompson (Ed), *The Oral History Reader*, Rutledge, London and New York, 1998.
13. The interview conducted on 13th Feb 2015 to Rupsing Ingti Kathar 50 yrs (M), village-Ronghang Rongbong, Hamren, Karbi Aglong.
14. The Interview conducted on 18th Nov 2015 to Babulal Phura 53 yrs (M)) village-Thailangso Phura Arong, Karbi Aglong.
15. *Thekar Arnivang*, Newspaper, 14th March 2016.

7

Divination through Chicken-Liver among the Galo Tribe of Arunachal Pradesh

Kiryi Potom

Introduction

Chicken-Liver omen (*Roksin-Kognam*) is unique identity among the tribal groups especially to Tani Clan of Arunachal Pradesh (India). The sub-clans of *Tani* group are Adi, Apatani, Galo, Nyishi, Tagin and Mishing Tribes of Assam. Still all the mentioned sub-clan of Tani in Arunachal Pradesh practice the Chicken-Liver omen but their ways of performing slightly differ from one sub-clan to other. It is believed that the Chicken-Liver omen was performed for diagnostic purpose during the early age but its scope increased later on. Now it is used for the prediction of the future, settling the disputes of lands and properties, marriage purposes, to find out the thieves, etc. The Chicken-Liver omen (*Roksin-Kognam)* could not be done by the common people except gifted person i.e. *Nyibu* (Shaman) and *Nyibe* (Orator).

There are three types of Chicken-Liver omen in Galo Tribe of Arunachal viz, *Kogek* (preliminary), *Kogja* (main) and *Kogyii* (conclusion). The *Kogek* is the preliminary form of Chicken-Liver omen (*Roksin-Kognam*) in Galo Tribe. The *Kogja* is done for details about main subject which is found in *Kogek* and the *Kogyii* is done to confirm the previous result.

I. Significance of the Study

This work will be beneficial to those who wish to do research on this and related topic in near future. The followings are the major significance of the study.

- The study will help the future researcher in their further investigation.
- The study will help in order to understand that this was dominant practice for diagnosing sickness and other related problems in the society.

II. Objectives

The purpose of the study is to attain the following objectives.

- To study the origin and historical background of Chicken-Liver Omen.
- To study the different types and uses of Chicken-Liver omen in Galo Tribe.
- To find out the present status of Chicken-Liver Omen in Galo Tribe.

III. Study Area

Galo tribe is one of the most prominent tribes in the state of Arunachal Pradesh who mostly inhabit in the West Siang district though some of them are also found in East and Upper Siang district. The Galo belong to the major Tani group. For present study the Galo of northern part like Darak, Liromoba and Kamba Circle have been chosen.

IV. Sources of Data

Both the Primary and Secondary source of data has been used to carry out the study. Sources of primary data was in the form of story narration, myths, etc. The primary data has been collected from the fields itself, interviewing the old persons, priests and shamans of some villages. The secondary data has been gathered through some published or unpublished books and journals.

V. Methods

All the information which is presented here is based on the ethnographic data collected by the author. The systematic field work and interview were conducted to obtain the required information from above three circles. The author used active participation, observation, using schedule and interview during the field study to get an in-depth understanding of their indigenous faith and beliefs. The camera and tape recorders were also used to record the discussion.

VI. Historical Background of Chicken-Liver Omen

At the very early days of human existence, there were three brothers *Riki* (ancestor of devils, who is also called *Taki*), *Rini* (ancestor of humans, popularly known as *Abo Tani*) and *Rinyo* (ancestor of animals, known as *Tanyo / Sonyo*). Taki and Tani had high spiritual power while *Tanyo / Sonyo* had less. Both the brothers, Taki and Tani had no mutual understanding in every step in their life and always clashed to capture each others powers. They lived their life with competition in every aspect. But in every step of conflict and fighting Tani always defeated Taki. Later on Tani even captured all the super natural powers and properties of Taki. Tani became most powerful creature. After that Taki remained frustrated and he always wanted to take revenge. He tried several times to take back all his lost spiritual powers and properties from Tani but failed.

One day, Taki was able to capture the 'Soul of Fire' (*Eme Yalo*) from Tani which was most precious thing among Tani's property and he trapped the *Eme yalo* at secret place. After capturing of *Eme yalo* Tani became helpless and he offered his properties to get back the *Eme yalo* but Taki didn't agree. In return of *Eme yalo* Taki demanded his spiritual power back. So, finally Tani agreed Taki's demand only to get back *Eme yalo* because his life was becoming incomplete without the fire (*Eme*). That was the turning point to Tani as he became spiritually powerless creature on the earth (*Sisi*).

After capturing all spiritual powers from Tani, Taki became most powerful creature on the earth and he escaped from Tani to protect himself from Tani's revenge. From that day, Tani became unable to talk and see him (Taki) and Tani could not take back all his lost power from Taki till his last breath. Taki's hatred towards Tani was still continued. Till today, he inflicts misfortunes to form bad incidents with humans.

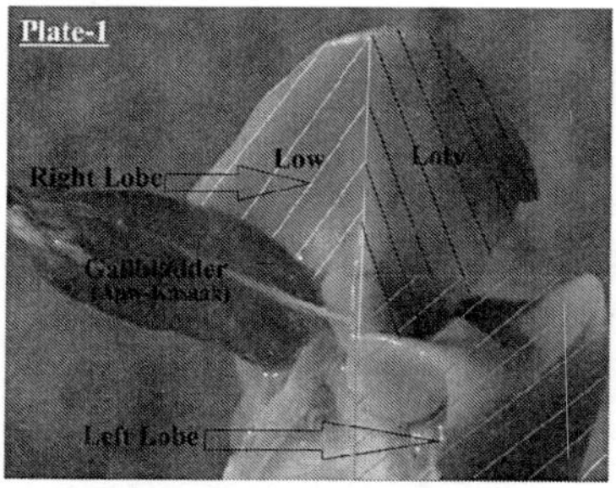

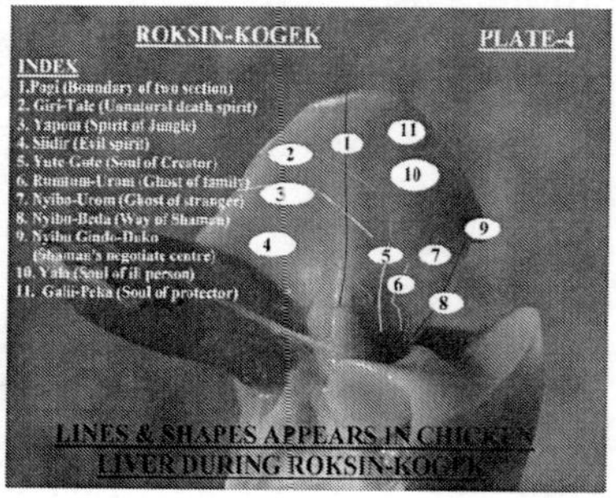

That was the most problematic situation for Tani; eventually he searched all possibilities to understand Taki's demand. In order to know Taki's demands, Tani used many things to communicate with Taki through examining various livers of animals and birds, leaves, pebbles, sticks, mushrooms etc. Among all he found Chicken-Liver Examination to be the most appropriate means to communicate with Taki. Later on Tani extended its scope by discovering of various uses such as marriage purpose, settlement of disputes of land and properties, agricultural purposes, settlement of thieves cases, prediction of future, hunting purposes etc. But common man cannot chant it except Shaman *(Nyibu)* Orator *(Nyibe)* and readers of the liver are also gifted one which is called *Roksin-Kone / Kane* (Reader of Chicken-Liver). Till today, the Chicken-Liver omen (*Roksin-Kognam)* is practiced among Tani group of Arunachal Pradesh.

VII. Chicken-Liver Omen in Galo Tribe

Galo Tribe used to read/observe only on the right lobe whereas the left lobe is used to read/observe by the other tribes of Tani clan which is shown in Plate-1.

The *Roksin-Kognam* is a chanting where Shaman requests the spirit to reveal the result in the form of lines or shape in chicken liver. After chanting, chicken is cut halfway open and after it is dead, the belly is cut open. The liver is then taken out for observation/read. The different lines, folds, holes, sizes and colours of the liver signify different causes. Brief explanations of different types of Chicken-Liver Omen are as follows:

1. Roksin-Kogek

In tribal's society of Tani Clan *Roksin-Kogek* played a vital role in their daily life. It can also be performed by Shamans *(Nyibu-Buuru),* Local Priest *(Nyibu),* and Orator *(Nyibe).*The *Roksin-Kogek* is performed in different fields such as:

(a) Illness *(Rame-Kogek)*: This is the process to find out whether it can be treated medically or traditionally. In case of traditional way of treatment, *Rame-Kogek* helps to know what types of spirit *(Uyu)* posses inside the body of ill person. The sections of spirit are shown in the picture (Plate-4) such as *Giiri-Tale Uyu* (Unnatural death spirit), *Yapom* (Spirit of the Jungle), *Siidir* (evil spirit), *Rumtum-Urom* (Ghost of family), *Agum-Urom* (Ghost of stranger), *Yute-Gute* (soul of creator) and *Gali-Peka* (soul of protector). *Rame-Kogek* is the process to find out the particular section of spirit (subject) in the form of indication on the liver. If any one of the indication which is shown in the figure appears in the liver, it is believed that, that particular section of spirit (Subject) is the reason behind the illness; later on that particular subject will be examined in detail in second Step *(Roksin-Kogja)*.

(b) Marriage *(Nyijir-Kogek)*: In the Galo tribe the *Nyijir-kogek* is a match making ritual by the boys parent's to different girls to whether the proposed girl will match the boy or not.

(c) Disputes of Land boundaries *(Rigri-kogek):* In the tribal societies the disputes on land and river was common in early time because of the absence of official written records. In order to settle such cases the tribal group of Tani clan as well as Galo Tribe used to perform *Rigri-kogek.*

(d) Thieves cases *(Dosso-Kogek)*: In the Galo society, *Dosso-kogek* is performed to reveal the thief by giving some clues. Sometimes, it gives false result.

(e) Agricultural Purposes *(Rigi-Kogek)*: *Rigi-Kogek* is performed before selecting the Jhum cultivation plot which is never cultivated by any person since long years. It is a belief Galo Tribe that, such jungles are reserved by *Yapom* (Spirit of Jungle). In case of positive result, the Shaman *(Nyibu)* propitiates with proper incantation, ceremonies and sacrifices before cultivating the plot.

(f) Prediction Purposes: As we know that, prediction of future is mostly done by the astrologers in Hindu society, likewise, the tribal community also believe in prediction of future but it is done in a different way. The Galo people also perform the prediction of their success and failure through chicken-liver such as war, hunting purpose, marriage purpose, student's examination result, carrier/job purpose, election result, commercial purposes like timber, canes, etc.

2. Roksin-Kogja

It is known as main process of *Roksin-Kognam* which is done after the preliminary process *(Roksin-Kogek)* is over. In this process Shaman *(Nyibu)* follows according to the subject which was indicated in the *Roksin-Kogek*. *Nyibu* as a mediator plays vital role to negotiate on the particular subject in order to solve the matter related to particular problems such as healing of sickness. The necessary ritual is performed to cure the sick person or any activity is carried out as per the result of the liver. All sacrifices are performed in a ritualistic way in order to heal the sickness of a person. Some time, it took many days to get to exact result in the liver and the process is continued until the positive result is obtained.

3. Roksin-Kogyii

It is the last and conclusive part of the *Roksin-Kognam*. Thus, after performing the main process of chicken-liver examination the *Roksin-Kogyii* is performed to confirm whether the main motive of chicken-liver examination is successful or not. It is also considered as a necessary examination in the process of chicken-liver examination in order to avoid any mistakes during the performance of the *Roksin-Kogja* (Main process).

Conclusion

Chicken-Liver omen *(Roksin-Kognam)* is unique identity marker of the tribal group in the world which is only practiced among the Tani group of Arunachal Pradesh and it believes that *Roksin-Kognam* is inherited since *Abo-Tani* (ancestor of Tani clan) itself. As per the study, indigenous beliefs and faith is rapidly declining in the tribal society of Arunachal Pradesh because of modernisation, with the introduction of Christianity in the region and education. It is also found that, the numbers of shaman are declining. Today, there is no replacing shaman. Villages are having few shamans today who may be the last shamans. Rural depopulation and access to modern medical facilities are the other factors responsible for falling importance of this system. The day is not far; this system will disappear from the society.

References

1. B. G. Deori, *Bamboo Art Work with Special Reference to the Traditional Ritual Altars of Galo Tribe*, Arunachal Pradesh, Northeast India, (No year).
2. J.N. Chawdhury, *Arunachal Panaorama* (Directorate of Research, Government of Arunachal Pradesh, Itanagar 1979.
3. Mibi Riba, Emerging *Religious Beliefs and Practices: A study on the Galo under Likabali of Arunachal Pradesh*, M.A. Dissertation, Rajiv Gandhi University, Itanagar, 2005.
4. Mohan Koyu, *Faith and Belief System of Adi, Continuity and Change: A Case study of Adi of East Siang District Arunachal Pradesh*, M.Phil Dissertation, Rajiv Gandhi University, Itanagar, 2011.
5. Muthu Kumaraswamy, *Voicing Folklore: Carriers; Concerns and Issues: A Collection of Interviews*, National Folklore Support Centre, 2002.
6. Nabam Tadar Rikam, *Emerging Religious Identities of Arunachal Pradesh: A Study of Nyishi Tribe*, Mittal Publication, New Delhi, 2005.
7. NEZCC- Northeast Zone Cultural Centre.

8. Oshong Ering, 'Philosophy of Donyi-Polo', T.Mibang and S K. Chaudhury (Ed), *Understanding Tribal Religion*, Mittal Publication, New Delhi, 2004, pp. 35-38.
9. P. C. Sharma, *Faith and Practices of the Adi in Traditional Customs and Ritual of Northeast India*, Vivekananda Kendra Institute and Culture, Guwahati, 2004, pp. 92-100.
10. P. K. Srutikar, 'Customary laws among the Nishings (Bengnis) of Arunachal Pradesh', in P. C. Dutta and D. K. Duarah (Ed), *Aspect of Customary Laws of Arunachal Pradesh*, Directorate of Research, Government of Arunachal Pradesh, Itanagar, 1997.
11. Rukbo, Talom 1998- Donyi-Polo faith and practice of the Adis, in Indigenous faith and practices of the Tribes of Arunachal Pradesh, eds. M. C. Behera and S. K. Chaudhury, Himalayan Publishers, New Delhi.
12. Verrier Elvin, *Philosophy of NEFA*, Gyan Publishing House (Reprint), Delhi, 1957.
13. Vishal Gupta, 'Jhum Cultivation Practices of the Bangnis (Nyishis) of Arunachal Pradesh', *Indian Journal of Traditional Knowledge*, Vol. 4(1), January, 2005, pp. 47-56.

8

The Politics of Identity and Culture: Tracing the Origin and Growth of Karbi Youth Festival

Bandita Teronpi

It is not unknown that India is a land of Unity in Diversity. It is this country where we find multi-language, multiplicity of culture, mixed economy, mixed government (coalition) and an overall plural society living together. The idea of unity of India is inherent in all historical and socio-cultural facts, as well as in its cultural heritage. India has one Constitution, single citizenship providing guarantees for people belonging to diverse religions, cultures and languages. It covers people belonging to all socio-economic strata.

The Northeast state of India is the house of diversity of ethnic community who are known either to have migrated from Burma, Tibet, China and Cambodia. The ancestral home of the various people speaking Tibeto-Burma languages was in Western China near the Yang-Tse-Kiang and the Howang-ho rivers and from these places they went down the coerces of Brahmaputra the Chindwin and the Irrawady and entered India and Burma.

This gives an idea that the Karbis might have come through the path described alone, and to know the history of a community or tribe lead us to the folklores of it. As to understand any people one must necessarily understand their creation story, which recounts how the world was formed, how things came to be formed and continued within creation stories.

Karbi Anglong is the largest districts amongst the 27 districts of Assam. History reveals that the 'Karbis', the then 'Mikir' were the earliest inhabitant of Assam who really constitutes an important ethnic group in the Hills Areas of Assam, but nevertheless, some Karbis also inhabit in North Cachar Hills, Kamrup, Morigaon, Nogaon, Sonitpur Districts and also in the neighbouring state of Arunachal Pradesh. Racially the Karbis belong to the Mongoloid group and linguistically they belong to the Tibeto-Burman group. But besides the Karbi tribe, there are also a large number of other communities residing in the district, such as Dimasa, Bodo, Rengma Nagas, Kuki/Thadou/ Hmar tribes, Tiwas, Garos, Mna-Tai speaking communities, some Khasi tribes in areas adjourning Meghalaya mostly in Hamren Sub-Division and some scattered Chakmas. There are also Assamese, Bengali, Bihari etc. groups of people throughout the District.

Talking about festival, it is very interesting to note that there are around 50 (fifty) greatest festivals in the world. It is the Harbin Ice and Snow Festival of China from January 5 – February 5 that lists the first. In this festival, we can witness the people build incredible things out of ice and snow, decorating them with lights and lasers. Next comes the Chinese New Year between January 21 and February 20. It is the biggest Chinese holiday with dragons, fireworks, symbolic clothing, flowers, lanliens and celebration, everywhere in China and even in other Asian countries. Likewise name can be taken of USA's Sundance Fun Festivals, Magh Mela festival of India, Up Helly Aa Fire Festival of Scotland, Holi of India. The carnival of Rio De Janeiro of Brazil which is quite famous and the La Tomatina Bund festival of Spain where people throw tomatoes at each other. What does all these festival around the world signify? What ideas do it gives to us? Or what impression does it imprint? Each of these world famous festivals gives the impression or the identity of the place or country it belongs, what is the culture or practice of that particular region, it is through the festivals the people, the location or the country gets recognition. It becomes a place of attraction to the global community thus, inviting more and more expatiators which ultimately results in the identity of the place, the people and the culture. It becomes a place of destination for tourist.

Coming to the point of our festivals of Northeast India. There are 11 popular festivals in Northeast India, which highlights the region's rich Indigenous culture with folk songs, tribal dances, food and crafts. Name can be coded of the Hornbill Festival of Nagaland, Sanghai festival of Manipur, Bihu festival of Assam, Brahmaputra Beach Festival of Assam, Dehing Patkai Festival of Assam, Torgya Monasty Festival of Arunachal Pradesh, Shillong Autumn Festival of Meghalaya, Nongkrem Dance Festival of Meghalaya, Wangala Festival of Meghalaya, Chapchar Kut of Mizoram, Kang Chingba of Manipur, Kharchi Puja of Tripura. The Hornbill Festival is held at Naga Heritage village, Kisama, 12 km from Kohima. The tribes of Nagaland celebrate their festival with appreciation and fervor. The objective behind the festival is to encourage inter-tribal interaction and to promote culture heritage of Nagaland, usually held between 1st and 7th of December. The Festival is named after the Indian Hornbill, the large and colourful forest bird which is displayed in folklore in most of the state's tribes. Assam, most famous for its one-horned Rhinoceros and tea gardens is also famous for its Bihu a national festival of the people of Assam, marked particularly on the agricultural period which is sub-categorised into three. The biggest and the most colourful of the three is Bohaag Bihu (also known as Bongali Bihu) celebrated at seeding time in Spring with lots of singing and dancing. Kaati Bihu, is another one, which is celebrated at the completion of paddy transplantation. The last is the Maagh Bihu (Bhogali Bihu) celebrated at the end of harvest season, with bonfires feasting, buffalo fights and pot breaking. Another festival of Assam is the Brahmaputra Beach festival, held at the bank of river Brahmaputra, entrance of Sonaram field, Bharalu in the month of January and February. In this festival one witness traditional Bihu Dances, food crafts, cultural exhibition, paragliding, boat cruises, canoeing, rafting, beach, volleyball etc.

Yet, another Assamese festival that is worth highlighting is the Dehing Patkai Festival. Name after the Dehing River and

Patkai range in Eastern Assam. Attraction of the festival includes fairs, tea heritage low, golfing adventures sports, wildlife and trips to Still Well road and World War-II Cemeteries. This festival is held at Lekhapani, in the Tinsukia district of Assam.

The fifth festival of Northeast India is the three day Monastery festival of Arunachal Pradesh. It is observed by the Monpa tribe of Arunachal Pradesh. The rituals, includes the performance of sacred dances by brightly costumed monks in the Monastery's country yard in a faith to ward off evil spirits and bring prosperity to the tribe. Likewise all those other festivals represents a particular tribe, a country, the traditionalism, the religion, the rich culture and how a festival is similar or different from the other, while each making a unique identity of its own.

When the discussion is on the festivals of Northeast India and of India, the Karbi Youth Festival cannot be left untold. As the Karbi Youth Festival is now 41 years old and it claims to be the oldest and the largest ethnic festival not only of Northeast India but the country itself. The Karbi Youth Festival is the festival of the Karbis, a Hill tribe of Assam. The Karbi's mentioned as the 'Mikir' once in the constitution order, Govt. of India, constitute an important ethnic group of Assam. Though sometimes the Karbis, called themselves '*Arleng*' which literally mean a 'man'? The birth of the Karbi Youth Festival has its own long historical background. This festival of the Karbis depicts the entire Karbi Culture. Before tracing the origin of the Karbi Youth Festival, let us know something about the youth. Youth has always shared a great place in the development activity of a race, a community or a nation. Youths are the backbone of a country. They are the future, who can materialise the dreams of a community. Dr Abdul Kalam spoke 'on the role of youth in realising the progress of India. For to the Karbis as well Society, the Karbi Youth has always played a very important and imminent role in the progress of Karbi culture and identity. It is because of those groups of youths, the Karbi Youth Festival has its existence. Prof. U.B. Pandey, commented on Karbi Youths that "this is much praiseworthy and mature on the part of the Karbi Youth that they didn't take to the culture of gun, guitar and girls which is very often associated with the tribal youth in the rest of the Eastern Indian region. I would call the Assam movement a turning point in the life of the Karbi Youth who made the presence felt at all India level and earned out a niche in the political history". But its origin history flash backs to 'The Roman Script movement' organised by Karbi Student Association (KSA) for Karbi language and demanding retention of English as the medium of instruction against the Gauhati University's decision to introduce 'Assamese' as the language of education in the colleges under its jurisdiction. A landmark decision was adopted for writing 'Karbi national literature' and Karbi text books to be used as Karbi Vernacular subjects in the lower Primary School Level in Roman Script. Accordingly a 'Script Implementation Committee' (SIC) was formed in 1973 with Bronson Engti as President and Roy Enghi as General Secretary. The 'SIC' through separate resolutions sent appeals to the council to adopt a resolution in the Council Session and the *Karbi Lammet Amei* adoption of Roman Script. But there was a difference of opinion between some groups of Karbi rulers.

A series of agitation programmes took place meanwhile; the leaders of the movement toured the entire Karbi Anglong district to mobilise the people. Karbi Adorbar was also parallel to oppose the Roman Script along the male and the Karbi female folk too were actively participating in the 'Roman Script Movement.' Section 144 was imposed in the entire district. It became a very hectic time; as volunteers all over the district were moving towards the district headquarter at Diphu. The volunteers arrived at a village named 'Kehai Timung' village (Presently Chotianala), where food was arranged and from where they could not move ahead to Diphu due to the imposition of 144. So, on 27th December, 1973, a procession was taken out from Kehai Timung village, but the police arrested the volunteers at Rongkhelan near present Donbosco School. Another procession took place on 28th December 1973, where the police again arrested some of the leaders of the procession including Dr Sarsing Terang, Sri Dhoniram Tisso, Sri Monsing Rongpi, Sri Mensing Rongpi, and Roy Enghi. They were all put in Diphu jail for two (2) days. It was in the movement that these youths first discussed about the necessity of a 'Youth Festival' of the Karbis. A house-to-house donation of Rs 10 was raised from Diphu for the preparation of it. The Diphu Government College students took active part in the movement. They smeard the signboards carrying Assamese Script (1972-73) with black paints. They also organised 'one-act plays' to expose corruptions and generated public opinion.

There was also the issue of Karbi dress code for Karbi girl students, raised by '*Karbi Lo Charli Asong*', which means Karbi Student Association. The decided dress code for Karbi female students was *Pini* and *Seleng*. Slowly cultural realisation started to take place among the Karbis. Harsing Engti wrote the first chorus for Diphu Government College Week, which Bagged the 2nd prize in 1973. Roy Enghi also took part in 'Youth against Famine Campaign' from Diphu Government College in 1973. Being an active performer, he became a great promoter of Karbi culture. His 'One Act Play' gained popularity as it was a form of exposure in exposing 'corruptions of politicians.' The then ruler of District Council enforced ban on his one-act-plays 'Kangship' and 'Kai Kirla', a full-drama. It is very interesting to note that the iconic chorus of the Karbis- "*Kardom dengtha o Karbi a*".... was composed by him and was first performed at Diphu Club in 1971. In spite of such setbacks, the leader of the Roman Script Movement became able to review the movement. Though many of those youths were behind the bars, yet their spirit never went damp. And there, behind the bars the 'idea' to launch a cultural movement, taking the shape to frame in the name of Karbi Youths Festival took place. Their goal was to do something 'New' in order to unite and rejoin the upcoming Karbi Generation, immediately after coming out of the jail; they started more vigorously mobilising the mass in general and youths in particular. So, after much hardship and complexity the first 'Karbi Youth Festival' was held by the end of January in 1974 at 'Karbi Club', Rongnihang, Diphu with about 300 participants. After that the growth of Karbi Youth Festival became visible.

The 3rd Karbi Youth Festival was held at Karbi Anglong Sport Association (KASA) playground as there was the demand from the growing participants throughout the district. On 30th January 1977, the Karbi Cultural Society (KCS), a body was instituted who takes the responsibility to organise, determine and redefine the Karbi Youth Festival annually in the month of February. The venue was also shifted to a permanent beautiful and evergreen hilly area of 1086 bighas, Taralangso, calling it the 'Karbi People's Hall'. Since then the Karbi Youth Festival has been regularly held at Taralangso every year in the mid-February month and has now become the largest ethnic extravagansa of Assam, Northeast and the whole of India.

Karbi Youth Festival

It became an important issue during those years of 1972's, when the Karbi youth took up the 'Roman Script Movement'. It was during the cultural movement and along the struggle for Karbi nationality that the psychology to create a common cultural platform was thought to be important and the idea to create and organise a 'National Festival' of the Karbis was adopted and thus the first Karbi Youth Festival was held in 1974. Beginning with some 300 people, now the Karbi Youth Festival welcomes expatiators nearly in lakhs. The Karbi Youth Festival is important as it has become a forum to determine and redefine the traditional Karbi Art and culture. It is also important because it is a celebration of Karbi heritage and rich culture. Karbi Youth Festival is also important because it is the 'dream come true' of those youths who dreamt of an independent identity for the Karbi's through this cultural festival, as the motto of Karbi Youth Festival says "Culture is always the face of the community (Karbi) and "The Literature the life of that community". Thus, when a culture is alive, that community to which the culture belongs is also alive. The Karbi Youth Festival is not only a festival for the purpose of entertainment but a wholesome reflection of the rich Karbi culture and heritage. If one has to study on the Karbis, the Karbi Youth Festival is the hub of knowledge. It is the knowledge of the traditional Karbi customs, knowledge on the Arts and craft which highlights the facts of how the Karbis were well equipped and sufficient. The various use of bamboo, right from making *Karbi Hemtun, Hemtaps*, i.e. the Karbi house and to the smallest useful objects of live is very fascinating, the knowledge of ethnic foods, the Herbal medicines, the *pindeng sumpot* i.e. the dresses of Karbis, the ornaments, which also highlights how rich the Karbi Society was and is. The knowledge of Karbi traditional political system, the presence of *Karbi Rechos* i.e. kings, the Karbi folk songs, the traditional dances, ways of cultivation displayed through dance etc is all witnessed and known through this youth festival of the Karbis.

Talking about the Karbi Youth Festival, it would be very significant to discuss the programmes of it. The program starts with "RONG KETONG", a traditional cultural procession, where participants from various twenty six (26) zones of Karbi Anglong, come in procession with their colourful traditional dresses each with their banner of identity and holding the *Jamili athong* from the Artists village (a place in Taralangso, where the participants are halt) to the *Hemphu-Mukrang-Rasingja Aklam* i.e. the stage named after the "God of the Karbis", He is the *Jutang Kuru*. After the traditional cultural procession, the *Tirim Kangduk* is observed which means paying homage to all the martyrs of Karbi's. This occasion is declared to be opened by the Karbi Recho (King). The *rong ketong* is the opening ceremony of the four days long festival. The Karbi cultural society's flag is hoisted by the President of the Karbi cultural society.

After that the different type of folk dances are displayed in the form of competition for the rest of the days. They are:

1. **Ritnong Chingdi and Hen-up Ahi Kekan :** It is a traditional dance form of the Karbis, which is related with one of the seed sowing festival a cultivating festival celebrated in the first part of the month of April. Both male and female perform together. This dance not only demonstrates but also gives the idea of the various stages of the process of cultivation sight from cleaning the cultivating area, sowing the seeds up to the reaping of the crops. In short, it displays the cultivation procedures of the Karbis. This dance is followed by the *'Hen-oop' ahi kekan*, which is again a fascinating folk dance of the Karbis. *'Hen-oop'* means bamboo shoot, out of the specific period of presentation and 'Kekan' means dance. In late summers, boys and girls from villages go to the jungle to collect the bamboo shoots and gather them in a place in their village. Though these are two different types of dance yet in the festival and

from the competition point of view the participants perform it in a mixed form.

2. Lingpum Sokchon: It is another dance form, which can be called as the 'Bamboo Dance' of the Karbis. Bamboo is the prop used in this dance. It is also a harvesting festival dance.

3. Nimso Kerung: It is the most colourful and fascinating dance of Karbi culture. It is performed during the occasion of *Karbi Chomkan* festival, held in the honour of the departed soul of the family. The word 'Nimso' means maiden and 'Kerung' means choosing and picking up the maiden for the dance. During this dance, the *Duhuidi-Duhuijang*, the two drummers, beats the drum.

4. Hacha Kekan: It is performed during harvesting. The Karbi community celebrates *Sok Keroi* Festival after the paddy is harvested. The *Lunsepo* is the singer, who sings song remembering the Great Social reformer *Rukasen* by singing the song of *Lokhi Keplang*, meaning the origin of wealth. This dance is performed by boys only.

5. Chong Kedam: It is an action oriented dance form of the Karbis. It is a warrior dance. It is generally equipped with *'Nok'*, and swords and a *'chong'* a shield.

6. Banjar Kekan : It is also performed during the *Chomkan* Festival. *Banjar* means a 'Bamboo Pole' and *Kekan* means dance. This *Banjar* Pole is skillfully earned and displayed, which lights on the richness of art and craft activities of the Karbis. A number of folk songs are also highlighted through the Karbi Youths Festival. They are;

(i) *Bong-oi Alun*: It means romantic song sung by young boys and girls in the form of dialogue between them, and exchanging their feelings.

(ii) *Mosera Kihir* : It is recited in the form of song during the 'Chomkan' festival recounting the past history of the Karbis.

(iii) Kurdidi by male and Oso Kebai (Female) is a song sung while making a baby sleep.

(iv) *The Sar Kebat Alun* (Male) and *Bor-et* (Male/Female) are songs recounting the historical events of the Karbis. The origin story and so on.

Through these dances and folk songs, we find that the Karbis in every occasion and parts of life has expressed its richness through these dances and folk songs. Imagination can be made how these traditional people could recite and memorize their history and can pass it to their generations without any written form but only through chanting. Besides the traditional forms, there are also modern songs and dance like *Lun Cheto*, means chorus, *Lun Chethak*, meaning a duet song, *Lun Sampung*, which means solo song, *Hamphang Kekan*, the modern dance etc.

We can also witness and be cherished through this festival, the performer playing the folk musical instruments like *Muri Tongpo*, meaning a flute like instrument, *Krong Chui*, meaning a lyre-shape musical instrument made out of bamboo and Iron, played by blowing with the mouth, *Kum Li-eng* means a wind instrument, like a violin, made out of gourd and wood. Besides music, song and dance, the traditional sports of the Karbis are also interesting. The traditional sports are:

(i) *Hambi Kepathu-* playing with hard seed.

(ii) *Kengdongdang Kekat-* a riding race on bamboos.

(iii) *Bathili Ke-ap-* means handmade tools to shoot or aim at some objects. It is more or less like a catapult.

(iv) *Hon Kejeng, bangphu Soktok Chingdi and Horling Kek* – Playing with traditional rice grinder.

Another attraction of Karbi Youth Festival is the traditional fashion show where we get the idea of Karbi traditional dress, like the male has a verity of costumes like *'Choihongthor'*-a jacket generally worn by married males. There are also other types of jackets like *'Choi-ang'*. *Choi kelok / choi umso, choi-ik*. Though *peseleng* is worn by both male and female, it depends on the heaviness of the design that differentiates and the patterns used on it while wearing between the male and female. It is generally white in colour. *'Rikong'* is a small or slim piece of cloth wear by males. It is generally used by elderly person and in villages. *'Poho'* is yet another product of Karbi worn. It is a head turban worn by Karbi men. The bachelor wears the white colour Poho while the married male wears the red one. The white coloured 'poho' carries more cultural significance as it is worn by the *Karbi Recho* (King), the *Pinpos*/the countries, *'Habe'* and the village Headman. *'Chepan'* is a longer piece of cloth with less broadness and decorated with beads and shells and straps around the waist by the Karbi male. *'Vojaru Ani'* is the head gear for bachelors who are in the statue of *'Klengsarpo'* and *'Klengdun'* or the chief of the youth dormitory or *'Tir'*. It is made out of the tail of a 'Racket tailed *drongo*'. *'Pelu'* is a thick women rectangular cloth used as traditional bed sheet and a important worn product in traditional wedding and death rituals. Differentiating in design, both male and female use *Pelu*. *'Pelu'* wore by male is called *'Pelu Marak'* and that for female is called *'Piniku'*. Though there is wide variety of female costume, the most commonly used are *'Pekok',* worn in upper body, slinging on the right shoulder to knee above length. There are varieties of *pekoks* based on the material and design texture. *'Pini kamphlak'* a rectangular piece of thick cloth worn over the lower body tied from the waist, by a *'Vamkok'*, a belt and same the purpose to fasten the *'Pini'*. *'Tir' ik'* is pieces of cloth shorter than a *'Piba'* worn by an adolescent girl till her marriage. *'jiso'* is a chest cloth worn in older days etc.

In the part of ornaments, Karbi man used to put on brass made ear-rings called *'Norik'*, a silver bracelet called *'Prinsoroi'* and heavy silver necklace called *lekrooa and lek-enji*. These items are rarely found at present. The women folks wore *'Nothengpi'*, big heavy ear-rings made of silver, with its diameter of about half an inch. Silver bracelets are called *'Rup-Aroi'* and the necklace made of white beads is called Lech-ho-so, and the other made of silver coin and coloured beads is called *'Lek-chike'*.

Another attraction of the Karbi Youth Festival is the *'Phu linglang'*, a rock concert competition earlier named as *'No toklet'*. The inclusion of the programmes highlights on the progressive mode of the Karbi Youth Festival towards modernisation. This has attracted a number of persons both as participants and the crowd. Thus, the Karbi Youth Festival holds the grip of tradition as well as modernity.

Thus, through this Karbi Youth Festival, we can know about the entire part of Karbi culture, through which each category would just lead to a research study.

Observing the origin and growth of the Karbi Youth Festival since its inception up to this date, we can feel its growth both in number, activity and publicity. There is a great growth of it. The Karbi Youth Festival was a challenge in reclaiming and repairing the rich Karbi heritage and culture. Focusing on the ritual infrastructure, the framing, the symbols, the ethnic nomenclature of the four stages viz. Long Mirjeng Achetai, Sing Mirjeng Achetai, Semson Sing Engti and Hemphu-Mukrang, one can depict the culturally rich Karbis. Question generally arises in our mind as to who is Sing Mirjeng or Long Mirjeng or Semson Sing Engti or Hemphu Mukrang-Rasinja. Hemphu-Mukrang, Rasinja. *Hemphu* is the legendary God of the Karbis, *Rasinja* is the sister of *Hemphu* and *Mukrang* to whom *Rasinja* got married. It is through them that the Karbi culture and identity flourished. Likewise Sing Mirjeng and Long Mirjeng by the name of whom the two stages of Karbi Youth Festival are named after the two sons of *'Songsar Richo'*. It is through them the Karbi song, music and dance flourished. Earlier, in the Karbi history, there was not any song, music and dance. It is also through them that the naming of the Karbi started like the name of person ending with the rhyme long, song, tong includes into the category of *'Senglong'* and the word rhyming *teng, meng* includes into *'cheteng'*, such as tot, not, bot, includes in *'bolong'* and to, *ko, lo* etc. includes in *'langno'*. The third stage is named after the founder of Karbi Anglong (earlier known as Mikir Hills) Lt. Semson Sing Engti.

Besides the stages, the bamboo traditional house built at several places of Taralangso, symbolises the social structure of the Karbi. How, a particular national resource becomes a part and parcel of a community can be understood. The Karbi house has two open space or the so called 'Varandas, one at the front and other at the rear. A bamboo ladder is used as an approach to the front varanda. Cattle are domestic animals and are generally kept under the bamboo platforms.

Since its inception, the Karbi Youth Festival holds in the name of certain important historical icons like one of them in the 41st Karbi Youth Festival-2015 was Dirchumai Arani which means *Dircumai's* Day. '*Dirchuma* is an' important personality as He was the first who held an important designation under the Traditional Institution of the Karbis. He was the first '*Jirsong Kleng Sarpo*' that means the first youth leader of the male dormitory of the Karbis. Not only that there was also '*jir Kedam*', the first traditional system established among the Karbi's, where young boys and girls go out for cultivation to other place. The '*jir Kedam*' has 10 (ten) office bearers with its leader '*Kleng Sarpo*' and its Deputy leader '*Klengdun*'. Though this '*jir Kedam*' became impossible with the changing of time, yet we find the tradition of '*Kleng Sarpo*' and '*Klengdun*' in each villages of Karbi Anglong.

The Karbi Youth Festival also tells us about the prevaling traditional political system of the Karbis. From the view point of habitation, the Karbis are divided into three groups namely, Chinthong, Ronghang and Amri. The Karbis shifted their Capital to Ronghang from Socheng, this place is also known as Ronghang Rongbong, situated about 16 kms from Hamren, a Sub-Divisional Headquarter of Karbi Anglong. There is a parliament called '*Pin Pomar*'. The '*Pin Pomar*' selects the traditional Karbi King '*Lindokpo*', who exercise the traditional authority in respect of socio-religious matters. The village headman is called '*Rong Sarthe*'. Several contiguous Karbi Kingdom constitute one '*Longri*' and the administrative officers of a '*Longri*' were called the '*Habe*'. The Kingdom has 12 (twelve) such Longri's and these Longri's were constituted into 4 (four) '*arthus*' and each '*arthus*' were governed by an officers called '*Lindok*' and the apex of the four *Lindoks* was the King called '*Recho*' or '*Lindokpo*'. The traditional political system of the Karbis is in the form of hierarchy.

But significant aspect of Karbis is that the Karbi Youth Festival gives the '*Jambilli Athon*'. A big '*Jambilli Athon*' is fixed at Hemphu-Mukrang Rasinja Aklam at Taralangso. The *Jambilli* is a wooden rod which carries a symbolical rod with the five Branches, at the end of each there is a wooden bird called in Karbi *'Vo-Rali'*. It represents the five clans of the Karbis. They are; the Terang, the Teron, the Enghee, the Engti, and the Timung. Each of these clans has as number of sub-clans. The *Jambilli* represents the unity of the all the clans of the Karbis. All the five clans are socially equal.

Thus, the Karbi Youth Festival has grown all throughout the years without any official recognition, state presence or patronage but it became successful in inspiring the passion of young generations ahead. Beyond the fun, entertainment and the festiveness, the food and the fashion, the music and the dance, the dream and the struggle of identity continued and flourished. The Karbi Youth festival became a resonant symbol of identity of the Karbi and a very unique way to presence, promote and showcase the rich Karbi heritage. This Festival is playing the role of an agent of socialisation of the Karbi culture, its history to the new generations. Each activity, the design, the farming, the symbols, the ethnic nomenclature of stages depicts the culturally rich Karbis. The Karbi Youth Festival signifies the particularity of the Karbis, its clans and kinsfolk and reinforces the Karbi identity as a unique tribe in India's federal Union.

Though, being such a cultural hub of the Karbis, the Karbi Youth Festival could not reach to the level of publicity compared to *Hornbill* and *sanghai*. There are many who recognises the neighbouring state festival of Assam, but do not have any knowledge about the 41 years old Karbi Youth Festival of the Karbis in Assam. The Karbi Youth Festival is never included as one of the major festival of the state. The electronic and print media also could played an active role all these years however the lack of publicity and improper government support has made this great festival of the Karbis a hidden and closed story to the other part of India and the World.

Since its inception in 1974, the festival mission has been to promote and share the culture and heritage of all the people of the Karbi descent with the Global Community. The 41st Karbi youth festival was sponsored by Karbi Anglong Autonomous Council (KAAC) and Assam Tourism, where we can say that it took 41 years for the state to recognise this largest festival of Assam. Now it is the pride and beauty of it. With the motive of unity and larger interest of the community, the Karbi Cultural Society had its theme composed.... *culture that unites and thrives through unity*. The Karbi youth festival has spread the sense of brotherhood among the Karbis through which the Karbis come under one roof of unity, despite different ideology, political background etc.

The first Assam Ethnic festival was also held at the very place Taralangso from March 13-15, 2015. With the greater interest to recognise, honour, unite, integrate and cherish all the ethnic groups of Assam. The holding of this festival at Taralangso, Karbi Peoples Hall, is a great honour and opportunity the people of the area and also signifies the importance of the place and the institution holding it which is the Karbi cultural society (KSC), the organiser and guardian of Karbi Youth Festival. It is because of this society that the Karbi culture stands bold and has kept its objective in organising and redefining and also educating the coming generation beyond all the political movements and instability.

As C. Hubert H. Pary said "folk –music supplies an epitome of the principles upon which art is founded". Russian classical musician told "it is the people who create music. We only arrange it", which the first one means that folk music narrates the entire principle from which the art and the culture are founded. Whereas the second statement reveals that it is the general people who create music but the musicians arrange it to the best. Both the statements just give one combination telling us the importance of traditional songs or music on the base of which the modern music beholds.

Thus, through this paper, the origin and growth is thoroughly traced, along with examining what the Karbi Youth Festival is all about. The '*Karbi riso nimso rong aje*' which means the Karbi Youth Festival shows us how the politics of culture played the role of politics of identity of the Karbi community.

The paper on the reclaiming of cultural identity of the Karbi through the Karbi youth festival concludes with its slogan,

"Jutang henlo khei aharchi

Kachingrum henlo khei atiri"

"Culture is the reflection of a society and the unification of the society is the pillar of it".

References

1. All the souvenirs published in the Karbi youth festivals since the year 1995.
2. An article on tribes and culture of Karbis from *Karbi Lammet Amei.*
3. Anthony Shay, *Choreographing Identities: Folk Dance, Ethnicity and Festival in the United States and Canada*, McFarland, 2006.
4. Boss Jacqueline, *Bucket List Festivals*, (E-book). http://www.escapenormal.com/2013/09/06/new-ebook-bucket-list-festivals-the-100-best-festivals-in-the-world/ (Accessed on 12th June, 2015).
5. Erich S. Gruen (Ed), *Cultural Identity in the Ancient Mediterranean: Issues and Debates*, Getty Research Institute, 201.
6. Interview with Chandra sing Kro, KCS President, Sanjay Killing, KCS General Secretary, Dharam Sing Teron, Independent Researcher, Diphu, Karbi Anglong.
7. Karbi Youth Fest's Blog.
8. Sharell Cook, *13 Popular North East India Festivals, India*, Travel Expert. http://goindia.about.com/od/festival information/ss/North-East-IndiaFestivals.htm (Accessed on 12th June, 2015).

III

Literature

9

Medieval Assam: A Reinterpretation of European Travel Writing

Monalisha Khakhlari

Introduction

The European writings reflect a chronological account of their trip, which usually began with a description about the preparation for expedition and then finally thriving themselves as a civilising mission. As "European discourses appear to separate their Self from the Indian Other-the essence of Western thought is practical reason, that of India a dreamy imagination, or the essence of Western society is the free (but selfish) individual, that of India an imprisoning (but providing) caste system" (Ronald Inden, 2000, 3). The European travellers show the idea of hardening European superiority leading to the manipulation of Orientalist theory which led Edward Said to coin the term *Orientalism,* describing the correlation between occident and orient as an asymmetrical one. Edward Said argues that the Orient "was almost a European invention" created by European scholars (the Orientalist) as a means of emphasising the West's hegemonic position (Procida A, Mary, 1996, 188).

I. Emergence of Exploration to Assam

Assam, though a fascinating state on a strategic frontier of India was not a popular destination in the earlier period. However, certain commercial interests and on rare occasions, a spirit of adventure attracted small number of foreigners including travellers, scholars, invaders, traders, soldiers, religious reformers and missionaries to this region. Since ancient times the particular region was visited and explored by many sages and travellers. Therefore, Assam like other parts of India received her due share from the writings of the classical Greek and Roman travellers (N.N. Acharyya, 1985, iii). The writings of Chinese travellers, Arabian travellers, and Persian travellers added valuable description to the limited picture of the ancient Assam history. In 1668 A.D., Teg Bahadur, the ninth guru of the Sikhs, visited Assam and established the 'Sikh tola' on the bank of the Brahmaputra at Dhubri. His account throws remarkable light on the history and geography of Assam (*ibid*, viii) European travellers have also augmented the history of Assam. Ralph Fitch, the first Englishmen to enter Assam in around 1586 describes about the administrative set-up with the system of legal affair. He also assessed the social and economic conditions. Two Portuguese Jesuit travellers named Father Stephen Cacella and Father John Cabral visited Hajo, Pandu and Koch Bihar in A.D. 1626. Their account describes the general condition of the land and people in the early seventeenth century A.D. (*ibid*), portraying new light on legal history of Mughal Kamrupa of that time. The Dutchman named John Van Leenen and a British merchant sailor named Thomas Bowrey, in the year A.D. 1661 and A.D. 1663 respectively, described the geographical area of 'Assam' bordering Bengal. In A.D. 1662, the Dutch traveller Frans van der Heiden, also known as Glanius, provided the aspects of Mughal period in Bengal and Assam. Two French travellers, Jean Baptiste Tavernier and Francois Bernier, who explored Assam during the Ahom period, wrote about the region in the sixties of the seventeenth century A.D. Jean Baptiste Tavernier was the one who provided significant information regarding the introduction of firearms by the Ahoms. Another French traveller, Jean Baptiste Chevalier who entered Assam in the year 1755, clearly reveals the mythical riches of Assam. Towards the end of the seventeenth century, Niccolo Manucci, an Italian soldier, who served in the army of Aurangzeb travelled in the neighbouring province of Bengal and collected information about Assam from the eye-witnesses. His account describes the military administration of the Ahoms and wealth and prosperity of contemporary Assam (ibid, ix). At the end of the eighteenth century and towards the beginning of the nineteenth century A.D. Assam has attracted large number of British civil and military officers. Alexander Dow, an English soldier wrote about Assam in A.D. 1769 (ibid). He gave a detailed description of the territorial invasion of Bengal by the King of Assam up to Dacca during the course of the civil war. Captain Thomas Welsh, a British military officer who stayed in Assam for two years (A.D. 1792 to 1794) underlined the account on Ahom administration and socio-economic aspects of Assam. John Peter Wade, a British Surgeon, who accompanied Captain Thomas Welsh to Assam in A.D. 1792, gathered clear information regarding natural features and historical accounts of Assam. He has left us a valuable account on the working of the Ahom administration and his article entitled *Geographical Sketch of Assam* is of vital importance to comprehend the history of Assam in the eighteenth century (S.L. Baruah, 2005, 51). During the period from A.D. 1808 to 1814, Francis Hamilton took on the survey of Assam as was commissioned by the East India Company for the same. Undoubtedly, he bestowed an important contribution to the study of political situation, economic resources and social life of the people of Assam just before the invasion of Burmese to Assam. Another European traveller, W. Robinson in his observation, *A Descriptive Account of Assam* (A.D. 1841), clearly describes the earliest traditions, ancient Kings of Kamarupa, Muslim invasions, rise of the Koches, the Ahom rule, insurrection of the Moamariyas, civil feuds and invasion of the Burmese (N.N. Acharyya, 1985, ix).

II. The Idea of Exploration

No doubt the accounts of European travellers such as Ralph Fitch, Father Stephen Cacella and Father John Cabral, Francois Bernier, Jean Baptiste Tavernier, Niccolo Manucci, Alexander Dow, John Peter Wade, Jean Baptiste Chevalier, and Captain Welsh had augmented the history of medieval Assam, yet we see the seeds of certain stereotypes being sow during this period that affected the received understanding of Assam later also. As Smith has argued that even eyewitness accounts 'cannot be accepted without criticism' because their bad intentions are 'clouds which obscure the absolute truth' (Ronald Inden, 2000, 16). Certain western representational strategies i.e. infantilisation, chronopolitics, gaze, eroticisation, degradation along with the practices of essentialising, stereotyping and classifying the other as backward, gloomy are clearly visible in the European writings which depicts the making of imperial meetings.

III. Representational Strategies

Infantilisation is a crucial representational strategy through which the 'Other' is rendered incapable of making decisions for it (*ibid*). The term chronopolitics is used to emphasise the relationship between the political behaviour of individuals and groups and their time-perspectives (Wallis.W George, 1970, 102). Chronopolitics, or the politics of time, has played an important role in Western representations of the non-western other. The other has been imagined as socially and culturally backward (in time) - medieval (feudal), archaic (like ancient Egyptians or Mesopotamians), prehistoric (primitive), or simply beyond the matrix of time (timeless). The colonial journey and travel of contemporary western commentators is often figured out as proceeding forward in geographical space but backward in historical time. This technique rendered non-dominant groups out of the present and legitimised control in the name of modernity. The notion of natives being backward, requiring the rule/control/guidance/assistance of more advanced "foreigners" to enter the modern era, was taken as uncontested fact (Anand Dibyesh, 2009, 31).

Gaze is not mere innocent curiosity: "to gaze implies more than to look at- it signifies a psychological relationship of power, in which the gazer is superior to the object of the Gaze" (Schroeder, 1998, 208). Though the gaze of European travellers might be taken into consideration as demonstrative or voyager, but it portrays an attempt of travellers to enforce Western beginning of instruction.

The idea of Eroticisation is an essential part to the westerners in representing the non-west i.e. other. The very language of exploration was marked by strong gender distinctions and drew much of its subconscious force from sexual imagery. The intent to subjugate indigenous people can be seen as the male's mastery of the female.

Throughout the ancient period, Assam has been related to degradation in the western imagination. Along with humiliation the westerners classified the non-west i.e. other as barbarian or uncivilised.

IV. Account of French Travellers to Assam

1. Jean-Baptiste Chevalier

Jean-Baptiste Chevalier, a French Governor in Chandernagore (1767-78) was an ardent defender of the French cause for the establishment of the Company's trade in India. He maintained close relations with the Indian princes. He was convinced with the notion that France could still create a sphere of influence in north India. Chevalier was given an important mission to go to Assam in order to acquire some land for the establishment of a factory. So, from here, it can be inferred that the main motive of Chevalier's visit was to establish trade relations with the north-eastern part of India. It is in this interest that this travel account could be looked upon.

Jean-Baptiste Chevalier, a European writer, had a preconceived notion towards Assam as he stated, "My instructions were that, in case Assem (Assam) happens to be as rich as it is believed to be, then I should leave no stone unturned to get an allowance for a plot of land from its prince in order to build a lodge there" (Dutta Baruah, Caroline and Jean Deloche, 2008, 23). As Edward Said argues, stereotypical images of the Orient's separateness- "its eccentricity, its backwardness, its silent indifference, its feminine penetrability, its supine malleability"- have been part of Western discursive practices for a long time (Anand Dibyesh, 2009, 20).

The notion of superiority of a European traveller is quite visible in his account when he refused to bow in front of the King. To him these particular rules in the kingdom were too humiliating for Europeans and therefore, he greeted the King in European style. Imaginative practices through which the imperial West came to represent the 'Other' can be interrogated through the various strategies of representation involved (*ibid*, 21).

Jean-Baptiste Chevalier describes the landscapes, flora and fauna of Assam. The landscapes on the riverbanks were monotonous (Dutta Baruah, Caroline and Jean Deloche (Ed), 2008, 14). On his journey to Assam, in the river of Banar i.e. one of the branches of the Brahmaputra that creates the Lakhya, he refer that "on both sides we saw only jungles, with no sign of dwellings" (*ibid*, 115). In the beginning of the journey, he did not find a scenic beauty. He came by a boat through the river and so, he could only see the sand banks, which made him give the description as monotonous. Going deeper in his journey, he says that the horizon on both sides presented the view of an impenetrable line of trees or reed, interrupted sometimes by human establishments. Here, he shifts from his earlier comment considering the beauty as monotonous.

Jean- Baptiste Chevalier was quite bewildered by the forests that made him say that the wild animals present in the place fronted an enduring risk to the cultivable land. This country is a land of misery and poverty instead of flourishing. In Rangamati, he noted down that "besides, the entire landscape along the route to get there is always the same: a deserted country full of jungles where tigers are the only inhabitants" (*ibid*, 131). It can be argued that the land in Assam was suitable for cultivation but the presence of wild animals made life difficult for cultivation. But, one thing to be remembered here is that numerous changes have occurred in this area since the beginning of the eighteenth century. Lands were being made cultivable at the expense of clearing the jungles. Later, he discovered the cultivation of jute at that land by comparing the land with Bengal, a place which enjoyed supreme monopoly in the world. He also mentions a strange hunt of fishing wild boars. During floods, the water rose up to 10 metres and many islands were submerged; animals that had settled during the dry season must then reach the bank by swimming, and at this point the people catch the animals (*ibid*,148-149). This shows a wild description of the people of the place, which can also be inferred that he did not see such people in the rest of India. The pre-conceived notion of the traveller comes in to account, which I had mentioned earlier.

He further mentions that apart from the hostility of the vegetation, there is the presence of unhealthy climate in the area. The climate was of extreme nature. He says- "Daily, about five to six times, we were passing from suffocating heat to bitter cold. If it was a bit windy by any chance, we had to cover ourselves as in winter and as soon as the wind stopped, we could scarcely breathe because of the heat" (*ibid*,146). Further, he says, "The fig during a part of the morning was so extensive and so thick that we had to wait until it cleared to start out. As we were going forward we felt the most biting cold, to the extent that all my people, Europeans and others, could hardly bear it" (Dutta Baruah, Caroline and Jean Deloche, 2008, 174).

In continuation, Chevalier further says that "during the rainy season that starts in April and ends only in September, the inhabitants are prone to a wasting disease that wears them down slowly and from which they die." (*ibid*, 134). This throws a bad light on the climate of Assam and in this process; he also compares it with that of France. He found a contrasting difference in climate of the two places, and this also applied in the case of India also. India had different types of climates, which he has described in his book.

To Jean-Baptiste Chevalier, the towns were not organised. They are badly described in his account. Only the picturesque site of Goaty (Guwahati, the capital of one of the main provinces of the kingdom) attracted him. As he stated, 'the city is located on both sides on the edge of the river behind a long mountain range forming a natural amphitheatre, all the more pleasant since it is natural' (Dutta Baruah, Caroline and Jean Deloche, 2008, 171).

He also talks about the trade in his account. The establishment of trading relations was the main motive of his visit. But, to the utter dismay, he only gives a summarised account of the trade. After talking with the border authorities in Rangamati, he came to the conclusion that it was easy to bribe the people at the border on the side of Bengal. This, he points out as one of the reasons for the snail paced progress of the trade between the two places. And as such, it was easy to divert the custom rules because of the disorganised administration of the province.

He talks about the Assamese border authorities. The *duaria barua* had the exclusive privilege of commerce with Bengal and received custom duties on all the goods. The chief item of import from Bengal was salt, which was in high demand in Assam. It was the perspective to earn big profits that attracted Bengali merchants to Assam. Jean-Baptiste Chevalier points out that salt were stored at Yogighopa and that merchants had to pay heavy taxes in Alamganj and in Rangamati, which was fixed at the rate of 20 per cent per transaction (*ibid*, 131-134).

Jean-Baptiste Chevalier further found that the Assamese authorities were less accommodating than the Bengali civil servants. But, he doesn't describe the reason behind this. He experienced this by not declaring the value of his goods, which were contraband for one part, but then he had to transfer them on Assamese boats (*ibid*, 151-161). After this illegal attempt, he was not able to trade in Assam. The tradition in Assam played the catalyst, which did not allow any person without the permission of the King to trade. He points out that the lack of confidence and distrustful towards outsiders of the Assamese made business transactions difficult. But, this cannot be taken as the reason for the Assamese being less accommodating than the Bengali civil servants. To him 'the people of the country are rascals. They are extremely crude and rash, besides being cruel and inhumane' (*ibid*, 141).

Finally, he mentions about the political administration of the Ahom. The Kings of Assam are called: *The God King who never walks on the earth, as he is worthy of being carried.* (*ibid*, 38). He says that the ruler was a despot; the King exercised despotic powers on his subjects and compares the subjects to slaves. However, Chevalier misinterpreted the administrative machinery as the king was not a despotic monarch, but was responsible to the Council of Ministers and they could remove the king if needed. He failed to take this into account. If the king was a despot, he would not have wine and food with his subjects. Also he misinterpreted the *Paik* system as slavery. No doubt, they were bound to the state, but cannot be compared with the European counterparts, which he did.

Chevalier also mentions that he was amased by the houses in the area which were made up of ordinary straw covering the room. But he concludes that they were made so because the area was prone to earthquake. On the contrary, the actual explanation for these types of houses is the economic factor, to which he was misled in his observation.

In his account, he mentions about the Kamakhya temple and the attachment of the people towards the temple. Yet he failed to give a proper description on the sources based on the temple. The hunting of animals by the king surprises him. He was amased to see the large number of people accompanying the king and drums were being beaten also. This tradition, according to Jean-Baptiste Chevalier, was totally absent in Europe. He was awe struck by the hunting expedition. Undoubtedly, he compared Assam with Bengal and Europe and in the end brought certain misleading conclusions.

2. Francois Bernier

Francois Bernier travelled to Assam with Mir Jhumla, the Governor of Bengal during the course of the Ahom – Mughal conflict. The expedition to conquer Assam started from Dacca in 1661 (Francois Bernier, 1997, 171). The Mughal army was marching ahead with victory and the Ahom King started to flee from one place to another place. Finally, the Mughal army could not move beyond Gurgaon. Francois Bernier goes on to describe about the place justifying the idea of exploratory on other. He mentions that Guerguon (Gurgaon, the then capital city of the Assam Kingdom) contained lots of wealth, which attracted the Mughal (Francois Bernier, 1997, 172). He also tries to bring in the economic importance of the city. The city was largely built and it was commercial in nature and the flow of trade was very visible in the city. Further, he mentions that the city was also popular for the beauty of its women (*ibid*).

Proceeding further, he mentions that Assam was very customary to rains. The rainfall used to be very heavy, inundating every spot of ground, with the exception of villages built on eminences. He talks about the mountains of the area which turned out to be barriers for the Mughal in their war against the Ahoms. He further mentions that the Mughal had to retreat as the waters and deep mud compounded the trouble (*ibid*, 172). Mir Jhumla was compelled to be confined to his camp during the whole of the rainy season and after the rainy season; his men were dispirited by their incessant fatigue. Finally, he had to abandon the idea of conquering.

3. Jean-Baptist Tavernier

Jean-Baptist Tavernier also explored Assam during the course of the seventeenth century. He procured first hand information about Assam through his visit with Mir Jhumla during the course of the Ahom – Mughal wars. He begins by bringing an ancient belief that gunpowder and guns were first found in Assam and it passed on to Pegu and from Pegu to China. But, before the beginning of the war with the Mughal, the people of Assam did not have any experience of war for 500 – 600 years. So, Tavernier thought them to be an easy opponent, (Jean Baptiste Tavernier, 1977, 217) as it is natural for the Europeans in linking themselves with eminence and superiority and other as weak.

While preparing for the war, Mir Jhumla came to know that the Ahoms were ready for the battle with a large number of troops equipped with guns, grenades and abundance of fire work. Mir Jhumla decided not to wage war at the moment for the reason that the weather was cold. Later he started his march and finally could not move beyond Azoo (Azo is a place near present Hajo).

Tavernier goes on to describe that the people of India cannot bear cold weather and Assam was not an exception to it (*ibid*, 217-218). A portrayal of the 'other' as incompetent can be seen in this description. Nevertheless, Tavernier has illustrated about the town and its customs. He starts by describing that the tombs of the 'kings of Assam' and the royal family are situated in Azoo. He says that the people of Assam are idol worshippers and do not burn the bodies of the deceased but bury them. He talks about the beliefs of the people of Assam, who believed that after death the deceased go to another world, which has two divisions. Those who were good during their lifetime enjoy a life full of pleasure and on the contrary, those who were bad suffer after death. Talking about customs, he says that after death the ornaments and the most precious possessions of the King were placed next to his grave. Some animals were also buried next to the King, which was believed that their lifeline ended with the King and they would come back with the King in the next incarnation. He used to be buried in the chamber built by him during his lifetime. He mentions that Mir Jhumla started digging these graves and found lots of wealth. He moves on to describe some acts of barbarism also in the form of wives of the king poisoning themselves Jean Baptiste Tavernier, 1977, 219-220). This description given by Tavernier is very difficult to understand. Yet the concept of imagining the 'other' as backward by the Europeans is visible in his account.

He proceeds on to describe the kingdom of Assam, by asserting that the kingdom was self dependent. It did not feel the need to search anything in the neighbouring places. He saw the silk production and described it as it is made from silkworm, which is round in shape and it remains in the tree for the whole year. The clothes made from silk are beautiful but he did not find the clothes to be enduring. With the silk production, he also describes about the gold and silver mines. Geographically, this lies to the southern part of the Kingdom (*ibid*, 220).

He also noticed the abundance of shellac in the kingdom, which were of two types. One is formed on the trees and is of red colour, which people use to dye their clothes. After dying their clothes, they use the lack to lacquer cabinets and other stuffs. They also make Spanish wax out of it. These lacks were exported to China and Japan for manufacture of cabinet. He found these lacks to be the best in Asia (*ibid*, 220-221). He doesn't describe about the other form of shellac found in the kingdom.

The gold and silver were found in the kingdom. Nobody was permitted to take gold out of the kingdom. Gold was not coined into money although it was a medium of exchange during trade among the merchants. The King used to keep it in vessels of different shapes. Silver was coined into money in the form of coins, which was octagonal in shape and it could be taken out of the kingdom (*ibid*, 221).

In the writing of Tavernier about food, the notion of uncivilised and naive characteristics' is reflected. He pointed out that the flesh of dogs was the favourite food of the people. The meat was sold in markets, which was brought from different places. He found grapes in the Kingdom, which were sweet but was disappointed when he could not find wine. Salt was manufactured in the Kingdom but the process of manufacturing salt started with the collection of the waste vegetables. The waste vegetables were dried and burned, and finally the ash was boiled and strained, which turned into salt. He also describes about another process of preparing salt, which is from the leaves of the tree. Comparing both the qualities of salt, he commented that the salt from the leaves was very harsh to consume so the people had to boil it before use. He also mentioned that these leaves were used in the dying process of silk (*ibid*, 220-221).

Finally, he describes about Kamrup. He starts by locating it as the residence of the King. The King did not take tributes from his subjects but all the gold and silver mines belonged to the King. He did not oppress his subjects to work in the mines; rather he would hire people from neighbouring Kingdoms to work in the mines (*ibid*, 222-223). This observation does not hold true in all cases. The natives were needed to work for the washing of gold. Describing further, he asserts that the people of Assam are well off. They have large areas of land and the houses used to be in the middle of the plot. A fountain was surrounded by trees and majority of the people used to keep elephants for their wives (*ibid*, 223). It can be argued here that Tavernier concluded about the living places of the people through the aristocratic view of the society and ignored the economically weaker section. In addition he moves on to describe that in spite of people believing in idol worship, polygamy was prevalent in the society. In order to maintain cordial relation among all the wives of a man, he used to signify wife for different works, which can be criticised as women being treated as objects in the eyes of Tavernier. But, if we look into the social set up of that particular period, we find that women enjoyed a much better position in the society. Adding to it, the practice of polygamy is also in doubt and the process of establishing cordial relations among the different wives of a man makes the whole process of observation of a foreign traveller a mockery.

Furthermore, he describes that the people are nicely built and found them to be olive coloured. They have a flat nose and they wear small pieces of cloth, which Tavernier described as 'calico'. The women pierce their ears and wear gold ornaments. Men used to keep their hair long till the shoulder and women keep it as long as it can grow. He also mentions the use of tortoise shell bracelets by both the sections. The bracelets were of yellow and coral. The bracelets were removed before they were buried (*ibid*, 224).

Conclusion

It can be asserted from the writings, that the European travellers to Assam had 'some' preconceived idea through which they tried to locate their journey in their notions. The travellers to Assam, with diverse intentions, outlined the character of its own identity. This clearly shows that the travel accounts cannot be taken singularly, it has to be corroborated with the other sources. Travel accounts should be studied with a dose of precaution and it should be verified with other sources. No doubt, the travellers entered Assam with different motives and with certain illusion, yet they throw light on interesting facts which nonetheless provides us information for the study of the period of their travel. The illusion created by these travellers cannot be taken as true in certain cases but the facts have to be studied carefully in order to get a precise history. This, in fact, brings out the importance of the travel accounts for the study of the past.

References

1. Ronald Inden, *Imagining India,* Indiana University Press, USA, 2000.
2. Procida A Mary, 'A Tale Begun in Other Days: British Travelers in Tibet in the Late Nineteenth Century', *Journal of Social History*, Vol. 30, No 1, 1996, pp. 185-208.
3. N.N. Acharyya, *North East as viewed by Foreigners*, Omsons Publications, New Delhi, 1985.
4. S.L. Baruah, *A Comprehensive History of Assam,* Munshiram Manoharlal Publishers, New Delhi, 2005.
5. Wallis W. George, 'Chronopolitics: The Impact of Time Perspectives on the Dynamics of Change', *Social Forces,* Vol. 49, No.1, Sep. 1970.

6. Anand Dibyesh, *Tibet: A Victim of Geopolitics*, Routledge, Tolstoy Marg, New Delhi, 2009.
7. Dutta Baruah, Caroline and Jean Deloche (Ed), *The Adventures of Jean- Baptiste Chevalier in Eastern India (1752- 1765)*, LBS Publications, Guwahati, 2008.
8. Francois Bernier, *Travels in Mogul Empire A.D. 1656- 1668,* (Second Edition Revised and Edited by Vincent A. Smith), Low Price Publication, Delhi, 1997.
9. Jean Baptiste Tavernier, *Travels in India,* Oriental Books Reprint Corporation, New Delhi, (Second Edition by William Crooke), Vol. II, 1977.

10

Off the Beaten Path: Critical Ethnography of Selected Narratives on Northeast India

Bhaskar Jyoti Gogoi and Narayan Ch. Gahatraj

"There is no power relation without the correlative constitution of a field of knowledge, nor any knowledge that does not presuppose and constitute at the same time power relations"

- *Michel Foucault, 1975*

The often quoted maxim "Knowledge is power" reflects how uncritical thinking process, narrow perception and limited modes of understanding diminish the capacity to envision alternative life possibilities and lead to a state of domestication. In this state, people will accept any form of dominant ideologies to be the one and only form of knowledge. Domestication will prohibit any new form of addressing conflict, and it will have the tendency to reject whatever is alien and different. Knowledge is power relative to social justice as it leads us to unravel and displace complicit systems and equips us with the tools to identify, question and act against the prevalent injustice.

But, how justified is any form of representation that is done by someone outside of the margins of a particular community. How authentic and true will be the report of an ethnographer or an anthropologist who comes into the contact of a particular tribe/ community/race of people and form a discourse of these people based on his experiences with these people? Do we even need to care about the authenticity of these discourses? Maybe the answer lies in a particular quote given by Stuart Hall. Hall quotes, "How people are represented is how they are treated"(Hall, 1997). Whenever a particular person is documented and represented by any other person, the reader or audience of that account meets the subject, learns of his/her experiences and the culture of the subject through the idiosyncratic lens of the interpreter's interpretation. In this interpretation is held a great deal of power and as such much care has to be taken regarding any form of representation of the "Other". Many questions arise in such an instance. How do we reflect upon and evaluate our own purpose, intention and frames of analysis as documenters and researchers? Who is responsible for any possible consequences of any misrepresentation whether intentional or unintentional? How can a systematic dialogue be established and maintained between the researcher and the subject/object of their study? How is the specificity of the local story relevant to the broader meanings and operations of the human condition? Moreover, also the major question of whether the work can or will make any justifiable contribution to equity, freedom and justice?

The answer to all these questions lies in the field of critical ethnography as the field of critical ethnography begins with an ethical responsibility to address processes of unfairness and injustice within a particular lived domain. Critical ethnography is a critical theory based approach to ethnography. It has been most aptly defined by Jim Thomas as "conventional ethnography with a political purpose". The main focus of critical ethnography is based upon focusing on unacknowledged biases that may creep up in ethnographic studies due to the implicit values expressed within it. The critical ethnographer takes us beneath surface appearances and disrupts *status quo* unsettling both neutrality and taken-for-granted assumptions by bringing to light underlying and obscure operations of power and control. Therefore, the critical ethnographer "resists domestication and moves from not only describing "what is" but also asks of "what could be" in order to disrupt text power relationships and perceived social inequalities. The critical ethnographer is inseparable from the context and speaks on behalf of the subjects. He/she have to attempt to recognise and articulate their own perspective. In doing that, their own shortcomings and biases also has to be considered and the bearings their own limitations, histories and institutional standpoints bear on their work. As such, critical ethnography must begin to extend its political aims and augment its notion of "domestication" and "politics". But, politics alone are incomplete without self-reflection. So, critical ethnography must extend its goals from simply politics to the politics of positionality. The question here emerges as to how to discuss the positionality of the ethnographer in their representation of the "Others"?

The discussion regarding the politics of positionality has been described by thinkers ranging from Jurgen Habermas (1971) to Michelle Fine (1994). These thinkers have bifurcated the social positions of inquiry to three positions:

1. The ethnographer as non-existent or invisible,
2. Vague presence of the ethnographer but not addressed in an adequate manner,
3. Clear and active presence of the ethnographer within the context of study and offering of alternative models for the existent ones.

Only the positionality is not enough for a realistic and justified representation but what is also required is a deep and abiding dialogue with the other as never before. The whole empirical basis of the ethnographer has to remain grounded in the world of the other. As such, the interrogation of the positionality has not to be only on the grounds of subjectivity but beyond that. The attention to the subjective self has to be in its relation to the other and is informed by our engagement and representation of the other. We are not simply subjects, but we are subjects in dialogue with the other. As such, critical ethnography is always a meeting of multiple sides with and among the others, one in which there is a negotiation and dialogue toward substantial and viable meanings that make a difference in the other's world.

I. Decolonisation:

The legacy of colonialism and the movements for independence continue to significantly shape political regimes around the globe. Anti-colonial movements critiqued and revolted against the unequal distribution of power in the world. They were less successful at generating alternative, more equitable modes of distributing power, which is what decolonisation, understood as truly ending the disparities of colonialism entail. Decolonisation is unrealised, but not necessarily unrealisable. Decolonisation, the dream of self-rule, is the most recent incarnation of the long-standing project to achieve political freedom and therefore deserves a prominent place in the discipline of political theory. Political theories of decolonisation provide extended ruminations about the challenges of finding a new polity that is more just, and they have the potential to deepen how political theorists understand core concepts such as freedom, equality, sovereignty, and the rule of law.

"Decolonisation" entered the lexicon in the 1930s but did not attain popularity until thirty years later. It is an awkward and inelegant word, therefore, in a way, appropriate to the subject it attempts to describe. Unlike the phrase "end of empire" which has a certain poetic economy suggesting a grand and sweeping occurrence, "decolonisation" is work a-day, rather like other "de" prefixed words that denote cleansing changes. Decolonisation was not a process but a clutch of fitful activities and events, played out in conference rooms, acted out in protests mounted in city streets, fought over in jungles and mountains. Its results pleased no one. It was too hastily done for some, too slowly carried out for others, too incomplete in effect for most. The subject is historically loose ended; there is no end to discussion of it. Not only does the old historical problem of mechanical physics here arise again the question of whether the European colonial empires were overthrown or collapsed because of their own weight—but continuing problems of political and social exploitation in the contemporary world beg this question: are these, too, the outcomes of decolonisation as a failed exercise in the transfer of power and nation-building?

Postcolonial political theorists and theorists of decolonisation focus on the particular moments in which new regimes get founded. They look into issues of how the political interruption of a political order came about and also looks for insights into how the legitimacy of the new regime was founded, asserted and eventually grounded. Persistent questions of whether such a change bring about progress and change or will it lead to the re-foundation of an old regime set up on new policies and new formulations. All the historical stories, fables and noble lies have been one of the foundational devices for the explanation of state policies and bestowing of legitimacy for state authorities. These stories are strategic and retrospective, inventing a past that serves the present. They provide a foundation for polities by making claims about the past, yet they also shape the present and the future. A study of these narratives on the de-colonial angle makes evident the struggle between the aspirations to change the course of history and the constraints that inevitably encroach upon human action. This tendency of the desire to change the course of history and assert self-determination, accompanied by a need to nonetheless reckon with the colonial legacies of colonialism becomes one of the central and recurring features of decolonisation theories.

Indian culture which is known for its religions and culture was recognised by the colonial powers. Colonisers considered Indian culture as the one that is in opposition to their Western culture and therefore thought there is a need to revive Indian culture to a large extent. For them Indian culture was the culture of the 'other'. And what Sebastian Conrad points out by tracing this historical past that today Indian culture has great amount of colonial influence and impact. Not only colonial past alone, but also Globalisation and Liberalisation have changed the image of our Indian culture. Sebastian Conrad points out that our legal structures, policies, systems of Governance and Education, etc. are heavily shaped by mimicking our colonial masters. Then, what is really "Indian" in it?

In Sebastian Conrad's view, 'culture' needs to be redefined and re-understood by placing it in our own context. For this, we have to come up with our own theories and frameworks about culture by taking into consideration our colonial legacies and also exploring new ways of understanding culture by our own experiences of everyday life. The rationale behind this write up is to make an attempt to understand our own culture by our own perspectives rather than to understand our culture from coloniser's point of view.

The British rule introduced the railways, the press, and the western system of education, clubs and associations all of which shook the prevalent socio-economic order. But the processes of exploitation unleashed by them destroyed the possibilities of development of industries and a modern economic system in India. The British rule rather systematically destroyed the native industries of India for the benefit of the industries in Britain and their market in India. Even though it sought to tie down the people it ruled to colonial backwardness, it released new historical forces within the Indian fold by throwing the traditional economic system and socio-cultural order out of gear. It gave birth to the desire of material advancement and better amenities and living conditions of individuals. Also it gave birth to a spirit of inquiry in the minds of Indian intellectuals who came in contact with western education. Both the social reformists and the conservatives took a fresh and critical look at their own society and culture as a reaction to western interpretation of the same.

The establishment of British rule in the late eighteenth century prompted British officials, missionaries and scholars to acquire knowledge of the classical languages of India, of the structure of Indian society and of values and manners of her people. The economic base was primarily agricultural, the tools and implements did not register any remarkable change through time, and arts and crafts mostly connected with poorly developed production grew. Socially the framework consisted of comparatively self-sufficient village communities in groups of contiguous villages. Caste was the typical Indian institution to accommodate various socio-economic strata and nascent classes, binding them together in groups and ensuring such constituents an occupational protection as well.

II. Colonial Ethnography

In the postcolonial context the study on colonial ethnography is in a way transforming into a diverse and interesting topic as it constructs as well as deconstructs diverse colonised identities. These identities by becoming a kind of referents produces diversified understanding of communities and ethnic groups, their ways of life and also brings forth various contestations. Unlike the meta-narrative of official documents, these ethnographic narratives (like travel writing, biographies, autobiographies, diaries etc.) offers a new mode of exploring textual resources and have contributed immensely in the construction of postcolonial discourses. These narratives provide a kind of alternative form of knowledge acquirement in the understanding of people and their customs and cultures. They have become a new kind of source which has brought the discourses of the marginal to the centre by deconstructing the colonist's attempts to give a voice to the native's mouth. As such, an examination of many of the colonised texts from the post-colonialist point of view attempts to understand how the natives and the colonised were constructed in these narratives.

III. Alternative Modernities

In recent times, the idea of alternative modernities has become a common word applied in the humanities and social sciences. Conceptually, it tries to negotiate a whole series of phenomenon that were unreconstructed and insists on the refocusing of some modernities that were considered primal, primitive, irrational and ancient and could not exist with the ever encompassing modernity that had been envisioned by the West. The terrain of alternative modernities across the disciplines of humanities and social sciences acknowledges the fact that western modernity project has led to the rise of certain other indigenous and traditional forms of modernities.

The annals of European social thought are abundant with accounts of modernity and its defining characteristics. The origin of modernity varies from person to person. For some, modernity began with the rise of the capitalist world-system whereas for some it begins with the colonial projects of intervention of the West in the continents of Africa, Asia and America. For many others, it begins with the construction/re-construction of secular states or in the rise of bio-politics. But, whatever may be the distinguishing characteristics, the modernity aroused by Europe has now gone global and it is no longer the all representing or the sole domain of the relatively few societies of the West. Modernity defines the whole society at large. But, to say that modernity has been globalised, is not to say that modernity has been globalised in the same way at all instance. Traditional knowledge system has always co-existed with the modern, and forms of religiosity and other cultural practices deemed primitive by the champions of modernity exist along the forms of production and exchange. This will be a bit rudimentary to term it as a failure of modernity. An important vein of contemporary also suggests that this can be accounted as signs of something else. Rather than viewing these as failures of the modernising impulse, these diverse practices can be best understood as signs and sites of alternative modernities and the complex dynamics of cultural and social modernisation implied therein.

Modernities are everywhere, at precisely the time modernity as the epochal discourse of the West appears to be on its last legs. This is one of the more paradoxical features of the globe. One might declare the end of modernity in a narrow sense as Jean-François Lyotard (and postmodernism in general) does, but to declare its end even as an epoch is either to fall into the fallacy that modernity has remained a Western phenomenon, or to colonise the world with the Western paradigm of the postmodern. The sense that modernity is at a turning point comes not, I would suggest, from its imminent demise either through the "end of history" (Fukuyama) or the "clash of civilisations" (Huntington), but from its global, transcultural, and variegated character. Globalisation may now be characterised by the multiplicity of its modernities and post-colonial theory provides a way to understand why this is so. How it does that will require a closer look at the journey of post-colonial theory itself and the pitfalls its alliance with globalisation studies has opened up.

The discussion with regard to alternative modernities is not a plea for a retrieval and reversal to indigenous knowledge systems. It helps in deconstructing the dominant knowledge paradigms to explore the possibility of other alternative paradigms. As a part of colonial modernity, several invasive processes such as deforestation, displacement of people, development of urban slums etc. disrupted the traditional knowledge systems of India. The Indian knowledge system was part of the ecosystem in which holistic knowledge system had been formulated. These were the consequences of a cumulative and fine turned pool of human experience, spanning over long periods that involved many complex cultural interrelationships. But the knowledge system of India has been accused to be not having a historical sense, but also as having antecedent phase traditionality for our colonial modernity. As has been argued by Marx (1853), "Indian society has no history at all, at least no known history. What we call its history, is but the history of the successive intruders who founded their empires on the passive basis of that unresisting and unchanging society." Thus, the concept of modernity needs to be understood within the spatial and temporal contexts in which it is appropriated as a concept. In that line of thought, alternative modernism, vernacular modernism etc. can be perceived as not continuities to Western modernism, but as deviant and subversive constructions.

IV. The Paradigm of Northeast

In Northeast India there amalgamates diverse ethnic and religious groups having different beliefs and customs. However, the land has been plagued by problems like unchecked militancy, insurgency, ethnic riots and killings etc. This rapidly suffusing violence has disrupted and paralysed normal life. This region has been, for generations, the battleground for sub-national identities confronting insensitive nation-states and internecine strife. It is a battle of ideas and arms, of new concepts and old traditions and of bitterness and compassion. This imposed nomenclature and constructed identity of Northeast generates a site for encounter; and therefore, within the region there are evidences of fractures: 'things fall apart' and 'the centre cannot hold'; marginalisation engenders further marginalisation.

Kailash C. Baral in "Articulating Marginality: Emerging Literatures from Northeast India" says the emerging literatures from Northeast are variously critiqued as ethnic writing, lacking in history and tradition, and often subjected to the virulent diatribe that it lacks in aesthetic virtuosity. These critical opinions are at best paternalistic and at worst, smack of ignorance in understanding the societies and cultures of the Northeast. Contemporary writers from this region aspire towards a vision beyond the narrow ethnic groove and represent a shared history. In these writings, the cultural memory is reprocessed in that the intensity of feeling overflows the labour of technique and craft. Tilottama Misra says that, "significantly, for mainland India, the region known as the 'North-East' has never had the privilege of being at the centre of epistemic enunciation... the imagination of the 'mainland' has even today not overgrown those constructs of the mysterious 'other'. Temsula Ao, says that the 'otherness' has helped them to overcome their isolation once their thoughts and feelings are textualised; yet the uniqueness of their cultural difference has not disappeared. In spite of this assertion, marginality defines the essence of that 'otherness.' It becomes a defining trope that signifies this literature's location as well as its reception by mainstream critics. However, literary marginality contests and problematised some of the universalistic assumptions of literature while factoring in and often valorising the unique ethnic and cultural experience that needs to be critically evaluated. The major factor has been the shift from "Master/Grand Narratives" to "Meta/ Local Narratives"; the metamorphosis from globalisation to glocalisation. Objectified history is rendered insufficient to understand factors and is replaced by "comparative history", moving dialectically between past and present, between concrete observation and an awareness of the heterogeneity and complexity of life.' A "comparative" literary history would not only try to keep in the fore ground this dialectic hermeneutic movement between past and present, but would try to do something analogous to what Braudel and the Annales school accomplished in their moving of history emphasis from the events of politics and diplomacy to, on the one hand, a study of the broader circumstances (demographic, geographical, climactic, etc.) conditioning such events and, on the other, a parallel and very detailed scrutiny of the concrete material data (quantified) of life of the past.

The Northeast region of India with the presence of over two hundred ethnic groups and about six hundred odd ethnic communities was perhaps one of the most difficult terrains for the colonial administrators. From the onset itself, the geographical territory of Northeast had been seen even by the British administrators to be a locale quite different and varied from the rest of India. The sensitive geo-political location along with the existence of diverse ethnic groups having different historical backgrounds distinguishes these states from the rest of the country. Predominantly, there are two views of the regions- one of the outsider and that of the insider. The former see the region as a relatively unitary entity, delimited by India's boundaries with other countries and the latter sees it as an extreme diversity of tribes, communities, languages, religions, customs, traditions and histories. As such, the study of any issue occurring in the Northeast has to be studied keeping in mind the diversity and multi-diversified context of the region. Tillotama Misra while referencing to the issue has pointed out the fact that the terming of this region under single umbrella term of the "Northeast" is indeed problematic. She further argues that '[o]ne has to recognise that there are many different communities in the region and the dynamics of each single movement have to be taken care of, if any solution is to be achieved'. Misra (2000) Hussain (2004) also formulates a similar observation and states that "[b]y bracketing the eight Northeastern states, with its diverse tribes, customs and cultures, into what is called the 'Northeast' we tend to ignore the distinct identity and sub-national aspirations of these ethnic groups". More so, such clubbing together of the region, in an attempt to look at it as a single entity, has led to stereotyping of the problem that plague the area (Haokip, 2011). "The North Eastern states of India may be looked upon as a political unit for the purposes of administrative convenience by the Government of India today, but historically at no point of time has it ever been a political unit, either culturally, economically or politically" (Sharma, 2004, 1). Haokip (2011) further makes an observation on the issue and states that,

It is true that the north-eastern region shares certain common problems like ethnic unrests, insurgency, immigration, drug trafficking, communication gap etc. However, there are severe intra-regional differences in social issues and ethno-political aspirations. The region is, in fact, one of the most ethnically and linguistically diverse regions in Asia and each state have its distinct cultures and traditions (113-114).

It is true that historically the region has witnessed high levels of violence, particularly armed insurrection and political violence directed, in equal measure against settlers, against different ethnic groups and the authorities, stemming mostly from ethnic and state subjugation. 'It was among the first regions to demonstrate, on the attainment of Independence, signs of severe political crisis in the form of nationalist movement' (Hassan 2007, 1). "Furthermore, plagued with dreadful inter-ethnic clashes, ever-growing separatist demands and criminalised insurgencies illustrated by the press, the Northeast soon got tagged with the unenviable epithet of the 'sick man' of India' (Egreteau, 2007, 5). However, there has been a continuous engagement on the part of the state to address issues and crises in the Northeast India but it remained unresolved till date due to its complexities and cross-cutting issues prevailing in the region.

V. Northeast and Dalton Hooker's *Himalayan Journals*

Colonial administrators were the first and foremost people who documented the terrain of the Northeast. Either for administrative purposes or for anthropological/ethnographical research they carried out surveys preparing reports, surveys and other materials. These materials became valuable sources for the documentation and source of information regarding the difficult terrain of the Northeast. Many documentaries ranging from the detailed history of Assam written by Edward Gait to hundreds of photos and videos taken by Haimendorf to the collection of artifacts collected by Hutton and Mills these books, reports, photos, videos, artifacts became valuable treasure for any anthropological inquiry into the territory of Northeast India. But, the valuable question regarding these colonial anthropologists/ ethnographers in the region is the logic of inquiry i.e. the methodology that was adopted by them. For example, the standpoint that had been taken by Verrier Elwin in the reporting and representation of the tribes of the Northeast has been questioned by many people in the recent times as Elwin is known to be not a professional anthropologist. As such, the ontology and epistemological premises of colonial ethnographers, and their framework remains questionable.

Though the number of colonial texts about Northeast is very few in number, some of the relevant texts throw light on various aspects of the life of the people of the Northeast and also lets us understand the process of colonisation in Northeast. One such text is Sir Joseph Dalton Hooker's *Himalayan Journals*. It is a botanical document that in a way introduced India's Northeast to the Eurocentric gaze. Hooker's text is a testimony of the travels of a botanist-traveller and of his experiences and interactions with the people who lived on his route. In a way, Hooker's journal can be read as a colonial document for historical understanding of the people of Northeast and particularly the Khasi people. His chapter on the Khasi people which he titled as *Khasia Hills* is an elaborate attempt to understand the Khasi people and can be justified to be revealers of history of those times. As such, Hooker's *Himalayan Journals* can be seen as an example of how alternative history could be produced from works of other genres and texts written by non-historians other than the official histories in order to highlight the colonial process of knowledge production and representation of the colonial Northeast.

Sir Joseph Dalton Hooker (30 June 1817 – 10 December 1911) was one of the greatest British botanists and explorers of the nineteenth century. Hooker was a founder of geographical botany, and Charles Darwin's closest friend. He was Director of the Royal Botanical Gardens, Kew, for twenty years, in succession to his father, William Jackson Hooker, and was awarded the highest honours of British science. Dalton Hooker visited India during 1848-1850 and came specifically to Cherrapunji, Meghalaya which finds mention in his journal *The Himalayan Journals* as the *Khasia* Mountain. With an annual commission of four hundred pounds and a directive to catalogue plants for the Kew Gardens, London, Hooker first arrived on the "Khasia Mountains" a 4000 to 5000 feet plateau on 1st June,

1850. Cherra was the traderoute and the point for the flow of oranges, coal, honey, lime and timber to Calcutta. Hooker finds the "Cherra plateau" almost barren and documents, "Cherra is one of the most barren places I have ever seen." (1853, 2) As Hooker ascended to Churra (Cherrapunji) he records and documents the Malayan character of the vegetation of Cherra.Hooker's *Himalayan Journals* takes into account the richness and variety of the colour, form and size of each blossoming plant. In his own words, "It is extremely difficult to give within the limits of this narrative any idea of the Khasi flora which is, in extent and number of fine plants, the richest in India, and probably in all Asia....I wonder whether in any part of the globe, the species of orchids outnumber those of any other natural order, or form so large a population of the flora." The cultivated betel nut raising its feathery crown and graceful stem is to him like an arrow shot down from heaven. Nothing in his experience prepares him for the breathtaking beauty of the cascades of water falling down the emerland green groves, 2000 feet below. His journal also records his visits to Lailangkot, Moflong, Myrung, Chillong, Nunklow, Jaintia Hills, Nongkrem, Jowai and Nartiang.

VI. The Northeastern World of Verrier Elwin

Another writer whose works throws much light on the tribal question as well as gives us a historical peek is that of **Verrier Elwin**. Elwin's extensive works on the tribes of the Northeast most specifically North-East Frontier Agency (NEFA) highlights many aspects on the history of Northeast as well. Elwin's works plays the double role of being a vivid commentator of the lives of the tribal people of the Northeast as well as being a kind of alternative history to the contemporary times. His works specifically like *Myths of the North-east Frontier of India, India's North-east Frontier in the Nineteenth Century, and The Nagas in the Nineteenth Century* etc. offer us an alternative history than that offered by mainstream textbooks and official historical documents. In order to strengthen the accommodative spirit of nationalist discourse, Elwin delved into the most important issue-that of protection of the native cultural ethos. He working in this direction constructed ethnographic canons of interpretations that self critically reflects on the nationalist discourse and its attempts to merge the northeast into its fold. By developing these canons which had historical, political and philosophical aspects imbibed into it, Elwin developed a 'human science of nativism' which helped to understand the Northeast Indian communities. And in a way it created a sort of significant break with the colonialist as well as the statist discourse embodying culturally loaded notions of primitivism and superiority.

Verrier Elwin (1902-1964) was an influential non-official Englishman who lived and worked in twentieth century India. Elwin's ethnographic studies and popular works on India's tribal customs, art, myth and folklore continue to generate controversy. Described by his contemporaries as a cross between Albert Schweitzer and Paul Gauguin, Elwin was a man of contradictions, at times taking on the role of evangelist, social worker, political activist, poet, government worker, and more. He rubbed elbows with the elite of both Britain and India, yet found himself equally at home among the impoverished and destitute. Intensely political, the Oxford-trained scholar tirelessly defended the rights of the indigenous and, despite the deep religious influences of St. Francis and Mahatma Gandhi on his early career, staunchly opposed Hindu and Christian puritans in the debate over the future of India's tribals. Although he was ordained as an Anglican priest, Elwin was married twice to tribal women and enthusiastically (and publicly) extolled the tribal's practice of free sex. Later, as Prime Minister Nehru's friend and advisor in independent India, his compelling defence of tribal hedonism made him at once hugely influential, extremely controversial, and the polemical focal point of heated discussions on tribal policy and economic development.

Verrier Elwin came to India almost eighty five years ago not to join the ruling class but by his gracious social conduct shared with the Indian people his deep philanthropic insights. This priest searched like the wild wandering wind and with his eyes he sought the aboriginals who lived on the horizons of mankind. Many of Elwin's observation on the tribes of India continue to be relevant even today. As had been foretold by Elwin, for most of the tribal societies, independence did not bring relief or freedom from exploitation and poverty. They continue to be alienated from the mainstream and also from the resources in which their livelihood depends. All major developmental projects like the building of dams, highways etc. and all environmental projects still contribute to the displacement of the tribes from different parts of the country, particularly Western and Eastern India. These were the issues which were fought by Elwin during his time which has not found its solution even today. He expressed deep anguish over the exploitation and assault on tribal institutions, beliefs, practices and a whole way of life by external forces. The colonial policy and the aggressive Christian and Hindu reformism were deeply responsible for the disruption of way of life of the tribal communities in his belief. He documented the changes and when he was in a position to make recommendations for developing a policy for the administration of the tribal's, he spelt out his ideas equivocally. He had deep respect and appreciation for tribal society and culture, and was most eager to protect it from forces that threatened to destroy it.

Elwin was the chief architect for documentation and the formulation of policies along with Nehru for the upliftment of the tribes of Northeast India. Of particular interest is the collection of anthology that had been edited by Elwin which was titled *India's North-East Frontier in the Nineteenth Century* (1959). India's North-east Frontier is a compilation of extracts from the reports of government officials and missionaries and the accounts of travellers written between 1825 and 1900. The collection relates to the Naga tribes inhabiting the hills on the eastern side of the Brahmaputra valley in Assam and the scattered tribes of the Himalayan foothills from Bhutan to the north Burma frontier: the Akas, Daflas, Miris, Abors, Mishmis, Khamtis, and Singphos. Talking of the compilation Elwin states that what he hoped from his book is the fact that it would work as primary source of general ethnographic information and, as the compiler states, are "in periodicals now impossible to obtain and difficult to consult."

But Elwin's book remains unfulfilling to its intention due to the meagreness of explanatory data and the lack of any clear statement concerning the basis or method of selection. The only reference to selective procedure is on the opening page of the Introduction which repeats the familiar doleful plaint that: "Very little has been written on the tribal peoples of the north-east frontier of India." Mr Elwin then states: ". . . I present a selection of passages from the older literature, down to 1900, which has a bearing on the history, people and problems of what is now known as the North-East Frontier Agency." He adds: "These passages are of unusual value, for they give us a picture of the country as it was before it had suffered any external influence. . . and despite all the faults both of fact and of taste their (the writers') work is of value to scholars and administrators alike."

Elwin's other book on the Northeast i.e. A Philosophy for NEFA was written from the vantage point when he was working as the acting advisor of Tribal Affairs for the North-East Frontier Agency (NEFA) under the Government of India. The book was presumably first written to formulate policy and a philosophy for the administrative and work staff of NEFA and to introduce new or uninformed NEFA personnel to facts about the area and its people. The philosophy of Verrier Elwin regarding tribal development in the Northeast has been formulated in this book, which is a midpoint between the stance of "leave them alone" to that of detribalisation. He states,

We are agreed that the people of NEFA cannot be left in their age-long isolation. We are equally agreed that we can leave no political vacuum along the frontier; that we must bring to an end the destructive practices of inter-tribal war and head-hunting and the morally repugnant practices of slavery, kidnapping of children, cruel methods of sacrificing animals and opium-addiction, none of which are fundamental to tribal culture. We wish to see that the people are well-fed, that they are healthy and enjoy a longer span of life, that fewer babies die, that they have better houses, a higher yield for their labour in the fields, improved techniques for their home-industries. We would like them to be able to move freely about their own hills and have easy access to the greater India of which at present they know little. We want to bring them into contact with the best people and the finest products of modern India. Above all, we hope to see as the results of our efforts a spirit of love and loyalty for

India, without a trace of suspicion that government has come into the tribal areas to colonise or exploit, a full integration of mind and heart with the great society of which the tribal people form a part, and to whose infinite variety they make a unique contribution. And at the same time, we want to avoid the dangers of assimilation and detribalisation which have degraded tribal communities in other parts of the world.

In another place he sums up his hopes and his advice in these words:

We see now that the tribal people will be of the greatest service to India if they are able to bring their own peculiar treasures into the common life, not by becoming second-rate copies of ourselves. Their moral virtues, their self-reliance, their courage, their artistic gifts, their cheerfulness are things we need. They also need the comradeship, the technical knowledge, the wider world-view of the plains. The great problem is how to develop the synthesis, how to bring the blessings and took advantages of modern medicine, agriculture and education to them, without destroying the rare and precious values of tribal life. We can solve this problem if we do not try to go too fast: if we allow the people a breathing-space in which to adjust themselves to the new world: if we do not overwhelm them with too many officials; if we aim at fundamentals and eliminate everything that is not vitally necessary; if we go to them in genuine love and true simplicity. (Elwin, 296)

For the achievement of these objectives what Elwin prescribes is a group of able and dedicated administrators who should strive to preserve the tribal lifestyle of the people of NEFA artistically and socially while transforming it materially. But, to talk in those lines is what Elwin has been accused of mostly-to be an idealist and romantic whose affiliation with the tribal people and his love for them made him less observant towards the realistic aspects of their life. The amalgamation which he talks about in terms of taking out the best of Western culture, the Indian culture of the plains and the tribal cultures is something of the aspirations of creating a heavenly abode in the hills of NEFA. And such a postulation is what Elwin has been criticised for in terms of the various policies that had been formulated by Nehru and Elwin in terms of tribal upliftment and development. These Nehru-Elwin policies are accused to be more segregationist than policies which act towards unification. But, nonetheless, Elwin's contribution towards the people of Northeast and his endeavour to bring anthropology closer to the common people highlights interesting facets of the lives, culture and problems of a terrain which was less visible to the rest of India and the world.

Conclusion

These counter/ alternative narratives of Dalton Hooker, Verrier Elwin, Furer Haimendorf and others presents to us a decolonised way of looking into certain colonised texts about the natives. They act as the silent narratives which do not adhere to the strict norms of studying history or ethnography and provide alternative routes to study and analyse certain moments of history. Deviant from the normative ways they also act like historical accounts of certain periods of the colonised times of our country. They also provide antecedents which allow us to introspect into the colonial narratives and as to how these colonial constructs differ from the constructs of the natives.

These ethnographies record multifaceted dimensions of the tribal communities including their everyday lives. These ethnographic descriptions constitute a corpus of knowledge that has enabled scholars and generalists, alike, to "discover", "inscribe", "imagine" and map India. Moreover, they also produce the consciousness as to how these ethnographic and anthropologist endeavours are intimately tied up with the imperial projects and reveal aspects of colonial mentality. At the same time, they depict the emerging template for interactions between different forms of knowledge colonial and Indian.

References

1. Ao Temsula, *These Hills Called Home: Stories from a War Zone*, Penguin Books, New Delhi, 2006.
2. Baral Kailash (Ed), *Earth Songs: Stories from Northeast India*, Sahitya Academy, New Delhi, 2005.
3. Conrad Sebastian, *Global History: An Introduction*, CH Beck, Munich, 2013.
4. D. Soyini Madison, *Critical Ethnography: Method, Ethics, and Performance,* Sage, 2011.

5. Desmond Ray, *Sir Joseph Dalton Hooker: Traveller and Plant Collector,* Antique Collectors Club, 1999.
6. Elwin Verrier (Ed), *India's North-east Frontier in the Nineteenth Century*, Oxford University Press, Bombay, 1959.
7. Elwin, Verrier, *A Philosophy for NEFA*. (Second Revised Edition.) Shillong: North-East Frontier Agency, 1959.
8. Hall Stuart, *Representation: Cultural Representations and Signifying Practices*, Thousand Oaks, California, Sage in association with the Open University, London 1997.
9. Jim Thomas, *Doing Critical Ethnography,* Sage, New Delhi, 1993.
10. Jones Julie Scott and Sal Watt, *Ethnography in Social Science Practice,* Routledge Press, 2010.
11. Joseph Dalton Hooker, *The Himalayan Journals,* Psychology Press, 2003.
12. Karl Marx, 'The Future Results of British Rule in India', *Marx and Engels: Collected Works,* International Publishers, New York: (1975) (2005), 12: 217 (Originally Published: *New-York Daily Tribune,* August 8, 1853).
13. Mibang Tamo, *Tribal Studies-Emerging Frontiers of Knowledge,* Mittal Publications, New Delhi, 2007.
14. Michel Foucault, *Discipline and Punish: The Birth of the Prison,* Vintage, London, 1995, (1975).
15. Soumen Sen, *Folklore Identity Development: In the Context of North-East India,* Anjali Publishers, 2010.
16. T.Haopik, 'Conceptualising Northeast India: A Discursive Analysis on Diversity', *Bangladesh e-journal of Sociology*, Vol. 8. No. 2, 2001, pp.109-120.
17. Tanka Bahadur Subba and Sujit Som (Ed), *Between Ethnography and Fiction: Verrier Elwin and the Tribal Question in India,* Orient Blackswan, New Delhi, 2005.
18. Tilottama Misra (Ed), *The Oxford Anthology of Writings from North-East India: Poetry and Essays,* Oxford University Press, New Delhi, 2011.

11

Identity Crisis as Reflected in the Novels of Siddhartha Deb

Tanushree Kulshreshtha

Identity is a concept which can be studied at various levels, probing deep into one's own inner psyche and search for the self, or look for one's identity in the society reflecting a particular culture, tradition and religion. In Psychology, Sociology and Anthropology identity is a person's conception and expression of his own identity (self identity) and others' individuality or group affiliations (such as national and cultural identity). Language and Culture differentiates a person's identity in a society. Language and ethnic identity are interrelated. Conflict in one's idea of identity takes place if insecurity rises for one's own language or culture in a diverse population. A person develops the concept of self and other if he feels discriminated on the basis of his language, appearance or culture. In a diverse country like India the concept of 'self' and 'other' has given rise to various evils infecting the society, creating differences and igniting issues like ethnic clashes, quest for roots etc.

India is a country of 29 States, Multiple Religions, Numerous Castes, Clans, Cultures and traditions, and today it stands apart for its kaleidoscopic existence. Each corner of the country reflects a distinct custom and culture, each tradition reflects colours of its own. And this diversity, if on one hand makes us unique, on the other hand it adds to the issues like thirst for the roots, crisis of Identity etc.

Northeast region of India also known as 'Seven Sisters' is a land enriched with abundance of nature and beauty in the form of beautiful hills, valleys, forests and diverse climatic conditions. A place enriched with various tribes and clans existing together and reflecting unique colours of traditions and culture. It connects India to various countries like Bangladesh, Bhutan, China, Myanmar and Tibet. Juxtaposing this richness of the region the chaos of ethnic clashes, and the race of establishing superiority of one's own traditions over another is disturbing the beautiful landscape and peace. The region undoubtedly adds to the alluring beauty of its country.

Literature however has been reflecting these facts since ages in some form or the other. Indian English Literature through its various genres fiction, poetry, prose and drama has been transforming these facts into a work of art and provoking thoughts and actions of the people regarding the same to bring an air of revolution and change. Upcoming Indian English writers are showcasing these truths through their works. Literature emerging from this region talks about various issues prevalent in these states which until recent years had remained under-represented. Manas Pritam Borah in his book on *Literature from North East India* writes: motifs like violence, insurgency, and activities of underground organisations, identity politics and people's responses towards those activities along with an assortment to cultural traits have produced the body of literatures within the ambit of a multicultural panorama (Borah, Manash Pritam, 2001).

Indira Goswami, Mitra Phukan, Siddhartha Deb, Mamang Dai, Srutimala Duara are some of the famous writers, reflecting the true picture of their home states. Siddhartha Deb (1970) is an Indian English writer who was born in Meghalaya and grew up in a small town in the north-eastern region of India, a border region near Tibet, China, Burma, and Bangladesh. He was educated in India and also at Columbia University, USA. Deb began his career in journalism as a Sports Journalist in Calcutta in 1994, before moving to Delhi to continue regular Journalism until 1998. He worked as a journalist in Calcutta and Delhi and has written for *Lingua Franca*, the *London Review of Books*,

New Statesman, the *Times Literary Supplement* and the *Boston Globe*. He went to the United States in 1998 on a literature Fellowship. He was well familiar to Literature and reading was one of his childhood interests. The place where he grew up always gave him something to ponder upon and scribble. He himself says, "This is an obscure and turbulent area, and it has informed much of my work, including my two novels, *The Point of Return* and *An Outline of the Republic*."

At present Deb is working as an Associate Professor at the New School in New York. He has been awarded PEN/Open Book Award for his book *The Beautiful and the Damned* in 2012. He worked as a fellow member in Radcliffe Institute of Advanced Studies, 2009-2010. His debut Novel *The Point of Return* was a New York Times' "Notable Book of the Year", 2003. His another book *An Outline of the Republic* was long listed for the "Impact Dublin International Award", and shortlisted for the "Crossword Prize" in India, and the "book of the year" in *Daily Telegraph*, London and he was also a part of Society of Authors (UK) grant, 2007.

Deb's novels are like a mirror to the contemporary society, as he explores the issues related to the life and society. His vision as a writer is not limited to the external conflicts and happenings, but he also focuses on the internal crisis and sufferings which a person acquires through his surroundings and his reactions to it which again intensify and bring new issues. His keen observation and writings of native land include facts related to politics, social norms and economic destitute and its impact on the life of a common man. Along with the contemporary conditions, Deb also brings out the historical facts related to politics and society and its impact on people at the present time. In an interview with *The Hindu,* when asked about his novels set in North East region, he answered, "That's where I grew up and because no one in mainstream India writes about it. There wasn't and still isn't any interest in the region" (Bhatt Shakti, An Interview with Siddhartha Deb, 2006).

This chapter focuses on how he projects the theme of identity, complications and conflicts related to it. His debut Novel

The Point of Return published in 2002 was selected as *New York Times* "Notable Book". The novel is Deb's apparently partly autobiographical and delves into the world of official corruption and ethnic violence in India's remote northeast. The social facts revealed in the novel are through the character Babu and his father Dr Dam. As the novel is partially autobiographical, we can see that Babu is projected as Deb himself and Mr Dam his father. The setting is an unnamed town which is presumably based in Shillong, where Deb grew up. The first section of the novel, "Arrival," which accounts for half the novel's total length, is written in reverse chronological order, starting in 1987 and finishing in 1979.

Deb focuses on the theme of loss of identity of people like Dr Dam and Babu. Dr Dam was forced out of what was to become East Pakistan after partition, and was later to become Bangladesh. But he and other displaced East Bengalees could not find a place within the large agglomeration that is India. Local tribes who wish to demarcate their own homeland and expel those who would contaminate their isolationist purity, were always after the lives of these Bengali people. Dr Dam tried to build a home for his family, but was frustrated at every turn, watching as his physical constructions succumb to the same fate as his mental conception of home, destroyed by either bad luck or the vicissitudes of bureaucracy and corruption.

The migrant, the person who doesn't belong anywhere, is a staple figure in recent Indian fiction, and in *The Point of Return*, Deb provides a disquisition on the subject through the persona of a family friend, Dr Chatterji. Discussing the forlorn state of the Bengali minority, Dr Chatterji contends that no matter how long they remain in their adopted home in the hills, they will remain foreigners forever. As he says: We are a dispersed people, wandering, but unlike the Jews we have no mythical homeland. Nor do we have their achievements that would make the world recognise and fear us one day. My two brothers have not been here for years. They left as soon as they could, but they found Calcutta too narrow, too alien, after their childhoods here. No doubt you face the same problem. One of them lives in England now, the other in Belgium. They send photographs of their houses, their cars, and their fair children with red cheeks who write *Shubho Bijoya* in English every year until the time comes for them to grow up and leave their homes (Siddhartha Deb, 2002, 287).

Babu recalls the time when he was called for an interview in Delhi, but was termed as a foreigner. He remembers how in the childhood days during a protest he heard the slogans like, "Go back foreign dogs, Go back Bangladeshis". He remembers that many times he was beaten by the people, for not speaking the same language they spoke, for having different features and colour complexions. He wondered, where his home was, Bangladesh, India or Pakistan. People like him were not accepted anywhere. There was no place which he could call home. Feelings of fear and alienation always surrounded him and he felt powerless.

Dr Dam who his whole life served the country and state considering it his own was at the end terrified at the point of gun by his head minister for not carrying out the schemes as per his wish and ultimately was threatened by such words, "corpse of one more foreigner will not make any difference" (*ibid*,276).

Deb in an interview by *Harper Collins Publishers* when was asked about the roots of these fractured relationships between tribals and non-tribals answered, The British colonial rule was superb at fostering divisions upon people on the basis of religion, ethnicity, class, and caste, and this is the point from which the fractured relationship originates. Add to that mass migration to the hills by Bengali Hindus fleeing their original homeland because of the partition of India in 1947 and the insecurity of the hill people because they are marginal compared to other groups in India, and there you have all the elements of a bitter misunderstanding (*ibid*).

The novel aptly brings out the sufferings of these people in the land in which they lived their entire life from the very childhood. They were homeless even after serving the country for years. These ethnic clashes resulted in the issues like the conversion of mass population into Christianity and adaptation of other religions by tribal people which later on further developed the feeling of insecurity among them.

Thus, in the Novel we come across various social and political issues polluting the environment and infecting the society, we see how people after partition who migrated back to India suffered in their own country, they kept looking for a name, an identity and respect but even after living for over a decade they could not establish their identity.

Deb's other novel, *An Outline of the Republic* or *Surface,* was published in 2005, and setting of the novel takes us back to 90s. The novel focuses on the various social issues prevalent in Northeast India. The insecure environment, problem of insurgency and other issues like ethnic clashes, drug use and highest rate of illiteracy are clearly revealed by the writer. Unlike his first novel protagonist here does not visit the land out of his nostalgic feelings and love but he probes in to investigate about a photograph, which seemed to him as a good story and an opportunity to establish himself as a successful journalist. In the novel he showcases how the issues of ethnicity become a cause of destruction, violence and hatred. He talks about the local tribal wars taking place in fight of acquiring more land and power, as he writes, "the Kuki tribe has been fighting the Nagas for all of last year. Villages burnt on both sides; passengers pulled out of buses and gunned down" (Siddhartha Deb, 2005, 47). Writer unveils that how government at both levels, central and local, were exploiting the natural resources and the benefits out of these resources was not even used in the development of the region. This created hatred in the minds of local people for outsiders and it too became a cause of their hatred for outsiders. Problem of insurgency is talked about by the writer, how insurgents and the violence created by them infected the entire area. As he writes, "The insurgents had been in the region in one form or another for nearly four decades, crystallising around different ethical and tribal identities as a distant government in Delhi alternated between complete neglect and brute force" (*ibid*, 31).

Deb focuses on the issues of violence, insurgency and corruption how it all collectively disturbed the peace and progress of the region. Ethnic clashes took place due to hatred and disputes between local tribes as well as hatred for the people living in the other parts of the country enjoying a better life as compared to people living in the region. He writes, "The politicians and administrators in Delhi who determined how the region would fare in fledging nation should have anticipated this barrier, but their knowledge was partial, their lack of imagination absolute (*ibid*).

Thus, in both his novels, Deb shows how the quest for identity can lead to violence and hatred. He reveals that in a country like India where multiple cultures, traditions and customs coexist together, in some parts of the country there are few who are still struggling to get an identity for their own culture and the roots attached to it. This struggle when not given proper weight age and attention to bring a change, turns into acts of violence, destruction and one starts loosing self and they start moving on the path of violence and shed blood of those whom they see as a threat to their own identity and culture.

References

1. Borah Manash Pritam, *Ethnicity, Identity and Literature: Reading Literatures from North East India*, Vikas Publications, Guahati, 2001.
2. Siddhartha Deb, *The Beautiful and the Damned: A Portrait of the New India*. Bond Street Books, 2011.
3. Siddhartha Deb, *An Outline of the Republic,* Harper Collins, New York, 2005.
4. Bhatt Shakti, An Interview with Siddhartha Deb, *The Hindu,* 3rd December, 2006.
5. Siddhartha Deb, *The Point of Return.* Harper Collins Publishers, London, 2002.
6. Siddhartha Deb, *Surface,* Pan MacMillan, London, 2005.

12

Linguistic Bases of Identity Politics: With Special Reference to Ethnic Assertions in Assam

Biplob Gogoi

I. Language and Identity- A Linkage Analysis

Language forms one of the pivotal components of one's culture and identity. The distinctive qualities that a culture possesses are its own values, customs, principles, faiths, ideologies and the ways of life which are embedded in its own language. Language reflects itself as a tool and operates as a means of connecting people of a cultural community which share the same collective identity i.e., a sense of belongingness whereby individuals identify themselves with a group or nation. People create their linguistic structure so as to bear a resemblance to those of the group with which from time to time they wish to identify. Our identities emerge from our transaction which is developed within a culture, whither essential. Sonja Lanehart (2009) relates language and identity through the concept of "language goals" where people construct their language structure so as to bear similitude with the cluster they want to identify with and want to become. "Language is a carrier of culture" and carries cultural identity which is defined as the product of social and historical background and which is constructed by way of individuals' categorisation of themselves with group, in addition to the social context and ethnically accustomed communicative structures in a particular society.

People who inherit a multilingual background face complex issues in adapting and assimilating their language to a cultural identity that they want to be identified with. Social perception that equates the choice to speak only one standard language creates a dilemma in most people who inherit multilingual background. In the process of such identity formation, language functions as a tool which holds the cultural identity that the language resembles. This perception and situation demonstrate that there is a significant connection between language and identity formation.

Kaili and Kaili (1998) claim that when individuals speak their mother tongue language with their peers, there is a sense of relationship, unity and bond that makes the cultural community more connected with each other. Ghose (2010) supports the idea of unity that language plays in identity formation in his article and he stresses that "language serves as a mean of unifying the country". However, if the role of language in uniting a cultural community is analysed in a different perspective, language can act as a tool that divides the people in a cultural community. Therefore, the role of language in the formation of cultural identity is always debatable because there are some cases when the individuals do not identify themselves as a group in particular ethnic term even though they master the language of that ethnic group. In this context, we can see two forces that drive the changes and divergences in identity formation: 'structures' and 'agency'. Structure is "the forces beyond our control which shape our identities" while agency is "the degree of control which we ourselves can exert as who we are". One cannot choose the language that he or she is born with because of the structural forces; however, as time goes by, identities change as a result of agency factor such as media, environment and social pressure and this induces a person to make changes in language and cultural identities they want to identify with. Thus, identities are not fixed and constant; they change too. It can be concluded that language is not the only tool that embraces identity; there are some other external factors that act as catalysts in the process of identity formation.

II. Assam: Genesis and Post Colonial Legacy of Ethnic Resurgence

In context of the Northeastern state of Assam, the six hundred years of Ahom Rule during 1200 AD to 1826 AD had fostered a generic interaction among different tribal groups to develop Assamese as a common language of local communication amongst people of the Brahmaputra valley. The valley was however distant in term of cultural contact with western Assam which shared similar ethnographic boundaries with the old Koch Bihar region. There is significant overlap between the cultures and dialects of western Assam and those of this region which now forms part of West Bengal and Bangladesh. The spoken language of North Bengal and Western Assam-that is undivided Kamrup and Goalpara districts was substantially the same as seems to form one dialect group. The cultural developments in the region comprising the eastern Koch Kingdom, i.e. Kamrup were more ambiguous. Those speaking Kamrupi and Goalporia adopted Assamese as the literary language but not without some hesitation in the latter case. Along with the legacy of the partition of the Koch Kingdom, there was a constant tussle between the classical Bengali literary group based at Calcutta and modern ethnic Assamese literary group based in Sibsagar to bring in local forms of speech within their sphere of influence. During the second decade of the twentieth century, a new group of Assamese elite with nationalist outlook entered into the Assam Association, the mouthpiece of the Assamese and it produced a radical change in Assam Politics in so far as it promoted pan- Indianism amongst the Assamese people to inspire them to join the national movement. However, like other regions of India, Assam too inherited the obvious tenuous conflict between pan-nationalist sentiment and sub nationalist tendencies. The Assamese sub-nationalist tendencies harped on the assertion of autonomy and distinctiveness of Assamese language and culture which was almost as old as the British conquest of India itself. The earliest assertion of Assamese sub-nationalism had taken root as a reaction to the British colonial decision in 1836 of making Bengali as a language of rule in Assam. As a result of the sustained reactions and efforts of the first generation of Assamese public intellectuals in the subsequent period, Assamese once again became the language of the schools and judicial proceedings in the province. The establishment of the organisation called *Axomiya Bhaxa Unnati Xadhini Xobha* in 1888 helped in consolidation of the movement for language standardisation, as a result of which by the late nineteenth century, Assamese spoken in Upper Assam was becoming accepted as standard modern Assamese to be emulated as a standard language all through Assam. It provided an "ideological marker by which the literate part of the population identified all native speakers as constituting the Assamese nation. In the cultural politics that ensued, one of the major agendas of the sub-nationalist movement was separation of the Bengali speaking district of Sylhet. The independence and separation of the district of Sylhet from Assam raised the pitch for the demand of finding a locus standi for an Assamese public identity which certainly precipitated the efforts of establishing a state language. The issue of Assamese public identity became more urgent than ever after the influx of a large number of Hindu Bengali refugees. The immigration issue inculcated in the Assamese mind a strong desire for cultural policies that would give them an advantageous position in Assam.

India had essentially inherited the legacy of pre-colonial past with a process of sub-colonial formation as against pan–Indianism, and therefore the problem of minorities within minorities made the task of reorganising India's states more difficult. Since the nation building efforts were at its peak, the Linguistic Provinces Commission was unwilling to make any Linstitutional accommodation to sub-nationalism. The Linguistic Provinces Commission constituted in 1948 had recommended against linguistic states in the context of reorganisation of India's provinces. It concluded that linguistic homogeneity in the formation of new provinces was attainable only within certain limits because it was very much prone to creating fresh minority problem. It revealed a pertinent observation that no more than 70 to 80 per cent of the total population speaking one language could be found in the provinces to be organised on linguistic basis, leaving a minority of at least 20 per cent of people speaking other languages.

As per the first census in 1951 after independence, Assamese speakers constituted around 56.7 per cent of the population of

Assam. The hill districts had indigenous languages and dialects like Khasi, Garo, languages of the Kuki-Chin and the Naga groups. Even in the plains districts, apart from Assamese, people spoke other languages and dialects mostly of the Bodos and Mising family. The most important challenge came from Bengali speakers which made up 16.5 per cent. of the total population of Assam. The states reorganisation commission had taken note of the ethno political reality of the state against the desired model of a linguistically based nation province, and therefore recommended that old boundaries of multiethnic boundaries be maintained and Manipur and Tripura, though not a part of the erstwhile colonial Assam, be merged with Assam.

However, like other parts of India, nurtured by years of colonial rule Assam too, for long a time, harbored the aspirations to acquire a cultural self in some public symbolic sense. It was soon to translate into a desire of acquiring an Assamese public identity. The implicit recommendations of the states reorganisation commission and the seventh amendment to the Indian Constitution in 1956 restructured many of India's provinces on linguistic basis. Following the pan-Indian model, the reorganisation of the state of Assam took place and the linguistic minorities speaking Bengali and tribal languages formed around 42.9 per cent of the total population of the state. As against the ethno-cultural reality, there was a desperate introduction of Assamese as the State Language of Assam through the State Official Language Bill of 1960 in the Assembly and it obviously reinforced the demand for separate political identity in the hills. The Bengali challenge to cultural policies that would define Assam as Assamese produced serious cultural wars that even degenerated into language riots the road ahead was beset with the realities of historical blending of language and sub-nationalism though it seemed axiomatic to most ethnic Assamese that Assam should have Assamese as its official language. The context of Assam could be primarily perceived in an influential set of essays entitled Axomot Bidexi (Foreigners in Assam) by Gyananath Bora, published in Ambikagiri Raychaudhuri's *Cetana*, an inspirational poet and lyricist where Bora also had argued that Indian provinces for hundreds of years have had their distinct languages and literature and have had maintained distinct religions, social customs and norms and have grown as distinct nation. Assam's multiethnic landscape-the product of colonial geography and of immigration as well as much older diversity was not conducive to Assam becoming a language based nation province. Moreover, the hill areas were historically unconnected to the plains and it was uncertain to what extent Assamese might be accepted in the hilly areas. The limited Assamese appeal came as a rude surprise to the ethnic Assamese in the hilly areas and the hills peoples, historically close to the Assamese and some plain tribes who had historically adopted Assamese culture and language eventually rejected Assamese. In case of the Bodos, the leaders apprehensively contended that clause 6 of the Assam Accord which had promised to protect the cultural identity of the Assamese people provided legitimacy to the imposition of Assamese language and culture on the Bodos. Student leaders like ABSU accused ethnic Assamese leaders of anti-tribal prejudices terming the first regional government of AGP as an Assamese government. Activists of the Bodoland typically used the term 'Bodo' to refer to not only Bodo speaking people but also all the other tribes who spoke Bodo or used to speak one of the languages of greater Bodo family which spanned other tribes such as Rabha, Deori, Dimasa, Kochari, Garo, Barman, Hajong etc. While it was plausible that the Bodos, hitherto inhabiting the foothills of Bhutan, had a total cultural disconnect with the Ahom rulers of the Brahmaputra valley, it was also discernible that their acceptance into the Assamese society was dependent on their acceptance of Hinduism which meant the loss of native speech in a few generations and adoption of Assamese language.

The contradiction between sub-nationalist vision of Assam and the reality of multiethnic Assam greatly facilitated the break up of colonial Assam. However, the union government with a unitary nature acted as a great facilitator in creating new states as it misperceived that territorial disintegration of the Assam province was necessary to preempt potential insurgencies in the Northeast. The formation of Nagaland was the first casualty for the nation province of Assam after the first phase of reorganisation of states in 1963; Meghalaya was separated from

Assam in 1970 and Mizoram in 1972. M.S. Prabhakara the well known columnist of Frontline magazine, conceded the fact that what more than four decades ago was just an ignition of fire among some of the Nagas of Assam had now spread like wild fire and it precipitated tendencies for all other similar kinds of insurgent resurrections in every part of the region. The 2011 population census demonstrates a different but substantial degree of similar ethnographic complexity which has ushered in existential interethnic contestation in modern Assam. The Assamese sub-national narrative has thus been subject to great contestation till contemporary times as tribes like the Bodos and Karbis continue to press the demand for territorial separation from the state.

References

1. Amalendu Guha, *Planter Raj to Swaraj: Freedom Struggle and Electoral Politics in Assam 1826-1947*, Peoples Publishing House, New Delhi,1977.
2. Benedict Anderson, *Imagined Communities: Reflections on the Origin and Spread of Nationalism*, Verso, London, 1991.
3. B.G.Verghese, *India's Northeast Resurgent: Ethnicity, Insurgency, Governance and Development,* Konark Publishers, Delhi,1996.
4. Census of India, 2011c Series, *Language wise Distribution of population in Assam*, Directorate of Census Operations, Guwahati, 2011.
5. Daniel Dor, Chris Knight and Jerome Lewis (Ed), *The Social Origins of Language*, Oxford University Press, 2014.
6. Hiren Gohain, *Dexopran Ambikagiri aru Dexapremar swarup (The Nature of Ambikagiri's Patriotism, in Gohain, Xahityor Xotyo (The Truth of Literature),* Baruah Agency, 1970.
7. John Edwards, *Language and Identity*, Cambridge University Press, UK, 2009.
8. Myron Weiner, *Sons of the Soil: Migration and Ethnic Conflict in India,* Princeton University Press, New Jersey, 1978.
9. Sanjib Baruah, *India against Itself: Politics of Nationality in Assam*, University of Pennsylvania Press, Philadelphia, 1999.
10. Udoyon Misra, *North East India: Quest for Identity*, Omsons Publications, Guwahati, 1988.
11. Yasmin Saikia, *Assam and India: Fragmented Memories, Cultural Identity and the Tai Ahom Struggle,* Permanent Black, Delhi, 2005.

IV
Politics

13

Challenges and Identity Crisis of Indigenous Bodo Community in Non BTAD Area

Hasib Md Iqbal and Diganta Biswas

Introduction

The North Eastern part of India in general and Assam in particular have witnessed a series of ethnic movements relating to the autonomous or separate state demands ever since the independence of the country. The question of distinct ethnic identity and the fear of either annexation or assimilation by the larger groups have been the prime factors responsible for most of the ethnic movements of the region. Assam itself has undergone several splits in the post-independence period only to satisfy the ethnic aspirations of the different ethnic groups of the region. Since millennia, Assam has been at the crossroads for interaction between several cultures and peoples. It was home to corporate groups of migrants, traders and smaller subsistence agriculture-based ethnic groups. These groups moved consistently between South Asia, Southeast Asia and Inner Asia. The Bodo speaking group was one among the many that settled in the region and these people are considered today one of the denizens of the 'Crossroads'.

This chapter proposes to examine the different stages of identity articulation among the Bodos who constitute the largest plains tribe of Assam, a state of Northeast India. An attempt will be made to explore the role of the educated middle class as a catalyst in the process of transformation and consolidation of Bodo national identity. The Bodos, also referred to as Kacharis in the pre-colonial historiography of Assam, are considered aborigines of the Brahmaputra Valley. It is generally believed that the Bodos inhabited the fertile plains of the Luit (Brahmaputra) river in the twelfth century and due to frequent skirmishes, with waves of migrating groups of people like the Tai-Ahom from the east and Indo-Aryan group from the west, they moved to Karbi and North Cachar Hills in the sixteenth century. The Bodos are a Tibeto-Burman speaking, Indo-Mongoloid ethnic group. In the present times, the Bodos are considered to be the largest plains tribe of Assam who inhabit the northern areas of the Brahmaputra Valley, namely, in places like Kokrajhar, Udalguri, Chirang, Baksa, Darrang, Sonitpur, Kamrup, Nalbari, Barpeta, and Dhubri among other places. Elsewhere, the Bodos inhabit the lower regions of Nepal, West Bengal, Meghalaya, and Tripura. According to Rev Sydney Endle, the Bodos are the autochthons of Assam. Historically, the Bodos came under different rulers at different points in time – more prominently under the Kiratas, Asuras, Mlechchas, and Danavas. In the comparatively recent history, the Bodo Kingdom was at its zenith during the reign of the Koch King Nar Narayan (1540-84). It was only after the assassination of Raja Govind Chandra in 1832 that the last Bodo Kingdom in Cachar fell with its annexation by the British. It was following this demise that the Bodos started feeling marginalised amidst the fear that they would be subsumed and submerged under other more dominant cultures. The Bodos have a glorious past, an ancient ancestry, and are thus, rightly proud of their roots.

The word ethnicity is closely related to the word "*ethnic*" which is increasingly used "to identify groups of people who have evolved from their primitive stages of tribe and clan identity in to a more cohesive group looking for a coherent political identity." On the other hand the word "*ethnic*" itself is derived from the Greek word "*ethnikos*" which refers to: (a) nations not converted in to Christianity, (b) races or large groups of people having common traits, and (c) groups of an exotic primitive culture. Ethnic identity on the other hand is an affinitive construct, where individuals view themselves and others view them as belonging to a particular cultural group. The growth of the spirit of ethnicity or ethnic self-assertion among various groups leads to the aspiration for a distinct identity for themselves. Generally, the ethnic groups with a small population and faced with the competition for subsistence with the larger groups tend to suffer from an identity crisis. This very question of identity crisis of the ethnic groups impel them to resort to various sorts of ethnic movements demanding either autonomy or separation from the larger groups so that they can preserve their distinct identity and also manage their own affairs without interference from the larger groups whom they fear as the invaders of their distinct ethnic identity.

I. Objectives of the Study

The Bodos are in recent times are very much interested in entrepreneurial works like-Handloom weaving, Piggery farm, Poultry farm, Dairy farm, DTP Computer Education, Handicraft etc. But it has been observed that in this type of business they involved in BTAD area. There are some basic problems in connection with the establishment in non-BTAD area from last few years. By considering all these sides the present paper is prepared with the following objectives:

(i) To examine the institutional enrolments of Bodo students in non-BTAD area.

(ii) To know about the socio-economic condition of Bodo people in non-BTAD area.

(iii) To verify official and organizational coordination/cooperation of Bodo employee with non Bodo employee in non-BTAD area.

(iv) To know about the involvement of Bodo people in different social welfare organization in non-BTAD area.

(v) To explore the existence and society status of Bodo people in non-BTAD area.

(vi) To examine the abolishment of traditional and local food items of Bodo people from Gauripur, Bongaigaon market.

(vii)To estimate the volume of Commercial transactions of Bodo people in non-BTAD area after the incidence of ethnic clash of 2012.

(viii)To evaluate or understand the real life situations in non-BTAD areas of the two districts in context of the security measure for the Bodo community people.

(ix) To assess the number of back to home Bodo people living permanently in the non-BTAD areas from BTAD areas who took shelter during the period of the ethnic clash.

An existing literature on Bodo identity assertion shows that significant work has been done by scholars like Udayan Misra, Mosahary, Snehamoy Chakladar, Ajoy Roy, Sanjib Baruah and so on. Udayan Misra (1998) in his book, *North-East India: Quest for Identity* critically discusses the struggles of different nationalities in northeast India, aimed at identity assertion. Mosahary (2002) analyses the factors behind Bodo identity assertion and the role played by different Bodo organisations in the process. Snehamoy Chakladar (2004) argues that the cultural movement of the Bodos preceded the political movement. He points out that the Bodos realised that they could not preserve their language and protect their land unless they acquired political power. He also discusses the methods used during different phases of the Bodoland movement. Ajoy Roy (1995) observes that pan-Bodo sentiment has a concrete basis and cannot be ignored in any study of the Bodos. Sanjib Baruah (1999), an eminent scholar on the northeast, examines the causes behind the growth of Bodo sub-nationalism and tries to analyse the Bodo political movement by applying the theory of relative deprivation. He points out the inadequate share of Bodos in modern occupations, a condition that Bodo activists attribute to discrimination by the ethnic Assamese.

Although the aforementioned literature focuses on different dimensions of the Bodo movement for self-determination, the issue of transformation of the Bodo identity and the role of the middle class in this process has not been highlighted in a significant way. This research, therefore, is an attempt to throw light on this theme.

The development of Assamese society requires full participation by all section of population including Bodo. Involvement of Bodo people in educational, organisational, entrepreneurial activities would ensure effective utilisation of labour generation of income and hence improvement in quality of life. It is realised that Bodo people are physically strong and they are efficient as a farmers, dexterity in handicraft making by which this community can renovate social and economic changes of all section of people. This study also seeks to examine the various social, political, economic activities and also problems faced by them in their various activities in the society. Thus, the study carries a great importance to study about the different aspects of Bodo people as it was mentioned earlier in non-BTAD area.

II. Methodology

While conducting the study, both the primary and secondary data were used. The primary sources of data includes the official records and were also collected through personal interview with some the leading person, farmers and retired employees of the two districts. The secondary data includes various books, journals and newspapers related to the topic of the study.

III. Question of Identity

During 1952-1967, the Bodo Sahitya Sabha, the most important literary organisation of the Bodos, played a significant role in the assertion of Bodo identity and the issues of language and script were integral to such assertion. This period was marked by the articulation of demands like introduction of Bodo language in the Bodo dominated areas and the replacement of the Assamese script by the Roman script. This phase of identity assertion was marked by the active involvement of the masses unlike in the previous phase. However, a major limitation of the politics of identity assertion during this phase was that the middle class leadership hardly made any radical demands for the improvement of the lot of the common man.

On January 13, 1967, Prime Minister Mrs Indira Gandhi made an important declaration regarding the reorganisation of Assam on a federal basis. This enhanced the prospects for the fulfillment of the political aspirations of the Bodo middle class which was reflected in the demand for a union territory to be called "Udayachal" for the plains tribes of Assam. A new political organisation, viz., Plains Tribal Council of Assam (PTCA) was formed to spearhead this territorial demand. The PTCA was, in essence, a Bodo political party although its name suggested a common political platform for all plains tribes of Assam. In this context, it has been argued by some scholars that the initiative to construct a pan-tribal identity of the plain tribes of Assam always came from the Bodo middle class leadership which was not only more organised, but was also likely to play a key role in any future power alignments. It appears that the Bodo political assertion during this period was accompanied by the emergence of a mass movement around the issue of territorial autonomy.

IV. Build up to Recent Violence-Brief Background

The build up to the present violence began with a string of protest programmes taken up by the non-Bodo organisations against what they have been long describing as the discriminatory policies of the BTAD administration against the other communities residing in the BTAD area. The Bodo leadership has been repeatedly accused of encouraging a policy of intimidation and extortion against non-Bodo sections of the population. It is significant that as long as Bodo militancy was at its height, efforts by non-Bodo communities to organise themselves did not meet with much success.

But, once militancy started ebbing with even the dreaded National Democratic Front of Bodoland (NDFB) faction led by Ranjan Daimary going in for a ceasefire and willing to open talks with the Government of India, the non-Bodo communities drew courage to organise themselves under the umbrella organisation called the Non-Bodo Protection Forum (NBPF) which included representatives from the ABMSU (All Bodo Minority Students Union), the All Assam Koch-Rajbongshi Students Union, Bengali Students Federation, the All Assam Gorkha Students Union and the All Assam Tea Tribes Students Union. Amongst these components, the ABMSU which was a wing of the All Assam Minority Students Union (AAMSU) and which represented the Muslim settlers was an influential presence. Beginning with May 2012, the NBPF initiated a series of protest programmes and made clear its opposition to the creation of a separate Bodoland state as demanded by the Bodo People's Front and other Bodo organisations. Along with the NBPF, the Koch-Rajbongshis, one of the major non-Bodo communities of the BTAD, too upped their ante for a separate state and scheduled tribe's status. They held huge rallies at Bongaigaon and other places on 22nd May. Within a week of this, the ABMSU called for a 24 hour Kokrajhar bandh on 29th May to protest against the administration's refusal to allow an Idgah maidan on government forestland near the Chakrasila wildlife sanctuary. During the ABMSU bandh, there was widespread violence and several government and public vehicles were torched and scores of people injured. In response to this, several Bodo organisations led by the ex-Bodo Liberation Tigers (BLT) Welfare Society and a faction of the NDFB held a mass rally on 30 May to protest the violence indulged in by the ABMSU and to reiterate the demand for the clearing of encroachers from forestland in the Bedlangmeri area. All this set the stage for a full scale confrontation between the Bodo organisations and the immigrant Muslim settlers now led by the ABMSU. The following month (June) was marked by isolated incidents in different parts of the BTAD, with the ABMSU blockading the national highway to be followed by a massive rally held by the Bodo People's Front to press for the demand for a separate state. As opposition to such a demand mounted from the non-Bodo organisations and primarily from the ABMSU, tension between the two communities kept on mounting and on 6th July two activists of the ABMSU were shot at in the Kokrajhar district. This was followed by the killing of four former BLT cadres in the Joypur area of Kokrajhar on 20th July. With this the mayhem may be said to have begun. Swift reprisals were carried out by the Bodo community and the violence soon spread to Chirang and Baksa as well as the adjoining Dhubri district. Within a week, scores of people were killed and nearly four lakhs were displaced. This has easily been one of the most massive displacements in the country's post-Independence history. Interestingly, this time the violence did not affect the Udalguri district which had been witnessed large-scale riots between Muslim immigrants and Bodos and other communities in 2008 when over 70 people were killed and over a lakh rendered homeless. One explanation is that during the present spell of violence the initiative has been taken by the former BLT rebels while the predominantly Christian NDFB factions have not been so proactive. Both the Muslim and Bodo refugees in the camps maintained that in most cases the houses were burnt but large scale killings did not take place. They also said that the nature of the violence was unlike that of a communal clash involving two communities. Rather, there seemed to be a pattern behind the entire violence as far as the burning down of both Muslim and Bodo villages was concerned. It is an undisputed fact that much of the violence could have been prevented had the security forces promptly moved into the affected areas. But there was a clear administrative failure in the deployment of forces and this resulted in the total erosion of confidence on the part of the people in the administration and the resultant fear and panic in which thousands from both the communities fled their homes. This partly explains the huge numbers of refugees in the camps. Another significant aspect of the present violence in the BTAD area is that, by and large, Assamese and Bengali Hindus, Nepalis, Koch-Rajbongshis and adivasis have not been affected. There has clearly been selective torching of houses by both sides and only occasionally have the other communities been caught in the violence. While all these communities are represented in the NBPF and one of its most vocal leaders is caste Hindu Assamese, yet the more organised group within the umbrella organisation is the ABMSU which has emerged as the representative of the immigrant Muslim community.

V. A New Identity Crisis

The question of identity assertion on which the Bodo people were hanging on/around during the period of movement for the separate state or independent nation or else. It was mostly political in nature and was confined to the areas firstly and the common non-Bodo people were mere victim of the conflict. The identity clash with the non-Bodo people that came into their way by accident or planned or was created, it was more to prove their existence of both political and economic power than real socio-political and socio-cultural gap of identity they felt for.

But the perspective changed to a great extent after the Ethnic clash of July 2012 that took place in place in different villages of Kokrajhar district. The worst sufferer of that incidence was the Muslim community of different interior villages, those who were mainly marginalised farmers and labourers. The victim had no other way out but to flee from the places and residence for a safer shelter and Dhubri district was one of the safest places followed by Bongaigaon district. This is not the end of the story rather here it is the beginning of the issues that this paper has tried to focus.

The Bodo people residing in the non-BTAD areas for a long time started to feel some sort of insecurity which was expressed in their behaviour and movement. The feeling of courageous and easy going nature was transformed into feeling of fear psychosis and confusion regarding their existence in a place where they were accepted as very much local. This abnormal behaviour was not for short period of time only but it somewhere was rooted into their mind and their existence has become thin in any kind of socio-political and socio-cultural involvement.

VI. Discussion and Findings

We are aware of the fact that like other sixth scheduled area the BTAD is not created comprising compact areas where Bodo people are exclusively dominant numerically. A large number of Bodos live outside BTAD area. During demarcation of boundary for BTAD area tribal belts and blocks and tribal sub-plan areas have been taken into consideration. However, Bodo national organisations like ABSU and Bodo Sahitya Sobha and political parties have been raising the voices for the interest of greater Bodo community including non-BTAD area.

In a society of composite nature during the practice of procedural democracy voters are polarised on the line of caste, community, religion etc. In such a situation in certain constituency particularly in Panchayat election political importance of Bodos outside BTAD has become insignificant as they turn into minority following the creation of BTAD. This is a political challenge of Bodos outside BTAD.

There were huge number of students in Colleges of non-BTAD area specially in Dhubri district, if we take example of Pramatheh Barua college of Gauripur, both male and female students of BTAD area usually came from Tipkai, Bashbari, Debitola, Kajigaon and Rupshi area to avail higher education from P B College and it was observed that most of the students studying stayed at relatives house or hostels. Few renowned personality of Bodo community studied from this institution, examples of those are Janaklal Basumatary IAS, Banen Musahary MLA took graduation from this institution. In student body election of college, Bodo students usually contested in different portfolio. Many times members from Bodo students got elected as members of student union body. But from last decades it was marked that member of student's enrolment in nearby institution of Gauripur is decreasing and now it is almost nil. The permanent inhabitant i.e. the Bodo people of Dhubri district, who are solvent and financially sound, send their kids/ child for higher education to Delhi, Bangalore, Dehradun, Guwahati and lower middle class family to Don Bosco School in Debitola and Kokrajhar.

In public vehicle the buses, mini buses those were maintaining communication in between BTAD and non-BTAD area, people of Dhubri district marked that either driver or conductor/handyman belong to Bodo. The buses of North Bank Contract Carriages (NBCC) runs in Dhubri, Bijni, Patiladah, Gossaigaon, Kasugaon, Kokrajhar, Basugaon, Salakati, Bhawraguri, Serfanguri, Ramphulbeel, Bashbari, Sapatgram, Tipkai.But there is no direct bus communication from Dhubri to BTAD area under NBCC as it was informed by Sohrab Ali, an employee of NBCC. One bus in between Dhubri - Gossaigaon, two star buses in between Dhubri –Kokrajhar, few Magic, savari runs in between Dhubri and Tipkai, Kajigaon, Rupshi area. Poor number of vehicle was indicative of the poor number of passengers' movement in between BTAD to non-BTAD area from Dhubri district.

It is also found that personal involvement in socio-organisational set up is decreasing day-by-day. Personal interview with Anjali Brahma, a retired Headmistress of

Gauripur Girls High School sorrowfully informed except her existence as President of Gauripur Lekhika Samaroh, no one can represent in high post of any socio-cultural organisation. There were few Bodo people engaged in Bihottor Gauripur Bihu Sanmilan, Gauripur Shakha Shahitya Sobha, Gadhar Kobi Chakra, and different Puja Committees, but now there presence is almost nil.

The study shows that the middle class has indeed played an important role in the consolidation of Bodo national identity as distinct from Assamese identity. However, it appears that the Bodo middle class will actually seek to protect its own interests in the proposed homeland instead of safeguarding the rights and interests of the masses. The bitter struggle for power among different sections of the middle class within the existing autonomous arrangements will bear testimony to this phenomenon. The deviation of the Bodo movement from autonomy to secession necessitates a critical relook into the role of the Indian State. Indeed, the response of the state is a major determinant that has shaped and transformed the nature of the Bodo struggle for self-determination.

VII. Suggestions

The following suggestions can be offered to solve the inner problems as well as development of relation between Bodo and non-Bodo people of Assam and BTAD area:

Firstly, there is an urgent necessity to hold frequent workshops and training programmes on value-based education in the educational institution of BTAD and its adjacent districts in non-BTAD area specially Dhubri and Bongaigaon. Such workshop and trainings should be free as well as to conduct in their own locality. Again the trainings should be regular but not for long duration, i.e. short-term trainings are more preferable for young generation.

Secondly, the prevailing education system of Assam should be revised as there is a primary requirement of inclusion of chapters like National Integration, History of Unification, Cultural Heritage, and Ancient Ethics in the syllabus. Again a proper environment should be created so that community clash, religious clash, disparity should be wiped out.

Thirdly, the marketing system in between Bodo and non-Bodo people should be developed. There should be an environment that the Bodo as well as non-Bodo should easily and freely purchase and sale their product without any pressure and fear. The government machinery should take initiative to coordinate both these communities to share same platform by arranging Fares and Exhibitions of traditional and handicraft product of both Bodo people and Non-Bodo people. There should be a proper mechanism of sale of their products at reasonable price.

Fourthly, the transportation system which is quite poor in between Bodo and non-Bodo area should be developed so that the people can easily move and transport their required materials for smooth functioning as well as development of their area.

Fifthly, common cultural programme to be organised specially in the places close to BTAD areas by the initiatives of both the Govt. and non Govt. agencies to cheer up both the communities and thus to create a feel free environment.

Sixthly, Bodo people are often seen as advance in games and sports and so they should be invited always in any sports event organised in non-BTAD areas.

Seventhly, intellectuals of both the locality should be given more scope to share a common platform in the name of Seminar, Conference, Symposium, Open Forum etc. in order to reduce the differences between Bodo and non-Bodo people taking the matter of incidences occurred in 2012 and thereafter.

Eighthly, some sort of ideas exchange programmes especially for women of both the places and community should be convened to address the universal issues of women which finally help to reduce and hopefully to forget the present situation of hatred and violence.

Ninthly, children are blessed with simplicity and they remain free from bias. So they should be given scope of free mixing programme in the form of Art Competition, Singing-Dancing

Competition, Quiz Competition, Fancy Dress Competition and many more entertaining events to create an atmosphere of relaxation and normalcy.

Tenthly, besides these soft mechanism of lessening tension and to bring back normalcy, the administrative measures to be sorted out for long-term solution such as a list of Bodo people who reside presently and permanently in non-BTAD areas to be prepared with full details of their identity as well as their local neighbour (specially non-Bodo people) with phone numbers for ready reference so as to take security and protection measure immediately involving the localities which will be more effective.

Conclusion

For a deeper understanding of the Bodo identity assertion, it is necessary to relate this assertion with the nationality question in India. The Indian State has always viewed this issue as a problem of all India national integration and has considered nationality aspirations as anti-national. This has further alienated smaller nationalities like the Bodos of Assam. Ironically, the Assam movement against foreign nationals had initially drawn the Bodos and other plains tribes under its banner, but it failed to accommodate the aspirations of these nationalities. Moreover, the Assamese middle class hegemony generated a sense of insecurity among the Bodo middle class and pushed it towards a path of self-determination for consolidation of the Bodo national identity.

References

1. Apurba K. Baruah, 'Communities and Democracy: A Northeast Indian Perspective', *North East India Studies*, 1(1), 2005, pp. 20-21, 131, 134.
2. B.B. Kumar, (Ed.), *Problems of Ethnicity in North East India,* Concept Publishing Company, New Delhi, 2007.
3. Paul R. Brass, *Ethnicity and Nationalism: Theory and Comparison*, Sage, New Delhi, 1991.
4. Joseph E. Trimble and Ryan Dickson, *Ethnic Identity,* Western Washington University, www.sagepub.com/cac6study/docs/Ethnic%20Identity.doc, (Accessed on 12th June, 2015)
5. H.K. Barpujari, *North East India: Problems, Politics and Prospects,* Spectrum Publications, New Delhi, 1998.

6. Sarthak Sengupta (Ed), *Tribal Studies in North East India,* Mittal Publications, New Delhi, 2002.
7. S.K. Chaube, *Hills Politics in North-East India*, Orient Longman, Patna, 1999.
8. Chandan Kumar Sharma, 'The Bodo Movement : A Preliminary Enquiry into the Role of the Middle Class and the State', in Girin Phukan (Ed), *Political Dynamics of North East India*, South Asian Publishers, New Delhi, 2000, pp. 128-129.
9. Susmita Sen Gupta, 'Identity Assertion by the Bodos of North East India: Exploring the Role of the Educated Middle Class', *Global Journal of Human-Social Science*, Volume 14 Issue 2, 2014.
10. Walter Fernandes, 'The Conflict in North East: A Historical Perspective', *Economic and Political Weekly*, No. 51, December 18-24, 1999.
11. Sanjib Baruah, *India against Itself: Assam and the Politics of Nationality,* Oxford University Press, New Delhi, 1999.

14

Ethnic Boundary- Making: Towards a Comparative Analytic Understanding

Sumit Kr. Sarma

Ethnicity has been debated by various schools of thought mainly on hyphenated and dichotomous terms. For the 'Primordialist' ethnicity is an essential characteristic of the social world which is acquired as a result of one's birth in a particular social setting. On the other hand, the 'Instrumentalists' sees ethnic identity as choice made by individuals to fulfill certain aspects of their social and individual life. The 'Essentialists' argues that ethnic group developed as a result of distinct culture and identity which was deemed essential to maintain basic social order in human life, while the 'Situationalists' maintains that it is the logic of a situation which compels an individual or a group of individuals to identify with a particular group. Another group of scholars, who take a perennial view of ethnic identity, believe that ethnicity has been a defining feature of human civilisation since time immemorial. At the other extreme the 'Modernists' are of the opinion that ethnicity has its genesis in the birth of the modern nation-states. Some recent writings on ethnicity considered it as a cognitive process with deep psychological roots and not just a primitive identity or interest based choice.

In the past two decades work on ethnicity has given importance to a synthesis view and attempts have been made to reconcile the contrasting theoretical approaches to ethnicity. But, at the same time it has been increasingly witnessed that the constructivism and approaches close to it like the instrumentalism and modernist view of ethnicity has found prominence over the earlier views like primordialism, essentialism and perennialism. This constructivist and schools closely allied to it lays emphasis on study of categories or discourses of differences rather than ethnic groups. It does not attempt to describe how an ethnic community travels down the historical memory; but tries to understand how it came into being and how it later changes or at times even dissolves into a new identity; instead of observing the everyday workings of the ethnic culture, the varying claims of cultural difference are studied (Wimmer, 2013).

This work takes a constructivist view of the growth of numerous ethnic identities in the northeast region of India.The ethnic categorisation initiated by the British paved the way for further divisions which many a times sowed the seeds of demand for a separate political entity in the form of home land states. Thus, we see the "Colonial propensity of fixing tribes to their supposedly 'natural habitats' has actually triggered exclusive ethnic homeland consciousness among the minds of the tribal people of the region" (Baruah, 2008, 61). The post-independent state too carried forward the colonial policy of drawing the boundaries on the basis of ethnicity. The granting of provincial states and autonomous regions based on ethnic affiliations further accelerated the growth of distinct ethnic identities.

A comparative study is necessary to see how and under what circumstances ethnicity becomes a major source of mobilisation in some society and not in the other. Such approach would help us to understand why ethnic identity is associated with inequality and discrimination in certain context regarding allocation of political power and economic resources. A comparative analytic of ethnic helps us understand why ethnicity matters to different degrees in different societies, different situations and different periods of time.

This work is built on the boundary metaphor popularised by Fredrick Barth (1969) in his seminal work 'Ethnic Groups and Boundaries'. His theoretical framework for the first time took into account the subtle and sinuous frontiers of ethnic boundaries, their underlying inter-connectedness and shifting terrains in the formation of ethnic identity. Formation of social and cultural boundaries takes place when the actors identify and distinguish between different ethnic categories and perceive the existing of an 'other' with a distinct social and cultural order. Such identification with a particular group gives birth to a categorical boundary which divides 'us' from the 'other'. At the same time, such a boundary also implies a corresponding act of discrimination against those who are at the other side of the fence. Therefore, focus on the social and categorical boundary would be more helpful to understand the formation and dissolution of ethnic groups than a sociological and anthropological approach which takes the existence and dissolution of ethnic identity to be granted.

At this point, we need to critically analyse the findings of Barth in order to show how such social boundaries emerge in the first place, and then what leads to their transformation in due process of time, how some new groups are included while some existing ones are excluded. Also at times, the boundaries become blurry, hasy, and porous and eventually dissolve; while at other times it might stand the test of time and persist over time. Ethnicity is a creation of a certain kind of inter-group relationship; it cannot exist in isolation, its continuation demands interaction with 'Others'. Barth while focusing at the formation and interaction across the ethnic boundary states that:

Categorical ethnic distinctions do not depend on an absence of mobility, contact and information, but do entail social processes of exclusion and incorporation whereby discrete categories are maintained despite changing participation and membership in the course of individual life histories. (Fredrick Barth, 1969, 9-10).

With due course of time cultural features change and individuals transfer their ethnic membership, the ethnic group continues and is maintained via the "continuing dichotomisation between members and outsiders" (Barth, 1969, 14). What is important for the establishment of ethnic boundaries is "the assignment of particular social meanings to a limited set of acts" (Blom, 1969, 74), social controls and sanctions, the construction of which is dependent on relationships with other ethnic groups - 'Us' and 'Them' - categories of inclusion and exclusion. The 'Us' and 'Them' exists by degrees, not necessarily in conflict and total opposition (Hummell, 2014).

Giving emphasis to the nature of practices of categorisations and social divisions not necessarily implies an exclusive focus on economic gains and political advantage. Sometimes, the gains may be in the form of honour, reclamation of lost prestige and power or the feeling of dignity; personal security as well as a sense of psychological stability at being member of a group. Also, factors like access to public goods, professions and political power form a part of the gain in being recognised as belonging to a particular group. Thus, ethnicity is not just about 'identity' or 'ideals', at times it can also be 'interest' and material 'benefits'. Such dichotomies are a product of western attempts to see ethnic process as creation of binaries in the society.

I. Towards an Integrated View of Ethnicity:

Ethnicity can be used in two different ways. In the narrow and more general sense it is understood as racial and linguistic groups. But this is too simplistic to understand a complex phenomenon like ethnicity. In the broader sense of term all types of ascriptive group identities qualify to be called as ethnic group. It includes race, language, religion, caste or tribe (Horowits, 1985). According to Weber, ethnic groups are 'those human groups that entertain a subjective belief in their common descent because of similarities of physical type or of customs or of both, or because of memories of colonialisation or migration' (Weber, (1922) 1968, 389). It can be considered as a comprehensive definition which attempts to highlight the important and defining aspects of ethnicity.

Recently, there have been attempts to undo the simple dichotomist view of understanding ethnicity with the prism of primordialism and constructivism. Scholars argue that social scientists should be concerned with using ordinary language definitions of terms, which are constructed by finding principles of attribution based on intuition and popular usage (Green, 2006). In their attempts to cover the groups intuitively understood to be ethnic while excluding those groups not normally considered as ethnic, Fearon and Laitin eventually come up with a definition of ethnic groups as groups larger than a family for which membership is reckoned primarily by descent, is conceptually autonomous and has a conventionally recognised 'natural history' as a group (Fearon and Laitin, 2000 cited in Green, 2006).

This definition relies into three important aspects of ethnicity namely, common descent, conceptual autonomy and a common history. The first and the third feature are common to all definitions of ethnicity and ethnic groups. Gerring and Baressi (2000) too try to take a "minimal" approach or definition of ethnicity by considering or taking into account only the least amount of descriptive features of an ethnic group. Use of such ordinary language to understand concepts like ethnicity helps academicians to discuss such difficult concepts with policy-makers and general public who are unversed in such theories. The ordinary language definition gives certain key qualities that must be present for an ethnic group to exist, thereby allowing researchers to construct data sets based on such a definition (Green, 2006). Such understanding allows one to eliminate the polysemy created by primordialist and constructivist approaches.

II. Drawing the Boundary

After adopting comprehensive understanding of ethnicity, it becomes important to define the 'boundary' as used in the context of making an ethnic identity. Explaining the notion of 'boundary' Andreas Wimmer (2014) writes:

A boundary displays both a categorical and a social or behavioural dimension. The former refers to act of social classification and collective representation, the latter to everyday networks of relationships that result from individual acts of connecting and distancing. On the individual level, the categorical and behavioural aspects appear as two cognitive schemes. One divides the social world into social groups- into "Us" and "Them" and the other offers script of action how to relate to individuals classified as "us" and "them" under given circumstances. Only when the two schemes coincide, when ways of seeing of the world corresponds to ways of acting in the world, we shall speak of a social boundary (Andreas Wimmer, 2014, 9).

This does not imply that the existence of such boundaries divides the world into water tight compartments. In fact, such boundaries at times can be blurry and soft allowing for easy movement of identities. Also individuals can make a choice among the several identities demarcated by the boundary. Thus, the concept of boundary neither represents clarity nor closure; it varies from society to society. It is an important challenge to the comparative study of ethnicity to take into account such varying degrees of boundedness.

Anthony P. Cohen (1994) sees boundary not just as a social barrier but also as a mental distance. He writes, "A boundary-crossing stimulates the awareness of a person as an individual, as someone who can step back and reflect on his or her position with respect to society. If we recognise boundaries as matters of consciousness rather than of institutional dictation, we see them as much more amorphous, much more ambiguous than we otherwise have done. It may be this very ambiguity which inclines societies to invest their various boundaries so heavily with symbolism" (Cohen, 1994). It is internalisation of the consciousness of belonging to a particular group that an individual uses to identify him or herself. Such understanding of boundary is important as most of the work on ethnicity has taken the boundary to be a cultural phenomenon. The fact that boundary can exist in terms of consciousness paving way for a mental distance can exist cannot be overlooked.

This study takes into account physical, social as well as emotional boundaries when it comes to boundary making in the construction of an ethnic identity. Taking a constructivist/ instrumentalist position of the formation of ethnic identity, the work is informed by the social, cultural and geo-political compulsions of the groups in defining and asserting their self-identity.

III. The Case- Study: The Bodoland and the Gorkhaland Movement

As mentioned earlier, this study tries to make a brief comparative analysis of the two important homeland movements and attempts to understand the compulsions and dilemmas faced by the groups in construction of a coherent identity.

1).The Bodoland Movement

The Bodoland movement has been of great importance and interest in recent times given the violent history it has been attached to. This movement has been exceptionally contested both in mainstream academic discourses as well as in political discussions. Ironically, most of the observers view Bodo movement as a separatist and violent movement and a challenge against the integrity of the state. Some scholars see it as an attempt to revive the ancient glory of the Bodo-Kachari kingdom which was uncontaminated by the Assamese culture (Baruah, 2012; Nath, 2013). While others see it as a resistance movement by a group to escape from a socio-political and cultural entrapment of communities perceived to be 'outsiders' (Vandekerckhove and Suykens, 2008).

What is evident in such scholarly debates is the failure to recognise the subtleties of the movement which also involves the state as well as the resistance put forward by other groups in the region to this movement. It does not either illustrate India's absolute inability to accommodate democratic political aspiration of the Bodos who remained outside the ambit of Constitutional protection till the creation of the Bodoland Territorial Council (BTC) in February,2003 (Mochahari, 2014). The movement has been in news for a very long time as being one of most violent statehood demands which led to a large scale death and displacement induced by both militants and state machinery.

(a) Constructing the 'Bodo' Identity: Rediscovering the Glorious History

The role of history, in both uniting and dividing a community is undeniable. History has been the powerful tool in reclaiming the self in the post-colonial period. Various subaltern groups which had been silenced by the powerful have been voicing their resistance through the means of history.

The 'Bodos' too have been engaged in a process of rediscovering and reclaiming their self by making attempts to construct a great Bodo-Kachari race. Mythological as well as historically documented evidences have been put forward to arrive at a common origin of the race in the region. The Bodos are a part of a greater and larger ethnic community called the 'Bodo-Kachari'. Bodos, Koches, Rabhas, Lalungs, Hajongs, Chutiyas, Meches, Dhimals and Sonowals of the Brahmaputra valley and North Bengal, the Dimasas of North Cachar, Hills, the Tripuras and Garos are considered to be a part of the grater Bodo- Kachari race (Barpujari, 1992). Racially, Bodos are a part of the Indo-Mongoloid race found all across Northeast India. According to Suniti Kumar Chatterjee, in the epic period the Bodos were known as 'Kiratas' and were considered to be the offspring of Vishnu and Mother Earth (Chatterjee, 1974).

The Bodos claim themselves to be the descendants of the Kiratas, a term used in the ancient Hindu epics to refer to the people of the Mongoloid stock. According to the Bodo legends, Mahiranga Danaba, a ruler of the ancient Kamrupa, was a 'Kirata ruler' whose original name was *Mairong dao*. *'Mairang'* is a Bodo word which means paddy or rice and 'dao' stands for hero (Mosahari, 2011). Another legendary king of ancient Kamrupa, Narakasura, also has been claimed to have Bodo roots. In Bodo, *'Narkho'* means stout and strong and 'sor' stands for iron in Bodo (*ibid*).

Bhagadatta, known as *Brog dao* among the Bodos, another contemporary king who ruled the present day Sonitpur had converted to Hinduism and also said to have taken part in the great war of Kurukshetra. In course of time, the Bodos came under the influence of Hinduism and the Bodo-Kirata royal families adopted Hindu names and titles like the 'Varman', 'Pala', 'Rai', etc. Historian E.H. Gait has observed that Varman (Varman : armouror defence) was a common Kshatriya title and was frequently appropriated by aboriginal converts to Hinduism of high rank (Gait, 1962, reprint).

The Kacharis living in the present north Bengal and western parts of Goalpara district of Assam are known as 'Mech'. It is believed that Bodo-Kacharis living on the bank of the river Mechi flowing through Nepal are called as *Mech* or *Meche*. The Kacharis of Cachar district (North Chachar Hills of Assam) call themselves Kacharis. They are simply known as 'Dimasa-Kacharis' means 'son of a big river', 'Di' means 'river' and 'cha' means 'children' (Brahma, 1989). They had inhabited the valley for centuries as the land being fertile enough for cultivation (mono cropping). By the second half of twelfth century, many Bodo chiefs started establishing different kingdoms in various parts of the region. From the Brahmaputra valley, many moved to north Bengal, Garo Hills, North Cachar and Tripura Hills and to a lesser extent had changed in physical features through intermarriages and also identified themselves with landmarks of their new localities (Bordoloi, 1984; Pegu, 2004).

A major deviation from the Bodo race took place during the medieval period with the establishment of the Koch-Rajbhanshi kingdom. This dynasty was founded by two brothers- *Bisu* and *Sisu*, who later converted to Hinduism and adopted the names Biswa Singha and Sib Singha. The Koch kingdom reached its zenith of its power during the reign of Naranarayan, whose army was under the command of his brother and the great warrior Chilarai. The Koch kings, the Bodos alleged that they discarded their tribal identity after becoming Hinduised and adopted the title of 'Koch'. The Koch kings soon became a great patron of the Hinduism and imported numerous Brahmans from Kanauj, Benaras and such other places in an attempt to make Hinduism a major religion of the kingdom. Subsequently, like the Koch- Rajbhangsis, the Tiwas, Karbis and a number of other tribes were assimilated into the Hindu fold. With this process of conversion, a great bulk of the Bodo and other Mongoloid population got assimilated into the Assamese fold. Several scholars are of the view that the genesis of the majority of tribes in Assam shows that they belong to the Mongoloid Kirata race of the great Bodo stock and their original language belongs to the Bodo group of the Bodo-Naga section under the Assam-Burmese branch of the Tibeto-Burma division of the Sino-Tibetan speech (Gait, 1905; Grierson, 1903; Shafer, 1955).

From the above discussion it is clear that the Bodo identity composed of a diverse range of communities, which in due course of time, being geographically isolated from the other developed their own distinct culture and language. Subsequently, the British ethnographers classified them as distinct tribes, based on their habitat they were divided into- Hill tribes and Plain tribes. The Bodos emerged as the largest Plain tribe inhabiting a large part of western Assam in the northern bank of river Brahmaputra.

Since the beginning of the twentieth century, the Bodos have been struggling to maintain their distinct identity as well as reclaim their political power by demanding a separate state. In the framework of a constantly declining situation of the plains tribal groups, a section of educated Bodos felt the need to come together to form multiple community centric organisations at different periods of time to work for the welfare of the community and negotiate with the powers that be for socio-cultural, economic, linguistics and political rights (Mochahari, 2014).

(b) Bodo and Assamese: Drawing the Lines

The present assertion of the Bodos cannot be seen as an isolated phenomenon. Their position vis-à-vis the Assamese language and culture is important in understanding their discontent. Usually, it is understood to refer to people speaking a particular language and living within a geographical area. In this regard, the Bodos seem to take a contrary position. It is seen as a language and culture which developed as a result of the *'sanskritisation'* of the region. Most of the Mongoloid groups lacked a written script; therefore it was readily accepted in the region and especially in the Brahmaputra valley. At the same time, the Bodo rulers were influenced by the Aryan civilisation and adopted Hinduism. With the advent of the Ahoms and their subsequent adaptation of the Assamese language most ethnic communities of the region began to learn and gradually adopted this language.

Expressing the views of the Bodos towards assimilation, Jadav Pegu (2004) notes that:

> *It is difficult to imagine a Marathi living in Orissa, pick up the Oriya language and start identifying himself as an Oriya. Or for that matter, an Assamese staying in Tamil Nadu, learning Tamil and calling himself a Tamil. In today's multicultural world, language is a vital benchmark in cultural identity and politics. Assimilation and homogenisation is hardly the accepted trend: rather the recognition of differences existing between people within a nation- state in terms of ethnicity, language, institutions, religion, texts and artifacts is advocated for the better understanding of the demand of indigenous people for accommodation of their cultural and political identities. The Bodo identity has to be seen in this light and as opposed to the homogenising Assamese* (Jadav Pegu, 2004, 7).

British scholar E.A. Gait who conducted extensive research on the Bodos writing in the year I905 had observed that the process of assimilation of Bodos into Assamese had made inroads into the Bodo society. By analysing the language data of 1891 census, he revealed that the languages/dialects of the Bodo group were dying out and would gradually be extinguished. He commented on the decline of number of speakers of Bodo language group from 1881 to 1891 census. The Bodo-Kachari (present day Bodos) speakers declined by 24 per cent from 2, 63,186 to 2,00,129 people, whereas Hinduised Bodos of lower Assam (Meche) increased by 19.6 per cent. According to him, most of the converted Bodo Hindus could move into some higher status Hindu caste. As a result, those joined the Assamese formation no longer identified themselves as Bodos (such as Koch Rajbongsis of Assam). Many of them such as Sonowal-Kacharis, Chutias, Rabhas etc. changed into different ethnic identity (Assamese under S.T. category), lost their original Bodo language.

Even after a long period of assimilation into the Assamese caste society there were groups who could maintain their unique identity, language and culture. Those groups who did not share any close geographical and political ties with the caste Assamese or the Ahom rulers were out of the ambit of the process of assimilation. Attempts to assimilate them into the Assamese society began only during the nineteenth century with the policy of official language and desire for homogeneity by the caste Assamese.

The language policy of the state government after independence has been a major factor in alienating the tribal population of Assam. The Assamese middle class who held the leadership of the state and dominated the politics subsequently held sway over the cultural manifestation of minority groups. The Assam Sahitya Sabha, the apex body for the development and promotion of Assamese language and literature was making untiring efforts to make Assamese the only official language of the state. It tried to make Assamese the sole medium of educational instructions as well as administrative purposes. Such a unilateral move was vehemently opposed by most of the non-Assamese speaking linguistic groups.

Prior to independence, the tribal leaders of Assam had formed a multi-ethnic tribal organisation in the year 1993 known as the 'Assam Tribal League'. The organisation included leaders from all over the state- Rupnath Brahma and Kalicharan Brahma (Goalpara), Jadav Ch. Khakhlary (Lakhimpur), Gopal Ch. Choudhuri and Rabichandra Kochari (Kamrup), Dhanbar Patar (Nagoan), Mohi Chandra Miri (Sibsagar), Bhimbar Deuri and Khorsing Terang (Mikir Hills), and so on. This conglomeration of tribal leaders shows the desire to come together and forge a united alliance against the injustice and discrimination meted out to them. The ATL, under the leadership of Bhimbar Deuri, made an appeal to all the tribal people of Assam to identify them as "Tribal", irrespective of their conversion to any religion in the forthcoming census of 1941. Consequently, the tribal population increased to 28,24,133 in the census of 1941 from a meager count of 12,39,280 in the year 1911 (Mosahari, 2011).

A major actor of the Bodo assertion and agitation has been the All Bodo Student Union (ABSU) which came into being on the 15th of February 1967 with the objective of raising consciousness among Bodo youth and students about the needs of their community and to actively raise demand for a separate homeland for the plain tribes of Assam. A new era began in the political life of the Bodos with the entry of Upendra Nath Brahma, the eighth president of ABSU. The quest for political identity with its separate entity for the Bodos found a new lease of life under the abled and dynamic leadership of U.N. Brahma.

He was able to effectively articulate the glorious past of the Bodos among the common people. He was able to bring the much required unity among the Bodos and mobilise them under the banner of ABSU. He attempted to carry out a non-violent struggle against the chauvinistic policies of the state government and safeguard the interest of the tribal population. At the same time he believed that the only a separate state could fulfill the aspirations of the Bodos.

During the same period various groups who advocated violent methods to achieve their objective came up. This also includes groups like Boro Security Force (BRSF), which was later christened as National Democratic Front of Bodoland (NDFB) and demanded liberation of the Bodo areas from the Indian Union. This set in a new political trend changing the very nature of Bodo unrest. In order to avoid in fighting, an umbrella organisation called Bodo People's Action Committee (BPAC) in the year 1988 in order to secure the support and participation of all sections of the Bodo society irrespective of their political affiliations was formed. The ABSU-BPAC combined movement continued for the next six years and culminated with the signing of the Bodoland Accord of 1993 which established the Bodoland Autonomous Council (BAC).

The BAC was unable to satisfy the aspirations of the Bodos as it failed to demarcate a clear-cut boundary of the Bodoland. Soon, ABSU disowned the Council and revived the movement for a separate state. This phase of the struggle was marked by violence due the activities of militant Bodo organisations like NDFB and BLT. The year 1996 in particular was marred with fratricidal killings in the Kokrajhar district which has the largest concentration of Bodos. The year also witnessed riots between the Adivasis and the Bodos, which displaced thousands of people and cost many lives. Violence against various communities living in the Bodoland region has been carried out by the militant armed groups since the inception of the armed struggle and it led to a considerable opposition by the non-Bodo groups to the formation of a separate state of Bodoland.

Finally, after a series of talks between the Central Government, State Government and the BLT backed by

ABSU-BPAC, a Memorandum of Settlement was signed on 10th February, 2003. This led to the creation of a self-governing autonomous body to be known as 'Bodoland Territorial Council' under the sixth schedule of the Indian Constitution. The demand for a separate state was withdrawn by ABSU as a support to the MoS. It has been witnessed at the later period that the political journey of the Bodos in Assam has been a turbulent one and continues to dominate public life in Bodo heartland in the absence of a pragmatic political solution to the problem (Mochahari, 2014).

2. Constructing the 'Gorkha'- The Making, Unmaking and Remaking of an Identity

The Darjeeling hills of West Bengal have been demanded as a homeland for the 'Gorkha' community of India. While the origin of Darjeeling is soaked in the imperial legacy of the British Raj, the Gorkha is a colonial construct which ironically have been used as a means to challenge the hegemonic rule of people who are perceived to be different. Although the Gorkha identity is deemed as representative of the Nepali community residing in India, it acquires special meaning and importance in the Darjeeling hills, where majority of the people suffer low wages, unemployment, underdevelopment and poverty (Chettri, 2013).

Demographically, Darjeeling is dominated by Indian-Nepali ethnicities, which are collectively identified as 'Gorkhas'. Unlike the celebrated 'Gurkha' regiments of the British Indian army the designation 'Gorkha' emerged not merely as a colonial military identification, but rather a twentieth century creation born of specific historical circumstances in Darjeeling and the political necessities of India more generally. Indian-Nepali communities today extend throughout northern and northeastern India. Having said this, the concern of this chapter, lies specifically with the formation and politics of Gorkha identity in Darjeeling. Since migrating to Darjeeling from Nepal in the early nineteenth century, their identity in India has remained in constant doubt. They have been deemed 'foreigners', 'hill tribes', and 'outsiders' for being geographically, racially, and nationally different from the Indo-Aryan majority of plains. Marginalised geo-racially, politically, morally, and economically, the Gorkhas of Darjeeling harbour deep seated anxieties over being in and being truly of the Indian nation state. Throughout the twentieth and twenty-first centuries, these anxieties of belonging, coupled with political interests and processes of ethno genesis, generated a range of identification forms (Middleton, 2013).

Darjeeling holds a unique place in the Indian imaginary, as being a tourist paradise. With its Himalayan landscapes, proximity to Calcutta, cool climate, and the mist, Darjeeling soon became the Britishers consummate hill station, mainly a sanatorium to escape the heat of the Empire. It was acquired from Sikkim in 1835 and in no time transformed to a tea-producing country and hill station in the nineteenth century. Construction works like clearing the rugged landscape, building roads, and providing workers to the region's budding tea industry required far more labour than the local Bhutia and Lepcha populations could provide. Colonial administrators turned to neighbouring regions of Nepal, where thousands from the "most vigorous and enterprising of the Nepal races" were willing to cross the border for work in colonial India (WBSA, 1888). The British had found an ideal and mostly loyal labour pool. But the Nepali Durbar was against this migration of its human resources. The British therefore encouraged the migration of labour from Nepal, but washed their hands of its doubtful legality by relying on informal labour recruiters known as 'Sardars' to move people across borders. 'Going to Mugalan', as India was then known or called in Nepal (Hutt, 1998), promised a life better than the autocratic rule of the Ranas and hard feudal toil in Nepal. The Nepali settlers soon became Darjeeling's demographic majority (Chatterjee, 2001; Subba, 1989; Subba and Sinha, 2003). But while the British offered food, clothes, shelter, and wage labour, they did not provide legal recognition as British subjects (WBSA, 1868, 1869, 1878 cited in Middleton, 2013). No longer Nepali and not yet Indian, these populations thus found themselves in an extended state of perpetual homelessness.

The postcolonial independent India brought little respite to the grievances of the Gorkhas of Darjeeling. They remained at the periphery of the political economy of the Hills. Racial and nationalist discrimination was apparent and they continued to be relegated from India's socio-political and economic agenda.

Thus, Gorkhaland, a separate state comprising of the three hill divisions of Kurseong, Kalimpong and Darjeeling, also with the districts in the plains and the Duars which has a substantial Nepali speaking population, is being demanded as a solution to socio-economic grievances of all the people living in those areas. But the ethnic connotation of this demand is not hidden; as it is highlighted as an assertion of a particular ethnic group the Gorkha. Even though there are other ethnic groups in the same region under the same socio-economic situation. Nevertheless, for political expediency and social solidity the term it has undergone dynamic shifts to incorporate everyone- Tibetan, Lepchas and all other groups living in the hills (Chettri, 2013).

The political history and turbulent years of Darjeeling is a witness to the repeated revival of the Gorkha identity as an instrument of mediation primarily with the state. Since the beginning of political realisation in the hills, the image and idea of the Gorkha has been utilised by all the political parties to orient their agenda around the attainment of Gorkhaland, using images and language commonly attached to the imagery of the Gorkha. As a product of colonial rule, the construction of the Gorkha identity can be credited to the process of 'making up people', whereby through casting and inducing insights people as well as their identities are created and promoted in a certain sense that never existed before. The Gorkha, in the Darjeeling hills is defined through the prism of ethnic suppression by the Bengali-dominated state.

Such identification marks the Gorkhas apart not just on the basis of cultural and socio-linguistic variances but also on the basis of exploitation and marginalisation, an identity which is hallmark of an unequal relationship of supremacy and control of one by the other. Such an approach has externalised the understanding of the Gorkha among the population of the Hills. Nonetheless approaches to understanding of the Gorkha, even in Darjeeling, range from passionate identification to that of hesitant acknowledgment, which is common amongst the urban population who are more comfortable with the idea of 'Darjeelingness' rather than that of a Gorkha. It might be a microscopic proportion, but it represents divergence from the mass attachment to Gorkhaland. Such approach is a reflection of an important aspect of socio-economic stratification of Darjeeling and the corresponding relationship between class and an ethnic category.

Even though it is represented and understood as an ethnic subnationalism, the Gorkha identity did not always exist as it is today. When groups like the Tamangs, Gurungs, and Limbus, which are now indispensable part of the Gorkha community, migrated to Darjeeling, they came with their own sociocultural and linguistic affiliations. They were in the understanding of modern academics distinct culture bearing ethnic groups. After being settled in Darjeeling, these distinct ethnic groups began to mix and fuse in exceptional ways. With Nepali or 'Khaskura' emerging as the lingua franca and intense inter-ethnic interaction, ethnicities like the Gurungs and Tamangs, in due course of time lost much of their linguistic and socio-cultural distinctiveness. Former practices were now replaced by new forms of ethnic consciousness and solidarity built around a common identity. Subsequently, these processes of ethno-genesis; thereafter, have reworked the social and political landscape of Darjeeling with far reaching consequences.

a. Quest towards a Tribal Identity

During the 1990s and 2000s, new ventures into Indian political scenario paved the way to redraw the lines of ethnic identification in Darjeeling. Individual communities like the Tamangs, Gurungs and Limbus looked for an alternate route to secure the rightful recognition and began to mobilising for recognition as Scheduled Tribes of India. ST status promised affirmative action advantages including employment quotas in governmental posts, lower standards of admission to education, eligibility for special tribal development packages, and hosts of entitlements (GOI, 2007). At the same time what was more important for the ambitious tribes of Darjeeling was the representative inclusion of these communities as the Scheduled Tribes of India.

Observing such phenomenon, political geographer T. Middleton (2013) writes:

"These claims of tribal identity marked an abrupt shift in the identificational practices and politics of the hills. The quest for tribal recognition necessitated an undoing of the Gorkhas on a number of registers. Politically, the go-it-alone tactics of aspiring STs atomised the Gorkha conglomerate and refigured the unit of ethno-political mobilisation. Socially, the exigencies of ST recognition amplified inter-ethnic competition and distinction. Analytically too, there were tensions. For while the Gorkha identity was predicated on hybridity, ST recognition with its mandates of cultural isolation, distinctiveness, and purity called for hybridity's undoing. That is to say, if groups like the Tamangs and Gurungs were to attain ST status, they would need to extract their discrete 'cultures' from an already melted melting pot. Many continued to self-identify as both Gorkha and say, Tamang, but it was clear that the Indian government had little provision for such segmentary configurations. And so, community 100-years in the making began to come undone. Once again, the making and unmaking of identity was proving derivative of the Indian state and its normative epistemologies of difference" (Middleton, 2013, 35).

b. Return of the Gorkha

Attempts to gain ST status were partially successful as few communities would gain it and the question of granting Sixth schedule to the Hills meet with vehement opposition. The passion of attachment to the Gorkha identity could be assessed by what came to be popularly known as the 'Prashant Tamang sensation'. In 2007, Prashant Tamang a resident of Darjeeling was selected in the 'Indian Idol', a national level singing reality contest. As a Nepali from Darjeeling, in no time he was taken to be a symbol of millions of Indian-Nepalis and their aspiration for acceptance and assimilation within the Indian nation. Campaigns asking for 'votes' were undertaken on a war footing, and it was led by Bimal Gurung, who taking the advantage of the situation formed the Gorkha Janamukti Morcha (GJM). Riding high on the emotions, the GJM renewed the demand for Gorkhaland and in 2011, after years of agitation, signed the Tripartite Treaty which led to the formation of the Gorkha Territorial Administration (GTA).

Writing on the requirement of constructing the identity of Gorkha, Mona Chettri (2013) notes:

The entrenchment of the Gorkha identity begins as a historical project and is accentuated by the political movement for Gorkhaland – thus in its present use it aims to serve three fundamental causes. First, apart from providing a basis for an ethnic collectivity, the Gorkha shields the insecurities of the Nepali community – an obvious phenomenon owing to the subservience and domination that generations of Nepalis have endured under colonisation and now neo-colonisation. Second, bravery and sacrifice in the battlefield is persistently highlighted by political elites as well as the general masses as one of the most important characteristics of the Gorkha. Valour, sacrifice and death for Mother India is celebrated and contribute to the display of patriotism and loyalty towards the Indian state in a bid to replace the negative image of the community as mercenaries and immigrants. Apart from enhancing group collectivity, the image of the brave Gorkha also negates the feeling and the colonial representation of Nepalis as 'coolies'/labourers thereby strengthening the identity further. Finally, the Gorkha as an ethnic group with its own distinct cultural markers performs the important act of differentiating the community from the mainstream, dominant Bengali population in West Bengal. This in turn justifies ethnic discrimination of the Nepalis and therefore the demand for a separate state of Gorkhaland (Mona Chettri, 2013, 10).

Conclusion

The above discussion clearly illustrates how an assertive ethnic identity, when fuelled by a sense of deprivation and marginalisation tries to unite the community by drawing boundaries at various levels. The demarcation of the boundary, most of the time is informed by the political and socio-cultural requirement of the groups. The role played by the ethnic elites in drawing as well as manipulating the boundaries is undeniable and requires further research. What is evident from this comparative analysis is that construction of ethnic identity, which attempts to draw a boundary between 'us' and 'them' is also a care construction of history which is required for the legitimacy of the identity. At the same time, the role played by the state and its policies cannot be overlooked when it comes to construction of identity in the contemporary times. Drawing the boundary line of identity requires the group to negotiate with the state and its agencies on a daily basis. Such an interaction can be both conflicting as well as cooperative depending on the nature of demand and the response of the state towards it.

Contemporary construction of the Bodo identity is based on a sense of alienation from the state due to years of economic neglect and attempts to assimilate into a common culture; which they resist as being a symbol of colonialisation over the tribes. One of the important planks on which the Bodo movement was based, according to the Bodo leaders was the "Assamese chauvinism" as being responsible for discords in a multi-ethnic state like Assam. Today, they desire to manage their own affairs without any dictation or interference from the state government which is perceived to be indifferent and unsympathetic towards the interest of the tribal's in general and Bodos in particular.

The study of the Gorkha conglomerate shows us that boundaries can be very effective when it comes to the politics of anxiety and belonging to the state. Such a quest for identity demands a broad drawing of the boundary line which would encompass a possibly large number of groups connected by some form of commonality (in this case it can be the race and the language as well as marginalisation by the state). Years of living together have given way to strong senses of shared history, group membership, and collective sentiment to these populations. Their repeated ethno-political aspirations and mobilisations based on the 'Gorkha' identity confirm their coming together. These conglomerate groups which makes up the Gorkha do not lack an identity; what they are awaiting is that sacred stuff of recognition to affirm their being in and of India and, in more Hegelian terms, their being in and of themselves (Hegel, 1977 cited in Middleton, 2013). Therefore, the crisis is not about lack of identity, but the lack of rightful recognition. In Darjeeling, the divisions, rejections, and (mis)identifications that have shaped ethnic politics here appear not as identity's shortcomings, but rather the by-product of a palpable politics of recognition, constitutive of real and lasting forms of exclusion. That these byproducts have fed back into an enduring and embodied sense of crisis among these groups only corroborates the power of the Indian state to affect, regulate, or otherwise deny those forms of difference that amass at and within its borders (*ibid*).

Marginalised communities like the Gorkhas and Bodos maintain intense desire for rights, recognition, inclusion, and belonging; at the same time they are dependent on the state to achieve those aims. Paradoxically, the conditions of life, even after the attainment of self-rule have altered very little. For people relegated to a non-descript and symbolic corner of the national geography, the desire for identity and its manifestations remains a 'thing' that must be lived at and lived with. Thus, the task of boundary-making as an integral dimension of both life and politics remains equally as generative as it is problematic.

References

1. Andreas Wimmer, *Ethnic Boundary Making*, Oxford University Press, London, 2013.
2. Anthony Cohen, 'Culture, Identity and the Concept of Boundary', (*Paper Presented at the Revista de Antropologia Social)*, Madrid, 1994.
3. D. L. Horowitz, *Ethnic Groups in Conflict*, University of California Press, Berkeley, 1985.
4. Elliot D.Green, 'Redifining Ethnicity', *Paper prepared for presentation at the 47th Annual International Studies Association Convention, San Diego, CA,* 2006.
5. Eloise Hummell, 'Standing the Test of Time – Barth and Ethnicity', *Coolabah*, No. 13, Observatory Centre d'Estudis Australians, Australian Studies Centre, Universitat de Barcelona, 2014.
6. Fearon J. Laitin, 'Ordinary Language and External Validity: Specifying Concepts in the Study of Ethnicity', *Presented at Meet Lab Comp Ethnic Politics,* University of Peninsula. Philadelphia. October 20–22, 2000.
7. Fredrik Barth (Ed), *Ethnic Groups and Boundaries: The Social Organisation of Culture Difference*, Allen & Unwin London, 1969, pp. 9-38.

8. George A. De Vos, 'Introduction', George Devos and Lola Romanucci Ross (Eds), *Ethnic Identity,* Mayfield Publishing Co, 1975.
9. J. Milton Yinger, *Drawing the Boundaries of Ethnicity: Source of Strength? Source of Conflict?,* State University of New York, New York, 1997.
10. John Gerring and Paul. A. Baressi, 'Putting ordinary language to Work', *Journal of Theoretical Politics,* 15(2), 2003, 201-232.
11. Max Weber, *Economy and Society* (Two Volume Set, with a New Foreword by G. Roth and C. Wittich (Eds), Bedminster, New York, 1968.
12. Micheal Hutt, 'Being Nepali without Nepal' in J.P.C. David, N. Gellner, and J. Whelpton (Eds), *Nationalism and Ethnicity in a Hindu kingdom*, Harwood Academic Publishers, Amsterdam, 1997.
13. Mona Chettri, 'Choosing the Gorkha: At the Crossroads of Class and Ethnicity in the Darjeeling Hills, *Asian Ethnicity*, Vol.14, Issue-3, 06 Feb, 2013, pp. 293-308.
14. Monjib Mochahari, 'State Hegemony, Identity Politics and Resistance in Bodoland', *.Journal of Tribal Intellectual Collective India*, 2 (2), (2014, pp. 76-96.
15. Monoj Kumar Nath, 'Bodo Insurgency in Assam: New Accord and New Problems', *Strategic Analysis*, 27 (4), 2003, pp. 533-545.
16. Montserrat Guibernau, 'Introduction', in Montserrat Guibernau and John Rex (Eds), *The Ethnicity Reader* (2nd Edition), Polity Press, Cambridge, 2009, pp. 1-10.
17. Nel Vandekerckhove and Suykens Bert, 'The Liberation of Bodoland: Tea, Forestry and Tribal Entrapment in Western Assam', *South Asia: Journal of South Asian Studies,* 3I (3), 2008, pp. 450-471.
18. Pemananda Mosahari, *Political Identity Crisis of the Bodos and the Bodoland Movement*, N.L Publications, Guwahati, 2011.
19. Sanjib Baruah, 'Territoriality, Indigeneity and Rights in the North-east India', *Economic and Political Weekly,* 43 (12), 2008.
20. T. Middleton, 'States of Difference: Refiguring Ethnicity and its 'Crisis' at India's Borders'. *Political Geography*, 35, 2013, 14-24.
21. Tanka B. Subba, 'The Last Word So Far' in n D. R. Nepal, G. S. Nepal, A. C. Sinha, and Tanks B. Subba (Eds), *Indian Nepalis: Issues and Perspectives*, Concept Publishing, New Delhi, 2009.
22. Tanka B. Subba, *Dynamics of a Hill Society: The Nepalis in Darjeeling and Sikkim Himalayas*: Mittal Publishers, Delhi, 1989.

15

Ethnic Movements of Mising Tribe of Assam: An Analysis

Thagendra Chutia and Anup Deka

Introduction

The tribe 'Mising' previously known as Miri, is one of the major group of tribal community in the Brahmaputra Valley of Assam. The migration of the Misings to the plains of Assam was as far as the early days of Assam History. Originally, the Mising came from Tani- a group of Tibeto-Burman race of mankind. Ethnically, they belong to the Tibeto-Burmese group of Mongoloid stock. They have their own tribal traditional beliefs and customs. They believe in "Po: Lo" the moon (as Father God) and the Sun (as Mother Goddess) respectively. Originally, the Misings belong to same groups of tribes namely Ghasis, Nishis, Miyongs, Padams, Adis etc. who are found in Siyang and Subansiri District of Arunachal Pradesh. However, they have possessed their own distinct language and culture different from the dominant section of upper Assamese society in respect of living style and socio-cultural traits as well. Their language belongs to the Tibeto Burma family of Indo-Chineses group which is akin to the Adi language. They want to preserve their rich cultural heritage and develop the community- socially, economically and even politically. In fact, they do not like to be sub-merged by the dominant Assamese caste Hindu culture. It needs to be mentioned here that the Assamese Culture does not necessarily imply the Culture of the Assamese Caste Hindu alone. Different ethnic groups of Assam also contributed their respective shares. The Assamese culture is a continuous process of socio-cultural fusion among diverse linguistic and ethnic traits for centuries. The tribals of Assam did not lag behind in this process. The Misings also contributed significantly toward this process.

Despite this fact, a section of the Mising elite strongly feel that they are markedly different from the Assamese Hindu caste who has been the dominant community in Assam. In many respect, they are more backward than other section of Assamese society. They also started to feel that they are humiliated and oppressed by the advanced Assamese society. For these reasons, the Misings tried to develop a sense of distinctiveness and gradually became articulate in the pursuit of preserving socio-cultural identity which culminated in the formation of the socio-cultural organisation among them. The Mising Bane Kebang as per reference of Leka Lakko a souveniour of special convention of Mising Bane Kebang on 27th and 28th April of 2002, it is clear that MBK is formally formed as Mising Paren Organisation on 20th December in 1939. Like it, various Mising organisations were formed namely TMPK in 1933, MAK in 1972, MDK in 1980, MMK in 1993, TMMK in 1990. However, the Mising educated elites felt the necessity of forming such socio-cultural and political organisation for the upliftment of this community. These organisation always struggle for the preservation of Mising language and culture as well as political safeguard for their society. The Mising organisations are demanding continuously for their specific cultural and socio-economic and even political safeguard for distinct identity of Mising community.

Methodology

The present study has covered the only the ethnic movements of Mising Community in Assam. This study is compiled with the help of the Secondary data. The Secondary data were collected after concerning various Books, Journals, Memorandum etc.

Analysis

Like other tribes, the Mising are also economically depressed and backward in terms of educational development. The problems faced by the Mising are in essence the problem of less developed communities living with a comparatively advanced group of people under a common political system. A greater portion of them is extremely poor. Although, the weaker section of the dominant Assamese and the Mising has been equally poor, the elite among the non-tribal population were larger, better equipped and better trained than the hitherto almost non-existent Mising elite. The conflict for economic and political power has been essential between the growing strength of the Mising elite on one hand and the non-Mising local elite on the other.

Today, it seems obvious that much of the Mising problems of Assam can be traced in their economic backwardness. Complication over possession of land seems to have prepared the ground for consciousness in Mising Community. It has been a long standing grievance of the entire plains tribal people including the Mising of Assam that their lands and property have been alienated and transferred ceaselessly to the hands of unauthorised non-tribal outsiders through process of illegal occupation, purchase, money landing and mortgage by their encroachment. It may be mentioned that the Mising have been easy targets for many glaring exploitation and injustices for decades due to their 'illiteracy' and 'simplicity'.

Like other tribal communities in Assam, a bulk of the Misings is also agriculturists. Agriculture is the main occupation of their livelihood. Thus, the President of the MBK mentioned, the Misings are prescriptive citizens and agriculture being the mainstay of their economy, their survival without land is unthinkable. He further asserts that "they are the best paddy growers in Assam and have the best cultivable land which might have aroused jealousy in other people". Thus, it seems obvious that the problems of land alienation have assumed a very alarming proportion. Since the inception of this century, immigrants from the East Bengal infiltrated in to their area swallowing up many of their old villages and the most fertile areas.

There is also resentment about the intrusion of immigrants in recent years who occupied patta land (government waste land) unclassified forests and even reserved forests of the entire northern part of the Brahmaputra Valley. Attempts to evict these immigrants have so far failed because of their strong financial standing and the tribal's including the Misings often lost their land through mortgage and litigation. Some Mising leaders suspect that certain political leaders of Assam are behind these developments. The immigrants are also supposed to have had other undesirable effects on the Mising e.g. the spread of tribal's belts or the habit of taking opium.

The Mising elite have tried to draw the attention of the government through letters in newspapers and representation for immediate measures to revive tribal blocks and belts to safeguard the interests of the Misings in particular and tribals in general in these areas and have appealed that delay in introducing such measures may frustrate the tribal's and lead them to take desperate action. In a memorandum to the Chief Minister of Assam in 1984, the TMPK has complained that the plains tribes including the Misings have been uprooted in a systematic and a planned way from their soil and that the 'Step motherly' treatment of the administration, dominated by the non-tribal people, have reduced them to the status of the second class citizens of the states.

The concrete steps toward the amelioration of the conditions of these weaker sections, started with the initiation of community developments schemes and especially multipurpose tribal blocks in the beginning of first plan period of 1952. Tribal land was sought to be projected through the application of Land Act of 1888 as amended in 1964, but it was not very effective.

It needs to mentioned that there has been a haste in the process of restoration of Misings land to their holders. Thus, the backward Misings have been made conscious about how they are being deprived of the vested interest of the tribal block areas. They have been ruthlessly exploiting and suppressing their aspirations and out numbering the tribal's in their traditional homelands including large number of influx into tribal block areas, illegal occupation of tribal lands by non-tribals.

Often the Mising elite alleged that they were not granted government loan or any other assistance because they have nothing to mortgage in exchange. There is extensive loss of land through sales by Misings to non-Misings not only for business purpose but for the erection of residential dwelling as well.

The Misings are also educationally backward than other non-tribal population of the state. As comparison to other sections of population in Assam, the Misings are also lagging far behind in the sphere of education. As per 1971 census, the percentage of literacy in Assam was 28.72 per cent. Among the scheduled tribe communities including the Mising community, the percentage of literacy was 26.02 per cent which was 2.27 per cent lower than the state percentage.

The present urges of the tribes in Assam, for maintaining distinct identity may be traced back ever to the period of British rule. In fact, the tribal's became organised and articulate prior to independence of the country. With the growing democratisation of the political system, the emerging educated tribal elite felt the need of organising their people in a bid to articulate their demands for all around development of the tribal in Assam. It may be noted that once Assam was much larger than today. As such, the tribal's of both the hills and plains made common effort to maintain their respective identity and anxious to preserve their heritage. Some of the tribal elite even thought of making their homeland (Assam) a 'Sovereign state' outside the Indian Union in the event of India being divided into Hindustan (India) and Pakistan. As a matter of fact, a section of the tribal elite didn't want that Assam should be a part of either Hindustan or Pakistan and they desired that it should maintain a sovereign status. They also thought that if Assam became free, the influx of non-Assamese Indians particularly into the tribal belt of Assam would be checked and more importantly, the tribal's would be in a better position within a sovereign Assam to protect their interests. In the middle of the forties, a feeling grew among some of the plains tribal elite in favour of an independent political existence for Assam as a means of safeguarding their distinct tribal identity.

In addition to this common effort, emerging educated elite of the Misings, gradually became conscious of their distinct Mising identity which culminated in the formation of separate organisations on the basis of their distinctness. The Mising leaders thought of improving the conditions of their people by raising identity consciousness among them. They are trying to find a way to raise their status and to meet the aspirations of their people. They are at the crossroads in the campaign to improve the conditions.

They want to improve their language to unite and develop the Misings. They sincerely believe that the development of Mising language and culture would ultimately enrich the greater Assam culture. The tribal culture such as the Mising, they assert, should be treated as a part and parcel of the composite Assamese culture.

The identity movement of the Mising, thus more or less emerged out of the movement for linguistic rights and it may be noted that language has been the favourite political issue in Assam. In fact, most of the similar identity movements of this region have taken place over the issue of language, especially after the enactment of the Language Act of the Government of Assam in 1960. The Mising language movement in Assam like any other tribal movement in the northeastern region is an aspect of the process of growing tribal consciousness for their self-development.

The political movement for an autonomous state is strengthened by the urge for maintaining and preserving their Mising identity. The political nature of the entire movement can hardly be denied especially when one examines the content strategy and tactics at every stage of this movement. Since the nature, the movement is political and their aspirations are based on political and economic principles. Thus, the identity movement can be appropriately characterised as a complex of socio-economic cultural and political factors.

Such movement for identity obviously emerged out of the socio-economic and cultural aspiration of the Misings. In fact, the memorandum issued by the various organisation of the

Mising reflected their feeling of socio-economic deprivation and grievances by and large; they want adequate protection against what they call 'economic exploitation' and 'land occupation' by the non-Misings. Moreover, the Mising leaders are conscious of the need for the educational development of the Mising community to achieve their socio-economic aspirations.

The identity movement of ethnic groups (Misings) is intended to strengthen composite Assamese culture and is in no way directed to make the latter weak. On the contrary, the identity movement of the Misings is being projected as undesirable for the progress of greater Assamese society. If the ethnic culture remains undeveloped, the vision of prosperous Assamese culture will remain a distinct utopia. As a matter of fact, we need a strong Assamese nation building as well as strong ethnic distinct identity. These are not contradictory but complementary to each other.

The second phase of Mising Movement for self identity started from 1947. After formation of the Mising Mimag Kebang in the session of 1993, 27th and 28th March at Jonai Morong Ghar as per memorandum taken by TMPK at Jiadhal Annual Conference, the main objective of the organisation is demand of Autonomous Council for the development of self socio-culture, political and economic grantees for the Mising community. They demanded Autonomy within the boundary of Assam. But, on 5th March 1995, a new socio-political organisation was formed by some educated Mising elites which is known as MADC (Mising Autonomous Demand Committee) under the leadership of Lakhinath Panging, demanding Autonomy for Mising for their self upliftment in socio-cultural, economic and political spheres. Their main issue was autonomy for Mising community and demand for political authority within the state of Assam. In this matter, the MBK and MADC submitted a memorandum to Chief Minister of Assam, demanding administrative authority to the Mising community for self development.

On 14th June, 1995, a Historical Mising accord was signed between Govt. of Assam and MADC and MBK which provided Autonomous Council to the Misings of Assam to provide for the establishment of an administrative authority for development of Mising Community which is known as "Mising Autonomous Council" (MAC). After signing this accord various Mising organisations like TMPK, MMK and TMMK were against the system of autonomy provided by the Govt. of Assam due to absence of specific boundary for the autonomous areas of MAC.

However, as per demand of the various organisations of Mising Community, the Assam Legislative Assembly passed a bill of amendment on MAC Act of 1995. On 14th June 2004, Five members of Mising Autonomous Committee (Cabinet Sub-Committee on Sixth Schedule), the various organisations of Mising submitted a memorandum for demanding creation of Mising Autonomous Council under Sixth Schedule. The present demand of Mising organisation is mainly, the creation of Mising Autonomous under Sixth Schedule under Indian Constitution. The three member expert committee on the plains Tribes of Assam (ECOPTA) led by Dr. Bhupinder Singh constituted during the Bodo movement describe this fact of exclusion of the plains tribal areas from 5th and 6th schedule as "Quirk of History". As a result of various reasons, the organisations of Mising also demanded for Sixth Schedule Autonomy as a whole. As a peace loving community of India, the Misings in 1982 on 14th and 15th September in TMPK's historic convention at All Assam Miri High School, firstly decided to demand Autonomy under Sixth Schedule for Mising Community and sound planning and well execution of the planned scheme by expertise of various subjects.

After the formation of Mising Autonomous Council, a tremendous ideological and issue base conflict occurred between the accord signed organisation and reactionary organisations like TMPK, MMK, and TMMK. Due to this conflict, the accord signed organisation MADC was collapsed and they lost organisational base in Mising society. However, MBK is still remain as parent organisation of Mising along with other organisations like TMPK, MMK MDK, MAK , TMMK and they are working for the development of Mising Community in this respective areas. At present the Mising organisations under the leadership of MMK is demanding for upliftment of Mising Autonomous under the Sixth Schedule provision of the Indian Constitution.

Conclusion

From the above account, it is to clear that the identity movement of the Misings started as a socio-cultural and economic movement but later it turned to the field of politics through which they wanted to develop their own community. The leaderships are provided by the tribal organisations. The MBK, TMPK, MAK, MMK have been playing an important role in the development of the identity movements and their activities are integrated towards a common goal of raising cultural, political, and economic status of the Misings within the lager Assamese society.

However, in the history of Mising movements, there is no any adoption of undemocratic means for their demand as peace loving people. They always tried to fulfill the demands for self identity through democratic means. They have no faith in extremist movement and never created any threat to the national unity.

The Mising is a peace loving tribe of Assam. The History of Assam bears ample evidences of its peace loving Character. It has always extended its sincere cooperation to all the government for the development of the India as a nation.

Now, the Mising people are demanding creation of an Autonomous state to restore their own Autonomous identity and for their survival. We should not be denied of the legitimate right to enjoy own culture, profess and practice own religion and use own language. The right to life, liberty, security and privacy of our nationality must be protected from inhuman derogatory treatment.

References

(a) English Sources

1. A.Bhuyan, *Political History of Assam (1920-1939)*, Vol. I, Guwahati, 1978.
2. B. Dutta Ray, *Tribal Identity and Tension in North East India*, New Delhi, 1989.
3. Barkataki M. Sharma, *British Administration in North East India (1826-74)*, New Delhi, 1985.
4. E.A. Gait, *A History of Assam*, Guwahati, 1981.

5. G. Phukan, *Assam's Attitude to Federalism*, New Delhi, 1984.
6. H. Barua, *Red River and Blue Hills*, Guwahati, 1962 (Reprint).
7. H. K. Barpujari, *Political History of Assam, (1826-1919),* Vol. I, Guwahati, 1971.
8. K.L. Barua, *Early History of Kamrupa*, Guwahati, 1966.
9. K.S. Sing, *Tribal Movement in India*, Vol.I –II, Manohar, 1983.
10. L. Devi, *Ahom Tribal Relation*, Guwahati, 1968.
11. N.C. Pegu, *The Misings of the Brahmaputtra Valley*, Digboi, 1981.
12. P.C. Chaudhury, *History of Civilisation of the People of Assam up to the Twelve Century A.D.* Guwahati, 1966.

(b) Assamese Sources

1. B. Doley, 'Bharatar Swadhinata Labhar Purbabhati aru Parbatia Misingor Bhumika' in *Smriti Gantha*, Mising Agom Kebang, Jorhat, 1987.
2. B. Doley, 'Mising Samajar Unnatir Samashya' in J.Kuli (Ed), *Murong*, Dibrugarh, 1978.
3. L. Gogoi, 'Mising Samajik Sanskritik Dikhat Abhumuki' in J. Kuli (Ed), *Murong*, Dibrugarh, 1987.
4. L. Padun, 'Mising Sanskriti' B. Kegyung (Ed), *Mising Sanskriti Alekhya*, Guwahati, 1989.

16

Negotiating Source of Power and Identity among the Konyak Angs of Nagaland

Jagritee Ghosh

Introduction

The Konyaks of Nagaland reside in present day Mon district, in the easternmost part of the state of Nagaland. This ethnic group also resides in Myanmar and Arunachal Pradesh. The Konyaks of Arunachal Pradesh are called Wanchos and Noctes and are found in the Tirap District adjoining Mon. The Konyaks therefore share international, national and regional boundaries. Konyaks have Assam in the north, Tirap district of Arunachal Pradesh in the east, Longleng district of Nagaland in the west and Tuensang district of Nagaland and Myanmar to its south.

Haimendorf argues that the Konyaks were different from all the other Naga tribes in the British administered territory (Haimendorf, 1939, 2). The hereditary chief or *Angs* are the major distinguishing factor of the Konyaks from the other "Nagas". According to Beck Jr., "Chiefdoms are complex social institutions and it is doubtful whether any one criterion or variation be it the administrative power structure or the number of levels of regional hierarchy is sufficient to account for this range of complexity" (Beck Jr. 2003, 642).The *Ang* structure is a complex organised structure. This paper would therefore, deal with the description, continuity and change in the *Ang* structure.

The paper could be divided into two different sections. The first is the account of the Ang structure given by Heimendorf during his study conducted in 1936-37. The second part would be a portrayal of the *Ang* structure in the present context. The study is chiefly a relook into the work done by Heimendorf in 1936-37. I would take the example of existence of village development boards and village development board members as state representation to understand the power negotiation of the *Ang* in a present day context.

I. Methodology

The amount of academic ink spent on the Konyaks is low. The major work done is by Christoph Von Furer- Haimendorf including the report of people of India project. This study is based on these literatures and on the basis of the ongoing field work carried out in Chui village. Interview schedule is used as the main technique of primary data collection. For this interview schedule, an optimum sample size of respondents is sorted out and interviewed by making use of both structured and unstructured questions. Stratified random sampling will be used to identify the respondents. And this stratification will be done on the basis of clans, *morungs*, age, sex. Other than these, church officials, pastor, village development board members, village council members, *gaonburras* and Ang/chief will form as the other key informants.

II. Konyak Social Structure

The Konyaks are divided amongst themselves into *Thenkohs* and *Thendus*. Thendu are the groups who have autocratic *Angs* and *Thenkoh* are the groups which do not. The *Thendus* have tattoos covering the face while the *Thenkohs* do not. The *Thendus* are the lower Konyaks bordering Assam on lower ranges while the *Thenkohs* are the upper Konyaks or the southern Konyaks. According to Haimendorf, amongst the *Thenkoh,* like in Wakching, the morungs are more important than the *Angs*. The *morungs* have their land which other *morung* members cannot claim their land and the *morungs* are exogamous among the *Thenkoh* but amongst the *Thendus* there can be *morung* endogamy, if clan exogamy is maintained. *Morung* is a boys dormitory and according to Haimendorf the most important space of socio-political discussions and negotiations. Conversely, for the *Thendus* the *morungs* are important but the *Ang* is the highest authority. The autocratic chiefs or *Angs* hold a unique position and are the undisputed ruler. The *Angs* are considered sacred and no commoner could ever reach the level of the Ang. (Haimendorf, 1939, 37).

Only pure blood eldest son of the *Ang* can be the rightful heir. The *Ang* clan is different from the commoner clan. Earlier the *Angs* were polygamous. They could marry as many girls from the commoner clan or pin along with their blue blood wife. Hierarchy is maintained in choosing the *Angya* or the queen. The daughter of a great *Ang* could only marry a great *Ang*. In most cases the marriages are fixed and constant between villages. For instance, the great *Ang* of Chui could marry only the daughters of the great *Angs* of Mon and Tang. The children of commoner mothers and *Ang* became royal clan but could not become Ang. On the other hand if pure blood women married men from the commoner clan she becomes a commoner. Godelier, argues that in order to understand tribe one has to understand the structure and function of its elementary groups i.e. clans. Morgan therefore, uses the term 'gentilities society' instead of tribal society. Morgan substantiates it by highlighting how certain chiefs are elected by gentes or clans (Godelier, 1977). Therefore, it differentiates in the clan which makes one a *Ang* or a *Pin* clan. The *Angs* have the largest share of land both in terms of agricultural and residential land. The order to sow and reap is given by the *Ang*. The commoners help in building the *Ang's* house and also work in the *Angs's* field. The Customary grants this difference in the ownership of land to both the *Angs* and *pin* commoners forms the identity of the both *Angs* and commoners.

The Konyak society is a hierarchal society. Society where the Angs are placed Heimendorf states that the autocratic chiefs or Angs hold a unique position in the hills. He defines them to be the undisputed rulers in their own villages. According to Heimendorf, "their position is sacred and no commoner can ever approach them upright" (Heimendorf, 1939, 37).

III. Land as Power and Identity

Identity is expressed as a person's conception and expression of their individuality or group affiliations such as national identity or cultural identity. Identity may be defined as the distinctive characteristics belonging to any given individual, or shared by all members of a particular social category or group. It emphasises the sharing of a degree of sameness or oneness with others in a particular area or on a given point. Identity is the label while identification refers to the classifying act itself. Identity is thus, best construed as being both relational and contextual, while the act of identification is best viewed as inherently processed. In case of Nagaland or for the "Nagas" village forms the core of their identity. Village studies in India have been about the caste Hindu villages and have not dealt with the tribal villages (Madan, 2002). The history of the "Nagas" is the history of village feuds. Naga villages are compact settlements and traditionally at the top of the hills. The strategic location of the village was for head hunting, security reasons and protection of village land. Therefore, the "Nagas" identify themselves with their village more than their community, geographical or administrative boundary. This identification with village is the identification with their land. These lands are village land, community land, clan land and agricultural lands.

The tribal's were traditionally dependent on land for their both agricultural and non-agricultural usage. Land is the centre of tribal life. Land as a resource is central to the livelihood of the tribal communities of India's northeast. The tribal workforce in the region as indicated in the census figures are engaged in the primary sector while their proportion in the secondary and tertiary sectors was least relatively. Such high dependence on land and forests is mainly because of the neglect of the secondary sector. Thus, changing land relations and its alienation in the northeast have to be situated within the context of high dependence on the primary sector that increases pressure on land (Shimray, 2006).

In the context of Nagaland, the term 'land' itself is comprehensive because it includes different types of land used for different purposes, as also for forests and water resources.

In an agrarian society, land can be of two basic types, viz. agricultural land and non-agricultural land. While agricultural land is used for cultivation, non-agricultural land includes house sites, grazing grounds, and land set aside for other non-agricultural activities. Land relations i.e. ownership of land regulated by customary laws needs to be understood and discussed. Ownership means the right to control, use and dispose off the things owned. Ownership involves socially recognised economic rights. The broad types of land ownership observed among the Naga tribes are: (a) village or community land, (b) *Khel* or *Thenu* land, (c) clan or lineage land and d) individual or family land. The types of land amongst the Konyaks are forest land, jhum land, home gardens, community land, *morung* land. There are clan owned jhum land, individual owned jhum land, and family/ancestral jhum land. Forest lands belong to clan, community lands belong to the village and it is residential area, *morung* lands are under *morung* members. Ancestral lands are inherited down from forefathers and are family land. The eldest son inherits ancestral land but cannot be sold at his own will. The consent of entire family i.e. younger brothers is required because the younger brothers cultivate in the ancestral land. The younger brothers can only cultivate but cannot own the land.

For a Naga tribal, land is always linked to one's identity. For instance, amongst the Angami tribal group, a person whose geographical identity is known but unseen is referred to as coming from '*mikhoshekemomiena*' which when translated would mean 'a person coming from a place whose smoke is not known'. Such a person commands relatively less respect, neither marriage to such a person is considered to be honourable too. Land thus, is very important to the Naga tribal communities. Persons who have more than sufficient land are considered to be rich irrespective of whether the person has money or not. A landed person is more influential, enjoys prestige and occupies greater status and social weightage than others. This higher status of the landed person gives them power. The legitimate power is the authority. When power is legitimated it has the consent of those who are dominated (Gupta 1996, 10). Therefore land is the most important factor which weaves power, authority and identity in one fold. In the context of Konyak *Angs* the Angs are the traditional rulers with the largest share of land and with highest authority. Next we shall move to the findings from the field.

IV. Coexistence of the *Ang* and State

The British Administrators derived the name Konyak from the word *keniak* which means man in the language of Tamlu (Heimendorf, 1969, 5). However, according to the pilot study that was conducted in Chui village, has a different version of the etymological origin of the term. It is believed that a British asked Yangpong Tamlu from Tamlu village what he was. To this, Yangpong Tamlu replied that they were human beings i.e. in local dialect of Tamlu as Khonyak, after which the British administrators named them as Konyaks, as also stated by Godelier in his book (Godelier, 1977, 77). But elderly Konyaks referred to themselves as Wanchos. Therefore, according to the narratives of Chui village, Wancho is the actual name of the Konyaks. Moreover it is also believed that the Wanchos migrated from Chui of Nagaland to the present day Tirap in Arunachal Pradesh.

The distinctiveness of Konyak Nagas is reflected in myriad ways to describe the socio-economic, political and religious setting of Chui village. Understanding of the people, place and the social life of the Konyak villages, therefore forces one to ask how customary rights evolved and established in different institutions of the Konyaks. All institutions are governed by their own specific rules and regulations. However, it has to be noted that the traditional structures have changed considerably and much of it has happened because of the changes brought about by Christianity. The field work in Chui village shows that after conversion to Christianity, they have lost their traditional rituals related to their birth, marriage and death. The practice of tattooing, which differentiated Konyaks from the other groups, has also died out and most importantly the *morungs* which, as described by Heimendorf, were important part of their social, political and cultural existence exist now as mere buildings. *Morung* the boys dormitory which formed the crux of Konyak society used it during Christmas and *Aoleang*. Earlier,

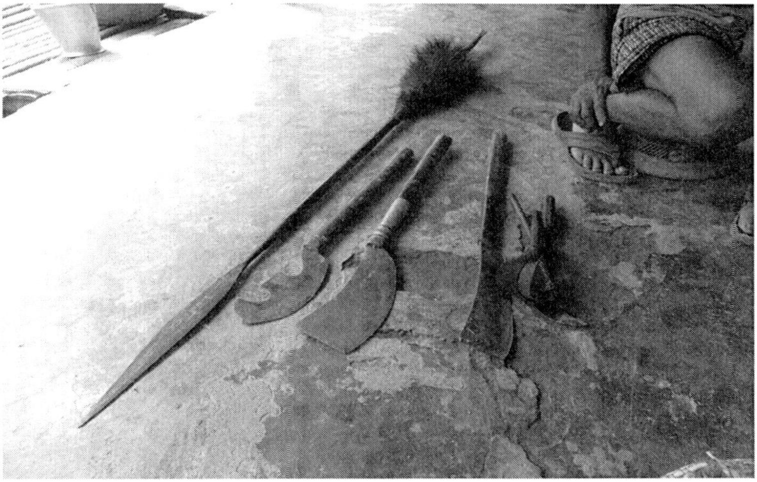

Aoleang was celebrated as the post-harvest festival that happened at different times during the year. But now dates of *Aoleang* are fixed from 1st April to 6th April. It is learned that polygamy existed earlier but it has stopped now. The rituals associated with birth and death has changed. Earlier the birth and death rites were conducted by the elders of the village but now are conducted by the Pastor. But the sanctity of the Angs continues in some form, as the first harvest and the head and leg of any animal hunted are still offered to the Ang. It is however, interesting to note that how in a situation where everything else is changing the customary laws related to land still exists. In this regard the Ang is of the opinion that land gives food and so the laws related to land has to exist.

Earlier there was the system of bride price. When the eldest daughter was married the husband gave the following (left to right):

- Pa
- Nongnan
- Khoshang
- Thuasang
- Yanhon
- Akoi

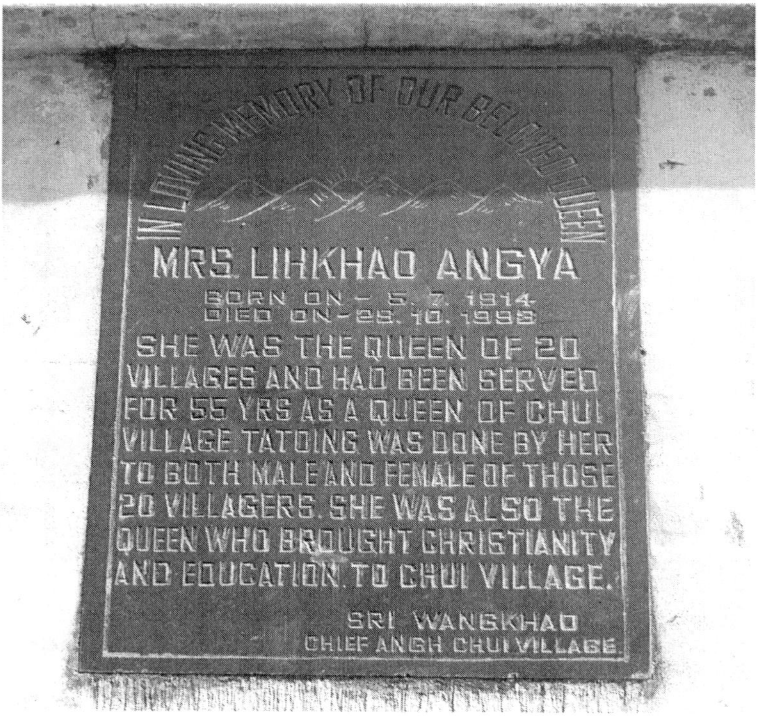

Therefore a lot rituals have changed with the advent of Christianity and modernisation. However, although, the power dynamics have changed due to Christianity and present day state formation, the Angs still enjoy considerable power. The ritual of offering to the chief and making the house of the chief is still continued amongst the Konyak Nagas. The authority of the Ang is continued in certain rituals but this legitimacy is also confronted by modern structures. A revisit is attempted in order to know the present scenario of their everyday interactions. It will help us map the transformations that have altered the old structures and emergence of new structures, their reproduction and institutionalisation. According to Veena Das, critical events are the points of leap, after which new modes of action come into being and traditional categories are redefined (Das, 1999, 6). Therefore, if one makes a comparison between Heimendorf's description of Konyak life and the present,

colonisation, Christianity and inheritance of the colonial position by the Indian state forms the critical events, which bring in changes in the traditional Konyak society and structure. Similarly, T.K. Oommen argues that the point of departure of cultural change in Northeast India is the colonial period and the advent of Christianity and Indian state, market and the civil society later on (Oommen, 2009, 7). The following pictures will further substantiate the argument.

(Queen who bought Christianity to the village. She was the grandmother of the present *Ang*).

The last Ang who followed traditional religion. But later in life converted to Christainity.

(The picture of the last believer of traditional language)

In this picture we can see the platform standing on which the Ang speaks. Behind it is the victory stone. Victory stone is the structure which was made after the Chui villagers stopped head hunting. All the enemy heads that were brought into the village were put in this place and the structure was created. We can also see the *Angpaan* or the *Angmorung*. To the right of the Ang morung is the water tank made by the NGO World Vision and to the right of the *Ang morung*s the Baptist church. This is the highest elevated point in the village from which the other nearby villages can be seen. This picture is very strategic because it speaks in itself how the *Ang* structure stands in contrast to modern Christainity.

Heads of enemies are a proud possessions. It is a symbol of pride for the villagers (Heimendorf 1939). But with modern ideas people treat it with shame and disgrace. The church has, therefore, taken the decision to demolish the structure and creat a children park in the place. The work of demolishing the structure has also started. The following picture shows it.

The present pictures were necessary to highlight how the changes in the structures are taking place amongst the Konyaks of Nagaland. In this background this chapter shall show the interactions between the state and the local power structures.

BAPTIST CHURCH

The village development council and village development board are institutions representing the state. The village development boards are unique to Nagaland. Village development boards are representation of state structures. The coexistence of the village development boards in a chief dominated society makes its manifestations interesting. The members of the village development boards are subordinate to *Angs* traditionally. However in relation to the village development board's decision, even though the *Ang* has a say, there exists a counter to his authority. The village development board works as an intermediate between the government and the village. The members of the village development boards can go to the government for certain schemes but the Ang has to give his final consent on what is necessary for the village. The Ang maintains his authority over the village development board's decision as he is the traditional chief and has the highest share of land. The Ang in his interview had said that land gives us food therefore land is the most important resource. The mode of production forming the social formations holds true in the Konyak condition. Thus, the Ang structure stands a contrasting form of governance to the governance of the state.

References

1. Christoph Von Furer-Haimendorf, *Return to the Naked Nagas: The Naked Nagas*. Methuen & Co, London: 1939.
2. Christoph Von Furer-Haimendorf, *The Konyak Nagas: An Indian Frontier Tribe,* University of London, New York and London, 1969.
3. Dipankar Gupta, *Political Sociology in India*, Orient Longman, New Delhi, 1996.
4. Robin A. Beck Jr, 'Consolidation and Hierarchy: Chiefdom Variability in the Mississippian Southeast', *American Antiquity*, 68, 4, 2003, pp. 641-661.
5. T.B. Subba, Joseph Puthenpurakal and Shaji Joseph Puykunnel (Ed), *Christianity and Change in Northeast India*, Concept Publishing Company, New Delhi, 2009.
6. U.A. Shimray, *Tribal Land Alienation in Northeast India: Laws and Land Relations*, Indigenous Women's Forum of North East India, North Eastern Social Research Centre, Guwahati, 2006.
7. Veena Das, *Critical Events: An Anthropological Perspective on Contemporary*, Oxford University Press, New Delhi, 1995.

V
Economy

17

Underdevelopment and Ethnic Identity Crisis: A Linkage Analysis with Special Reference to Assam

Tarun Gogai

Colonial processes and socio-economic conditions have always created identity crisis by deepening divisive roots and dimensions of multifarious identities in a society. The legacies of a colonial economy were naturally adorned by the newly independent but centralised Indian state and this aggravated the already existing cultural and economic hiatus between different communities of different regions in the same country. Being trapped in the transitional phases of a decolonised economy, the Northeastern region and particularly Assam remained at the periphery of capitalist development; the crisis was profound in polity and socio-cultural life as well. The developmental fruits of an emerging economy have been poorly distributed, thus creating a sense and feeling of alienation amidst people of the peripheral region of the country. The region has always been at the receiving end of the modernisation process taking place in the entire country. Moreover, much of the regional economic underdevelopment has hitherto been believed to be caused by the intrusion of the outsiders and the control of the state's economy by the migrant and non-indigenous business communities. Particularly in Assam, such a cultural and economic hiatus has percolated down to different 'ethnies' and is now profound between the tribal peoples and the people of the plains.

In this background the objective of this chapter is to find out the specific roots and causes of underdevelopment which may provide panacea to the long standing ethnic identity crisis and movements in the state.

I. Background of the Study

Assam is considered as the gateway to the Northeast India and connected to the mainland India by a narrow corridor in West Bengal called the "Chicken's Neck". It is located south of the eastern Himalayas. Present Assam comprises the Brahmaputra Valley and the Barak river valleys along with the Karbi Anglong and the North Cachar Hills with an area of 78,438 sq. km. It is connected to six other Northeastern states and has a long border with Bangladesh and Bhutan. In many respects, Assam is a miniature India with different national, ethnic, religious and linguistic and tribal groups living together in the region for centuries. It was never a monolingual or single nationality region at any point of time. A considerable number of people speaking Assamese, Bengali and other languages and dialects live in Assam. Hill tribes like the Karbis and Dimashas live in the hilly districts of Karbi Anglong and North Cachar hills with their own dialects and cultures and many plain tribes like Bodos, Mishings, Deuris, Tiwas, Sonowal Kacharis, Mech Cacharis, Rabhas, Koch Rajbanshis, etc. live in plain areas. There is also a mixed tea garden population with their own language and dialect basically concentrated in Brahmaputra valley. The process of assimilation of diverse ethnic groups of Assam became weak under the British rule. It led to clashes of interest among them and they continue to live and think along ethnic lines. The ethnic identity consciousness by various ethnic groups is further energised by the complex history of immigration into Assam.

II. Historical Consequence of Immigration

The continuous flow of immigration into Assam started ever since the British occupation. The economic transformation of Assam during British colonial period caused an enormous demographic shift. The British colonial officials actively encouraged immigration into sparsely populated Assam located next to a densely populated region of the Indian subcontinent

Bengal. Like the colonial officials a few Assamese middle class personalities also favoured immigration to Assam. Thus, due to the encouragement of British officials and support of Assamese middle class personalities immigration to Assam took place in a vigorous manner. The demand for labour in the tea plantations was the first major reason to turn to immigrants. In the absence of a strong local labour force, Assam had to face mass-migration of labour, mostly from the Jharkhand region, to serve the interests of the British capital. Tea labourers' massive migration transformed the demographic structure very significantly in Assam. By 1921, the population of tea-labour has become 1.3 million or one-sixth of total population of Assam (Gait 1994, 362). However, it was not only tea plantations that had to depend on immigrant labour. Other enterprises that developed during Assam's economic transformation in the nineteenth century such as coal and oil fields and the construction of roads, buildings and railways, also attracted immigrant labour. There were, in addition, immigrants who came to Assam to occupy the new middle-class positions that required new skills, such as the knowledge of English, and to take advantage of the expanding opportunities for trading. Among them the Bengalis migrated to Assam to occupy the secondary positions in the colonial administrative set up. The Marwaris from Rajputana migrated to Assam as collaborators of the colonial state. Besides many Biharis came in search of livelihood and were prepared to do any toilsome job. On the other hand, many Nepalis came to Assam as a result of British colonial expansion and consolidation (Gohain and Bora, 2007, 10). The situation became more critical when the virgin and fertile soil of Assam has attracted a large number of immigrants from East Bengal (now Bangladesh) in early parts of the twentieth century. The colonisation of land by settlers from East Bengal began in a big way in the second decade of the twentieth century to supply food grains and other agricultural products to the growing modern sectors in Assam. The immigrants gradually subjugated the vacant *chars* and forest lands of Assam. So rapid and large was the immigration that C.S. Mullan, a British Census Commissioner, commented in his Census Report of 1931 that immigration was "likely to alter permanently the whole future of Assam and to destroy more surely than the Burmese invaders of 1820 the whole structure of Assamese culture and civilisation." (Census Report, 1931, Vol. III, Part-I, 49) The influx of Muslim peasants, which peaked during the first three decades of the twentieth century, came to a halt with independence. The Assamese people also expected that the immigration would come to an end with the partition of Bengali dominated areas from Assam with independence. But contrary to their expectation, the Bengali Hindu 'refugees' from East Pakistan found no difficulty in crossing the porous border and settled down either by themselves or through their relatives unchecked and undetected to escape communal violence. Of about twenty lakh refugees who entered India during 1947-1950, undivided Assam had to give shelter to some three lakhs (Misra, 2000, 111). This flow of refugees was also seen during the liberation war of Bangladesh in 1971 in which more than 12 million refugees poured into India, of which one million stayed back in Assam (Franda, 1982, 109). The nationalist organisations of Assam like AASU fear that even today the immigrants from Bangladesh continued unabated to Assam through the porous borders (AASU, 1980) and these dimensions of immigrants still continued to be a factor in Assam politics.

Added to this, the annexation of the whole Northeast India to British India facilitated structural change in material conditions in Assam. Penetration of foreign capital, growth of tea plantations, development of railways and roadways, introduction of English education, emergence of private property in land and common subjection to a highly centralised political authority, brought drastic changes in its socio-economic structure (Srikanth, 2000, 4119). It was during this period that lakhs of migrants, some representing more advanced nationalities and ethnic groups, settled in Assam. The migrations that took place during the British period, apart from creating the ground for cultural and linguistic conflicts, generated competition among different groups for new economic and political opportunities. The natives did not feel threatened for the wage labourers who came to work in the tea plantations, but they became highly apprehensive of the educated Hindu Bengalis, the hardworking Muslim Bengali peasants and the enterprising Marwaris, who entered the bureaucracy, agriculture and business respectively. The natives, who could not compete with the new immigrants, began to worry about domination by these new immigrants in all spheres. Their sense of insecurity and feeling of alienation made them conscious of their own identity vis-a-vis the Bengalis. They felt that together with the British, the Bengalis were responsible for many of their economic miseries. The English educated Assamese middle class gave political expression to the collective fears and suspicions of all the natives. By projecting the Bengalis as enemies, the Assamese leaders attempted to promote Assamese nationality consciousness amongst other tribes living in the Brahmaputra valley. Overshadowed by the fear of new immigrants, other native groups also supported the Assamese elites' crusade against the Bengalis. The Assamese leadership, in turn, did not take positive steps to develop closer ties with the tribal people to rid off their fears and ethnic prejudices (*The Assam Tribune*, 28 October, 1947; Phukon, 2003, 18). As a result, internal differences and conflicts among the tribes and between the Assamese and other native ethnic groups remained unresolved.

III. Language Issue

Historically Assamese language developed as a result of interaction among different tribal groups in Assam. It was during the Ahom rule that Assamese became the *lingua franca* of the Brahmaputra valley. But during the British rule, the colonial rulers imposed Bengali as the official language of Assam. Projecting it as a deliberate attempt on the part of all the Bengalis to dominate the Assamese people, the Assamese middle class leadership mobilised the Assamese people and demanded that Assamese should be made the official language of the region. Simultaneously efforts were also made to develop Assamese language and literature. The immigration issue inculcated in the Assamese mind a strong desire for cultural policies that would give them an advantageous position in Assam (Baruah, 2010, 91). The growing numbers of migrants in Assam were viewed by a large section of the Assamese people as a threat to their socio-cultural, political and economic life. The heavy immigration since the first decade of the twentieth century from erstwhile East Bengal and the influx of a large number of Hindu Bengali refugees after independence made the issue of Assam's cultural policies more urgent than ever. The Assamese middle class elite became assertive of their socio-cultural and linguistic rights. With this objective in view, they intended to adopt certain measures to establish their language in its rightful place. *The Assam Tribune,* the daily newspaper of Assam which generally champions Assamese sub-nationalism, made inquiry in its editorial as to whether "Assam has no right to exist as the land of the Assamese people." It further criticised the government for its "intention to turn the Assamese people into a minority community in their own province and jeopardise their language, culture, and their very existence" (*The Assam Tribune,* 1949, May 27). The *Asom Jatiya Mahasabha* led by Ambikagiri Roychoudhury submitted a memorandum to Assam Government in September 1947 appealing it to defend Assamese interests. The *Asom Sahitya Sabha* also campaigned for recognition of Assamese as the State language and language of education in 1950 and celebrated July 16 as "State Language Day." Thus, "the *Assamisation* design of the governing Caste-Hindu Assamese elite caused nightmarish experiences" (Datta, 1993, 19) for the non-Assamese ethnic groups in Assam. However, the *Asom Sahitya Sabha* gave an ultimatum to government to declare Assamese as the State's language in 1959. These developments were described by H. K. Barpujari in the following way:

> A chauvinistic section of the Assamese went further and sought to hasten the process of 'Assamisation' or extension of Assamese influence in the neighbouring hills. They could make no distinction between integration and assimilation and here lies the tragedy – the fragmentation of Assam. Constant harping of assimilation and 'Greater Assam' alarmed the unsophisticated hill men of losing their culture; language and even their main prop namely land. The Khasis and the Garos who fought jointly with the Assamese leadership against the Cabinet Mission Plan of grouping, gradually developed a lurking fear of being exploited and outnumbered by their neighbours in the plains (Barpujari, 1998, 16).

Amid intense controversy, the Government of Assam finally introduced the State Official Language Bill of 1960 in the Assembly. The introduction of Assamese as the State Language of Assam had reinforced the demand for separate political identity in the hills and in due course Nagaland, Meghalaya, Arunachal Pradesh and Misoram were formed reducing the size of Assam. Besides, Assam's diverse ethnicity and multilingual character was not conducive to the creation of a language based province. The hill districts had indigenous languages and dialects like Khasi, Garo, and languages of the Kuki-Chin and the Naga groups. Even in the plains districts people spoke other indigenous languages and dialects, mostly of the Bodo and Mising family. No sooner had the Assam Official Language Bill been introduced in 1960, the Bengali speakers, who constituted 16.5 per cent of Assam's population, sharply reacted to it (Baruah, 2010, 96). The Bengali challenge to Assamese cultural policies produced serious cultural conflicts which even degenerated into "language riots". There were violent conflicts between ethnic Assamese and Hindu Bengalis, and deaths as a result of inter-ethnic conflicts as well as police firing to control protest demonstrations and riots. In 1972, again riots occurred over the decision of Gauhati and Dibrugarh University to switch to Assamese as the language of undergraduate education. Again the decision of the AGP government to impose Assamese language as compulsory third language upon the non-Assamese medium students in secondary schools, through a Circular given by the Secondary Education Board of Assam on February 28, 1986 was resented by All Bodo Students' Union (ABSU) and later the government suspended the same. This language policy bred a feeling of insecurity among the tribal and non-tribal ethnic organisations within a greater Assam. It added to the ever increasing unhappiness among the emerging tribal middle class in the hills and the plains which had existed vis-à-vis the dominant leadership of the plains since the colonial rule. The sense of deprivation and exploitation of the hills and plains tribal's by the dominant leadership of the plains reached its senith with the introduction of Language Bill. The hill elite complained that "The Assamese who happened to be the single majority community in a heterogeneous State try not only to dominate others in all affairs of administration of the State, but also try to impose their language on the non-Assamese" which was regarded by them as "imperialist policy of the Assamese over the non-Assamese" (Phukon, 2003, 100). This turmoil on language ended with a compromise initiated by Congress leader Lal Bahadur Shastri. But, the 'fear of domination of the Assamese over the tribals' never subsided. It was reflected in the memorandum submitted by the Mikir and North Cachar Hills Leaders' Conference to the Prime Minister of India in June, 1973. In the minds of the plains tribal's too 'the fear of domination of the Assamese' continued. The ABSU raised the issue through a booklet titled *Why Separate State* submitted to the President, Prime Minister and Home Minister on November 10, 1987, in which it maintained:

> The arguments of the Assamese people and Assam Government are like that, the Assamese language is the official as well as regional language of Assam, a link language among different communities of Assam, a language for the integrity of Assam and that is why everyone must read Assamese, must speak Assamese, must know Assamese, those who live in Assam must speak Assamese and those who do not speak Assamese they are not Assamese or indigenous people of Assam, Assam is only for Assamese – they think (ABSU, 1987).

Thus, the tribal elite of the hills and the plains and the non-tribal's too alleged that "the Assamese people always try to impose Assamese language upon the non-Assamese people including the indigenous tribal people." As such here arises the clash between the Assamese speaking people on the one hand and tribal's and other linguistic minorities on the other. It is argued that the colonial Assam had to be reorganised due to the aggressive cultural policies pursued by Assam's mainstream leadership. Udayon Misra observed that the rigid stand of establishing the Assamese as the sole Official Language of the State had contributed significantly to the desire of Assam's "tribal" populations to opt for separation (Misra, 1988, 122).

IV. Post Independent State and the Politics of Development

In addition to this, in independent India, the capitalist path of development has generated severe regional disparities. In Assam too the pace of development has been extremely slow and lethargic as compared to the developed regions of India.

The legacy of the colonial economy has continued in the post-colonial Assam. Financially Assam depends heavily on the Centre, a result of centripetal constitution, to discharge its responsibilities. Assam failed to evoke any systematic response from the Centre for a long period. It has been argued that Assam is an endowed region, gifted with many natural resources, but the endowments have not translated into economic growth and development. Again Assam is located in a strategically sensitive region which faces perennial floods, political disturbances and severely underdeveloped infrastructure of roads, railways, communication, power, terminal and institutional facilities and abject poverty (Hussain, 1993, 67). Hence, Assam fails to draw worthwhile private investment for its economic development. "Instead of investing in the region's infrastructure and allowing market forces to do the rest", Subir Bhaumik argues, "the country's federal government pumped huge quantum of funds to sustain the region's economy" (Bhaumik , 2009, 231). Terming Assam as "colonial hinterland" Tilottama Misra stated that "there has been a systematic exploitation of the rich resources of Assam, before 1947 by the colonial rulers, and since then by the Indian State and Indian capitalists who have continued the colonial tradition"(Misra, 1980, 1357-1365). Thus, Assam continues to remain an agriculturally and industrially backward State in spite of having rich resources. It led to the growing awareness among the Assamese people of being subjected to gross economic exploitation on a scale comparable to, and even sometimes worse than in the pre-independence days (Phukon, 1984, 114-115).

Thus, the policy of strengthening the Centre at the cost of the States has led to the opinion that "Assam is being subjected to colonial or 'quasi-colonial' exploitation by foreign imperialists and by the Indian State and the big industrialists" and "has been progressively sucked dry of its natural resources" (Misra, 1980). Despite being the country's largest producer of tea, oil, plywood and forest products, Assam is one of the poorest and industrially most backward States of India. After decades of independence, Assam is 'lagging far behind the rest of the country in most important parameters of growth.' Its economy remained predominantly agrarian. Assam is affected by increased pressure on available land due to demographic transformation.

In addition to this, Assam faces perennial floods. The failure to control the Brahmaputra and other rivers contributed decisively in keeping Assam agriculturally backward in spite of its fertile soil. The growth in agricultural sector in Assam was virtually stagnant leading to dependence on other States for food grains.

The development in industrial sector is also not encouraging. Tea has been the biggest 'extractive enterprise' of Assam founded in the colonial period. The total area under tea cultivation in Assam is accounting for more than half of the country's total area under tea. The tea production in Assam constitutes more than 50 per cent of the total production of the country. But Assam is deprived of her legitimate share and benefits because of the practice of concealment of real profit of tea earned by the foreign as well as big Indian capitalists (Borgohain, 2012, 45-46). Moreover, except the Assam Tea Corporation which is a public sector organisation owning a few sick and unprofitable tea gardens, the overwhelming majority of the big gardens are under foreign and Indian companies which are controlled from London and Calcutta. As a result, a large share of profits from the Assam gardens flow out to foreign and Indian big companies. In this regard Amalendu Guha asserted that 'the stranglehold of foreign capital on the economy of Assam remained very much there' (Guha, 1977, 329). Even Assam did not have a Tea Auction Centre till September 1970. Before commissioning the Gauhati Tea Auction Centre, the State exchequer did not receive a single paisa by way of sales tax from Assam tea. Even the main office of the Tea Board, which is the highest authority in relation to the tea industry and which besides implementing the Tea Act of 1953 is also responsible for approving grants, loans, and labour-welfare projects, is situated in Calcutta though most of the gardens it controls are in Assam. Besides, in the post-independence period majority of the gardens were bought over by Indian big capitalists such as Tatas and Birlas. Therefore, it is argued: "The demand for the nationalisation of the tea industry and the shifting of the head offices of the tea companies to Assam cannot be dismissed as merely 'parochial' demands" but must be seen as reactions against "the protracted colonial exploitation in the tea sector" (Misra, 1980).

Another important natural resource of Assam is crude oil which has become a cause of contention between Centre and

Assam in post-independence period. Assam has an estimated reserve of 1.3 billion tonnes of crude oil and 156 billion cubic meters of natural gas (*The Hindu* 2009, November 14). Assam accounts for about 15 per cent of India's crude output. The wells at Digboi, Duliajan, and Sivasagar etc. also produce natural gas accounting to about 50 per cent of India's total onshore production. But, the oil industry did not develop in Assam contrary to the expectations of the people of Assam for two basic reasons: first, the foreign capital played an important role in oil industry till the beginning of the Assam movement; second, the Government of India was not interested in establishing refineries in Assam until the vigorous movements started by the people of Assam. Apart from the question of the establishment of refineries, the people of Assam have been feeling that the State is not getting adequate royalty for crude oil. There could have been no other reason except vested political interests for the establishment of the large public sector refinery for Assam crude at Barauni with more than 30 lakh tonnes, it is argued. Mass movements protesting against this unfair decision of the Centre were staged in Assam in 1956-57, as a result of which the Centre tried to appease the people by establishing a small refinery at Gauhati with an annual refining capacity of only about seven lakh tonnes. The decision of establishment of refinery at Barauni was criticised by the Public Undertaking Committee of the Indian Parliament as "an entirely wrong decision to have located the refinery at Barauni, a decision taken in spite of the strong objections on technical grounds both from the Indian and Russian experts" (Gohain and Bora, 2007, 45). Another refinery movement shook the State in 1969, demanding the setting up of a second public sector refinery. But even this time the new refinery-cum-petrochemical complex fell far short of the size and capacity of the Barauni refinery, its refining capacity being only about 10 lakh tonnes a year. Further, Assam has been deprived of her due share of royalty on the crude produces. This trend of deprivation continued till today and this was reflected again in a memorandum submitted to the Prime Minister on April 20, 2012 by the Government of Assam in which it urged the Central Government to provide the State government a portion of Oil Development Cess and maintained that "Oil and Natural Gas have always been a sensitive issue in

Assam" and it requested the Government of India "to take urgent necessary action so that the State gets it due share of benefits from its natural resources in the form of royalty and tax revenue, thereby removing the persisting sense of deprivation and alienation of the State."

In addition, there was much possibility of establishment of petro-chemical and some other ancillary industries on the basis of natural gases extracted from the oil fields in Assam. But, the growing importance of natural gas as a source of energy and as raw material for a variety of modern industries does not seem to impress the Central Government much. Therefore, the Centre as well as the State Government has not adopted any clear policy in this regard. For, over 50 million cubic feet of natural gas is being flared off daily at the different oilfields of Assam for several decades. According to an estimate during the period of 1970-1987 an amount of natural gas worth Rs 1900 crores was burnt up in Assam (Gohain and Bora, 2007, 46). Only about a very little amount of natural gas is utilised in Assam and most of it is being used in the Namrup thermal plant. Of late, as a result of Assam Accord the Assam Gas Cracker Project registered as 'Brahmaputra Cracker and Polymer Limited' on January 8, 2007 is coming up at Lepetkatta in Dibrugarh which has been approved by Cabinet Committee on Economic Affairs in its meeting held on April 18, 2006 with a project cost of Rs 5460.61 crores which was expected to start commissioning from the year 2014.

Further the colonial pattern of industrialisation is evident among the plywood and other forest based industries of Assam. Assam earns very little compared to the sales tax earned by the Government of India from Assam's plywood. Eighty per cent of the produces of the plywood factories of Assam has been transferred by roads and rails to depots outside Assam. On the other hand, most of the plywood industries of Assam are owned by big Indian capitalists. Only a few plywood factories of the State produce tea-chests for the tea garden of Assam and they produce only 50 per cent of the total requirement of these gardens. Besides, Assam has some other major Central public sector industries like Brahmaputra Valley Fertiliser Corporation

Limited (BVFCL), Cement Corporation of India Limited (CCI), Hindustan Paper Corporation Ltd. (HPC), and North Eastern Electric Power Corporation Limited (NEEPCO) etc. BVFCL Plant of Namrup produces around 45 per cent of the total output of its parent organisation Hindustan Fertiliser Corporation. The production of the Namrup plant is expected to increase further with the commissioning of new plant. The Namrup unit is the largest in Hindustan Fertiliser Corporation. Yet, the headquarters of the HFC is set up in Calcutta, notwithstanding the repeated requests of the Assam Government to locate it within Assam. Similarly, the headquarters of the HPC have been set up in Calcutta in utter disregard of the legitimate claims of Assam. Again, Assam in spite of being the third largest jute producing State in India has not been able to draw sustenance from development and diversification of jute products. About 70 per cent of total jute produced in Assam is purchased for processing outside the State. Unfortunately, the State's efforts for starting and operating jute mills have not borne happy experience, in spite of having a good potential for the same.

In the field of power generation too, the position of Assam has been low in the all India list. Although Assam, as a State criss-crossed by fast mountain streams and rivers, has a large potential of hydel power in Assam, there have been very few hydroelectric generating plants in Assam at present i.e. Karbi-Langpi Hydro Electric Project (100 MW) and Kopili Hydro Electric Project (275 MW). Assam has only three thermal generating plants at Namrup (134 MW), Bongaigaon (240 MW) and Lakwa (126 MW) and a few diesel generating stations producing about 15 MW of power. Of course, some new hydro electric projects are coming up in the Northeast India like Lower Subansiri Hydroelectric Power Project (2000 MW), Dibang Hydroelectric Power Project (3000 MW) etc. However, these projects have experienced several problems during construction due to landslides, re-design and opposition.

In addition to this, Assam has a tremendous potential in tourism that has not been exploited at all. It has diverse ethnicity, varied climatic conditions, national parks like Kaziranga and Manas, rain forests, beautiful hilly landscape, tea gardens and rivers like the Brahmaputra and Barak and its tributaries. Assam has each and everything from topographical diversity to scenic beauty and from rich historical background to unique ethnic life-style. In spite of its identification as a tourist destination it lacks the infrastructure and the marketing drive to attract tourists. Richly endowed with flora and fauna, landscape and ethnic diversity, Assam can be developed into a viable tourist hotspot (Bhaumik, 2009, 240). Therefore, the government should spend on developing tourism infrastructure.

Another cause for the slow pace of economic development of the State has been the inadequate transport facilities. Even after decades of independence Assam has been far behind in railway network. The British constructed the existing meter-gauge railway line in Assam in 1881 to facilitate the transportation of tea and troop movements whenever necessary. So, Assam's single main railway line passes through the tea-belts of the State without touching most of the important towns and villages. It is interesting that, even today, important Assam towns like Nowgong, Jorhat, Sibsagar, and Dibrugarh, have been connected only by branch lines and there has been no direct rail link between these towns. The railway map of Assam has remained the same since the British days, and the motives which impelled the British to construct the railway in this region appear to be shared by the administrators from Delhi. Assam was linked by Broad Gauge railway with the rest of India after mass agitations in the State. Due to poor train services in the region, MP from Assam Pankaj Bora described the North East Frontier Railways as the 'North East Forgotten Railways.' Regarding railway services Biren Baishya, another MP from Assam, observed that 'Northeastern region is nothing but the story of negligence, nothing but the story of ignorance and nothing but the story of discrimination' (*The Assam Tribune,* May 13, 2012).

These arguments of the members of parliament from Assam have, indeed, justifications. They pointed out with evidence that the Centre did get benefit out of Assam's resources while Assam has not been getting her due share. Assam remained backward in spite of enormous wealth due to post-colonial capitalist nature of economy of India. The legacy of colonial economy has continued in post-colonial Assam and it continues as 'colonial hinterland'. It appears that in post-colonial period the nature of Assam politics manifests a neo-colonial trend generated by the new group of elites which emerged in independent India. As a result of India's weak federal structure and capitalist path of development, Assam financially depends heavily on the Centre to discharge its responsibilities for which, many times, it suffers from the "step-motherly attitude" of the Centre. Centre's failure to fulfill the local demand for adequate share of natural and economic resources led to perpetuation of anti-centre feeling among the Assamese people. The sense of frustration of the people of Assam further aggravated as a result of worsening of the unemployment situation in the State and the upsurge of allegations of discrimination against local youth in recruitment for Central Government undertakings located in the state. Therefore, the people of Assam participated in large scale in several movements viz. oil refinery movement, Assam movement etc., against the centre in the post-colonial period. Actually the problem of economic underdevelopment of Assam is a colonial legacy. This legacy of exploitation and neglect towards Assam continues in the post-colonial period.

Owing to the combination of above factors such as the geographical location of the state, neglect of the central government, unabated migration, incompetence of state leadership, and unwillingness of the Indian monopolies to set up industries in Northeast, Assam remained a backward state with growing competition for limited social and economic space among the diverse communities. As alternative sources of income were very limited, the demand for cultivable lands and government jobs started mounting up. The people at large were dissatisfied with the Congress party. They have been experiencing frustration, dissatisfaction, tension, competition, conflict and violence in varying degrees in the different socio-economic and regional milieu. Such a situation is conducive for the emergence of various kinds of social movements through which the masses try to seek alternatives, betterment and satisfaction (Hussain, 1993, 7-8). The regional press took up the cudgels and highlighted the Centre's exploitation of Assam.

It led to a state-wide agitation by All Assam Students' Union in 1974 on the issue of the economic development of the state. The increasing pressure on land and jobs ultimately found expression in the anti-foreigner upsurge 1979-85. While the problem of continued influx and the ever-growing pressure on land coupled with the fear of the Assamese losing their socio-political identity seemed to be the immediate motivating factors of the movement, it was in actuality a popular outburst against decades of economic neglect of the state by the central government (Misra, 2000, 122-23). The Assamese chauvinists started raising slogans about culture and identity, which was at stake due to Bangladeshi immigrants settled in Assam. By attributing a high rate of growth of population in Assam due to foreign immigration and by creating a bogey of the Assamese people becoming a minority in their own land, the leaders of the Assam agitation were able to mobilise lakhs of people in the Brahmaputra valley in support of their demands (AASU, AAGSP, 1980). While a moderate section of the leadership demanded detection and deportation of all foreigners settled in Assam, the radicals who later formed the militant outfit, ULFA, tried to direct the movement against the Indian state. Many Assamese intellectuals also justified the movement on grounds of nationality, federalism and internal colonialism. The leading role of the students and youth in the movement and their apparent patriotic slogans attracted public attention and sympathy even outside Assam. The agitation continued for about five years and came to an end with the Assam Accord in 1985. Assam Gana Parishad (AGP), a political party floated by the leaders of Assam agitation, came to power in the subsequent elections in 1986. But within a few years, the Assamese found their hopes shattered. The AGP government could not solve any of the basic problems of the people of Assam.

From the time the Assam government attempted to impose the Assamese language, the Bengali citisens in the Barak valley started looking at every move of the people in Brahmaputra valley with suspicion and caution. The attacks on the Bengalis during the Assam agitation has only helped in further widening the gulf between the people of Brahmaputra valley and the Barak valley. Their opposition to the Assam agitation took the form of the student's agitation for a separate central university in the Barak valley, which subsequently materialised in the year 1994. After coming to power, the AGP government sought to impose Assamese as a compulsory third language at school level and knowledge of Assamese, a pre-requisite for government jobs. But in the wake of opposition from the Bengalis and tribal groups, the government had to repeal the order. Further, the attacks on Hindu and Muslim Bengalis during the Assam agitation gave birth to United Minority Front (UMF) representing the interests of the minorities. With the Bangladeshi immigrant issue gradually turning communal, several communal organisations seeking to fight for the cause of the Muslims made their appearance in recent years. More than these, in the aftermath of Assam agitation different ethnic groups, like the Ahoms, the Bodos, the Rabhas, the Koch Rajbanshis, etc, who at one time supported the Assamese cause against the Bengalis, have now begun using similar slogans, against the Assamese people. The Bodos began claiming that they were the indigenous people of the land and demanded a separate Bodoland state for protecting Bodo identity, language and culture from extinction (Dutta, 1993; Choudhury, 1995; Srikanth, 2000). With the demand for an autonomous state picking up in North Cachar and Karbi Anglong Hills, the plain tribes like Rabhas, Mishings and Koch Rajbanshis became conscious of their own identities (Hussain, 1994; Bhuyan, 1989; Srikanth, 2000). Even the Ahoms, who were instrumental in creating an Assamese identity, express their regret over losing theirs and are urging the government to recognise them as a scheduled tribe. Far from ensuring the unity of tribes, the growth of ethnic identities has aggravated intra ethnic fears and prejudices. The Assam agitation has, thus, resulted in exasperated inter and intra ethnic tensions and conflicts in Assam.

Again the issues relating to political and financial autonomy and centre's continued neglect of Assam have turned a section into sympathisers of militancy. Unabated immigration from across the border, the ever-increasing pressure on land, the changing demographic pattern and the moribund state of economic progress of the state have been contributing towards sustaining insurgent politics in the region(Srikanth, 2000).

The ULFA was only an offshoot of these kinds of situation. The birth of ULFA showed the way for other ethnic groups to float their own militant outfits to realise their demands. Today in addition to ULFA, many other militant organisations like NDFB, Karbi National Volunteers (KNV), Dima Halam Daoga (DHD), United Peoples' Democratic Solidarity (UPDS), Koch Rajbanshi Protection Force, Rabha National Security Force, Muslim United Liberation Tigers Association (MULTA), etc. are active in Assam. Apart from these Assam-based militant outfits, a few other militant groups active in the bordering states also have their bases in Assam. However, it is true that given the present national and international realities, the insurgent groups' attainment of their goal may appear quite remote.

The tenuous inter-ethnic relations coupled with the historical legacy of a moribund state of economy beholds enough explanation as to why the post-colonial period saw growing competition for limited social and economic space with resultant hostilities and prejudices among different ethnic groups in Assam. Like other parts of the country, in Assam too, educated Assamese middle class expressed solidarity with the sub-nationalist aspirations of the people and they unleashed a sustained campaign over language and immigrant issues but at the same time, failing a great deal in winning over the confidence of the tribal people and involving them in the nationalist movement. Because of this limitation, certain tribal groups could not fully identify themselves with the Assamese or with the Indian nationalist leadership. After independence the dominant Assamese leaders, who got hold over the state Congress and took over the reigns of government in Assam, tried hard to make Assam a monolingual state. The sustained efforts of these leaders to extend Assamese hegemony over other national and ethnic groups living in the state through *Assamisation*, however, received retreat leading to greater assertion of other linguistic and ethnic identities in the state (Srikanth, 2000). The Congress governments, both at the centre and the state, did very little to develop the economy of the state. Owing to limited industrialisation, low level of urbanisation and weak transport and other basic infrastructure in the state, alternative avenues for employment for people are severely restricted. Under the circumstances, land becomes the main source of livelihood for the majority of people. As a result, there developed competition and conflicts amongst groups for control over limited resources and opportunities. The continuation of immigration in a situation of stagnation and underdevelopment generates competition and hostilities among different ethnic groups. It is not difficult to realise that behind all talk of threats to language, culture or identity, every national or ethnic group evinces simultaneously a strong desire to grow and a fear of losing control over the limited resources that they already possess. In pursuit of its interests, every ethnic group form their own political parties or pressure groups for articulating their demands. Later on, insurgent groups took up those demands and gave a radical twist to them. Although there are differences in the style of functioning, in substance, there is little difference in the ideology of the insurgents using non-constitutional methods and those of regional or ethnic based political parties and pressure groups taking recourse to parliamentary means. They, from two sides of the same coin, indulge in politics of identity for creating and consolidating its respective identities. Their efforts finally motivate and guides identity politics in Assam. In Assam, the much claimed struggle against exploitative Indian state or indifferent central government ends up as fratricidal conflicts with other communities living in the state. The politics of identity in Assam draws its strength from prejudices and misconceptions of groups about themselves and others. Feeding on the fear of the 'other', it pits one community against the other and mobilises the people along ethnic lines. Again, electoral politics in a society dominated by identity politics further consolidates ethnic loyalties and identities. Not only regional and ethnic groups and parties, even national parties encourage identity politics to the extent it serves their narrow political objectives. In a society where identity politics becomes the norm, there will always be people tempted to take recourse to militancy, when their demands could not be met within the legal and constitutional framework. Until and unless the toiling masses of Assam identify the material roots of their insecurity and alienation and involve in common struggles for the elimination of poverty, unemployment and underdevelopment, it is not possible to ensure economic development and promote peace and harmony in the multi-ethnic and multi-national state of Assam.

In Northeast India, especially Assam, ethnic crisis or the demand for separate statehoods, primarily, have sprung from distinct historical and structural setting. The crisis of 'identity' reflects upon age old economic deprivation and colonialism owing to the existential legacy of a state structure which retained a separate and distinct sense of identity for a long time. It is the consequence of developmental imbalances which failed to promote integration and cohesion. A given structural imbalance is likely to produce consequential impact in any particular polity, or economy. Actually, ethnic autonomy demand is a reflection of intra-regional, intra-state contradictions, which have generated because of wrong policy of assimilation and integration. Unless, the fruits of modernisation and development are evenly distributed, the identity 'crises' will continue to linger on in terms of intra state rivalry and factionalism in the state.

References

1. AASU, *Memorandum to the Prime Minister of India*, February 2, 1980.
2. ABSU, *Why Separate State*, (A Booklet submitted to the President, Prime Minister and Home Minister of India by All Bodo Students' Union), November 10, Kokrajhar,1987.
3. BC Bhuyan, *Political Development of the North-East,* Part 1, Omsons Publications, Delhi, 1989.
4. Baruah, Sanjib, *India against Itself: Assam and the Politics of Nationality,* Oxford University Press, New Delhi, 2010.
5. Edward Gait, *A History of Assam,* LBS Publications, Guwahati, 1994.
6. Girin Phukon, *Assam's Attitude to Federalism,* Sterling Publishers, New Delhi, 1984.
7. Girin Phukon, *Ethnicisation of Politics in Northeast India*, South Asian Publishers, New Delhi, 2003.
8. Guha, Amalendu, *Planter-Raj to Swaraj: Freedom Struggle and Electoral Politics in Assam 1826-1947,* People's Publishing House, New Delhi, 1977.
9. H. Srikanth, 'Militancy and Identity Politics in Assam', *Economic and Political Weekly*, Vol. 35, No. 47, Nov. 18-24, 2000.
10. H.Gohain and D.Bora (Ed), *Asom Andolon Pratisruti Aru Falasruti,* Banalata, Guwahati, 2007.
11. H.K Barpujari, *North-East India: Problems, Policies and Prospects,* Spectrum, Guwahati, 1998.

12. Homen Borgohain, *Aoupanibeshik Soshanar Viroddhe Asomor Sesh Sangram*, Vintage Books, Guwahati, 2012.
13. M. Hussain, 'The Tribal Question in Assam: A Sociological Appraisal', Milton.S Sangma (Ed), *Essays on Northeast India*, Indus Publishing Company, New Delhi, 1994.
14. M. Hussain, *The Assam Movement: Class, Ideology and Identity,* Manak Publications, Delhi: 1993.
15. Marcus F. Franda, *Bangladesh: The First Decade*, South Asian Publishers, New Delhi, 1982.
16. P .S Datta, *Autonomy Movements in Assam (Documents),* Omsons Publications, New Delhi, 1993.
17. Subir Bhaumik, *Troubled Periphery: Crisis of India's North East,* Sage, New Delhi, 2009.
18. Sujit Choudhury, 'The Bodos: The Tribe for Whom History Failed', *The Window*, No 4, March, 1995.
19. Tilottama Misra, 'Assam: A Colonial Hinterland', *Economic and Political Weekly,* August 9, XV(32), 1980, pp.1357-1365.
20. Udayan Misra *The Periphery Strikes Back,* Indian Institute of Advanced Study, Shimla, 2000.
21. Udayan Misra, *North-East India: Quest for Identity,* Omsons Publications, Guwahati, 1988.

18

Economic Stabilisation of Women: A Case Study with Riverine Population of Five Mouzas along the Dhansiri (South) River, Assam

Shashwati Nath

Introduction

Stabilisation means the act of steady or sturdy something or making anything more stable in favour of better enhancement for sustainability. Stability in monetary system refers to an improved economic condition that experiences constant growth and low inflation. Compensation of having a stable economy comprises increased productivity, improved efficiencies and low unemployment. Economic stability is beneficial for society by means of bonding social unity and prosperity. A survey by Neilson reflects that Indian women are more stressed out in the world: 87 per cent of Indian women feel stressed. Even in workaholic country USA, only 53 per cent women feel stressed.

In a spiritual land like India, at an extreme, girls are aborted before they are born, girls upbringing are neglected, tortured, molested, sold, raped and got killed. A very common in the habits of Indians are that they exploit the people much, particularly women who are not in power. In an International Women's Day celebration in Assam on 8th March 2015, a report was made public, which reveals that in Assam itself (Bengali News Paper, *Dainik Jugasankha*, 9th March, 2015) 15,206 numbers of women were the rape victims and 23,829 numbers of women were abducted during last ten years i.e., from the year 2005 to August 2014. If this is the scenario of only one state, we can well imagine the extent of sufferings in whole of the country.

A famous modern Indian writer Shri Chetan Bhagat very truly said: "Indian women are the most beautiful in the world. As mothers, sisters, daughters, colleagues, wives and girlfriends, we love them. Life cannot be thought of, without these ladies. It would be a universe full of messy, aggressive and egomaniacal males running the world, trying to outdo each other for no particular reason. There would be body odor, socks on the floor and nothing in the fridge to eat. The entertainment industry would die". Considering such facts, if more eligible women are made to be in power, many unwanted odds from the day-to-day occurring can easily be eradicated.

Attempts should be made to bring the economic stability among women which will assist to identify their self-concept and self-confidence and help them to spend an empowered self-dependent life. When women are empowered, a nation's stability improves and democratic participation goes up.

Women's empowerment refers to the capability of women to acquire control of their lives, follow their own ambitions and live according to their own values. Women's economic stability predominantly describes women's power over their own finances, financial well-being and a voice in the financial decisions that shape their lives and the lives of their families. Moreover, women play some vital roles for the society with particular concentration given to admittance to finance, participation in food security as well as nutrition activities and access to sway governance and decision making arenas.

Considering the vastness of the issues, riverine population of five mouzas along the Dhansiri River, which is one of the south bank tributaries of the river Brahmaputra in Assam calls for attention. In this connection, riverine or bank line population especially women is the focus with special reference to the economic stabilisation. The stable economy and its impact on their lives have been studied more closely and suggested some helpful measures that could possibly ameliorate their living condition and survive successfully.

I. Study Region

The study region covers Golaghat and Karbi Anglong districts of Assam (Location Map 1). The concerned area has a total population of 14 lakhs according to the 2011 census. Out of thirty-six villages in the concerned area along the Dhansiri river from 25^0 North to 26^0 30' North latitude and 93^0 30' East longitude to 94^0 East longitude, nine villages has been the area of observations and sample have been taken from these villages (Fig. 2). The study area covers eight villages according to five mouzas(Mouza maps Fig. 3-7) from Rowduar to Borpathar of Golaghat district which are Kuruabahi, Rowduar, Halmara Tup, Kathkotia, Dhuliagaon, Moinapara, Simoluchapori, No.1 Dubarani (lower part of Dhansiri (s) river) and one village of Karbi Anglong district i.e., Puroni Borpathar. The selected villages have a total population of 10,716 persons according to the 2011 census.

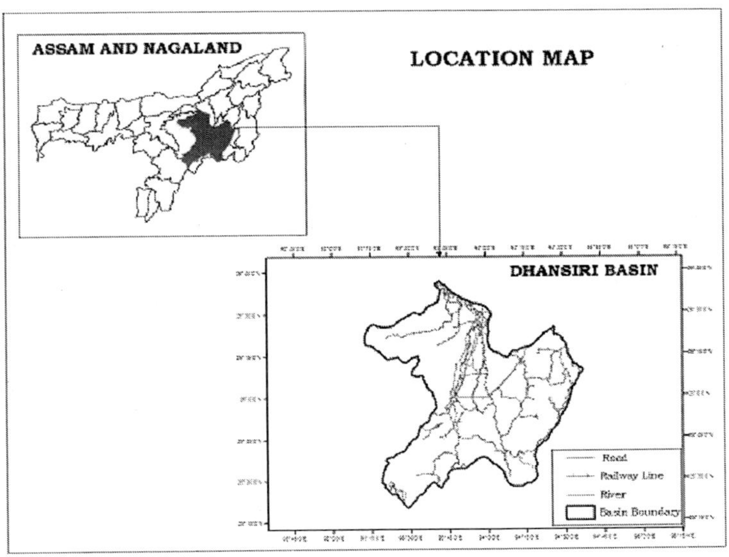

Fig. 1: Location Map

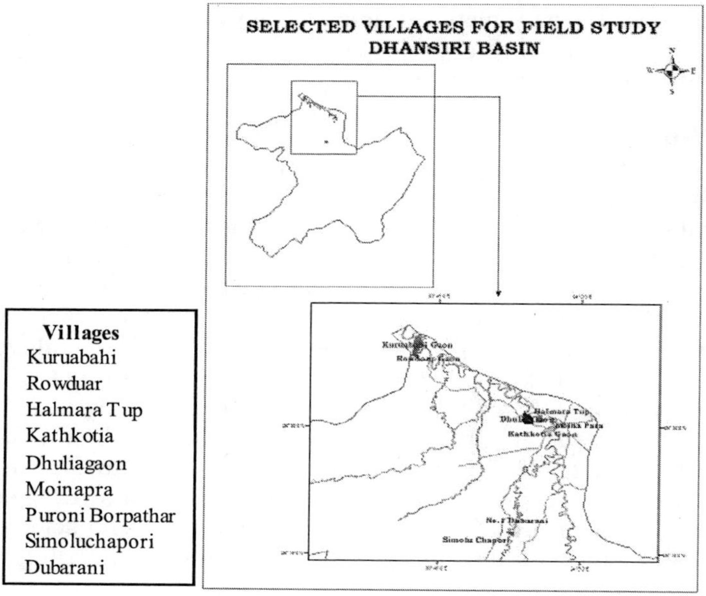

Fig. 2: Selected villages for field study

The study region is primarily inhabited by peasant families. About 88 per cent of the total population lives along the valley and 70 per cent of the population is engaged in agricultural activities. Other than this, fishing is another source of income of the riverine people. Different groups of settlers like indigenous Assamese people, Scheduled Caste people and immigrant people from Bangladesh and Nepal are identified along the riverine belt.

II. Objectives of the Study

The major objectives of the study are:

1. To study the number of male-female population of the selected villages with their literacy rates according to mouzas.

2. To assess the skills of the rural women for economic empowerment.

3. To study the types of economic activities prevailing in the study area in addition to the role of women for their economic strategies.

4. To analyse the result from findings and suggest some policy measures for women in the concerned area.

III. Data and Methods

Data is collected from both primary and secondary sources. To collect primary data from sampling unit, both stratified and random sampling methods have been adopted and for this purpose a suitable questionnaire with a view to collect information from the sample villages. A central aspect of methodology through interview has been its participatory nature, ensured through the organisation of workshops and public forefront in which various sectors of civil society expressed their perceptions of the impact of stabilisation and adjustment policies on their lives. The sample size has to been taken as 30 per cent from each of the villages and wherever the size of population is very small such as Rowduar (315), Kathkotia (478) and Simoluchapori (204) every household has been covered with the help of sampling techniques. The research process too incorporates qualitative and quantitative methods. The first stage implicates consultations, which provides a qualitative analysis based on the participation and thoughts of a wide range of people of the region who take part in the mass awareness programmes and workshops. The second phase of research focused on quantitative analysis by means of statistics and secondary sources. Secondary information is collected from books, journals and government officials.

IV. Male-Female Population with Their Literacy Rates of the Selected Villages of Five Mouzas

Kuruabahi and Rowduar villages are fall under Bokakhat Mouza and sub-division, which is bounded in the north by Sonitpur and Lakhimpur districts. These villages cover a total population of 1,788 and 315 comprising of 873 female and 915 male and 152 female and 163 male respectively. Out of the total population in Kuruabahi village, 70.58 per cent are literate which is considerably high. One interesting point is that the literacy rate of Rowduar village is also very high, which is 77.46 per cent (244 persons).

Halmara Tup village is located under Dhekial mouza and Golaghat sub-division. The village is bounded in the north by

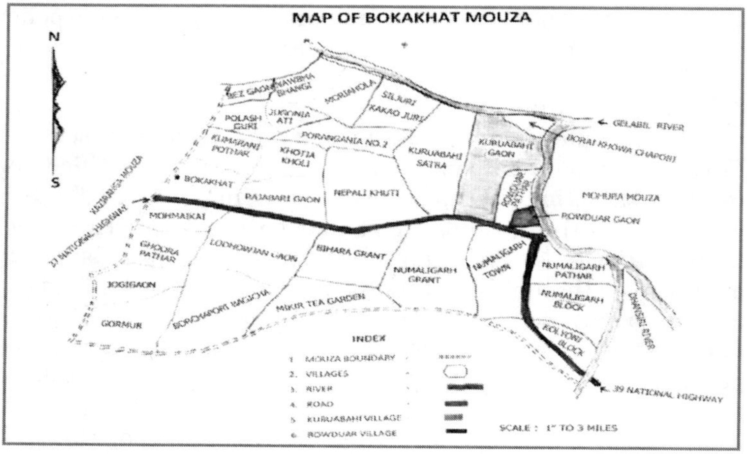

Fig. 3: Bokakhat Mouza

Lakhimpur district, in the south by Sarupathar Sadar sub-division, Golaghat town and Jorhat district in the east and Karbi Anglong district in the west. The village comprises 750 female and 790 male persons (total population1540) where 28 per cent

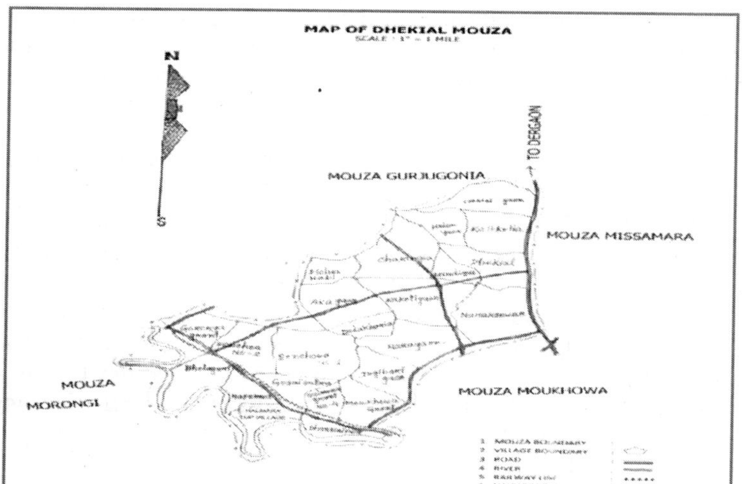

Fig. 4: Dhekial Mouza

(431) is literate due to tremendous riverine hazards caused by the river Dhansiri.

Kathkotia village falls under Moukowa mouza and Golaghat sub-division. It is bounded in the north by Golaghat town, Lakhimpur district and the Brahmaputra river, we have to the south Sarupathar Sadar sub-division, east by Jorhat district and west by Karbi Anglong district.

During field study and conversation with the people, it has been known that fishing is a prime source of income of the villagers because one of the small tributaries of the river Dhansiri named Thorajan flows through the village and cause heavy floods and bank erosion. The village has 478 numbers of total populations where 270 male and 208 female persons and 51.88 per cent people are literate.

Dhuliagaon village is under Morongi Mouza and Golaghat Sub-division. It is bounded by Sonitpur and Lakhimpur districts in the north, Sarupather Sadar sub-division in the south, Golaghat town and Jorhat district in the east and Karbi Anglong district in the west. Out of the total population (2500), 1425 are male and 1075 female and 25 per cent people is literate, where 17 per cent male and only 8 per cent female.

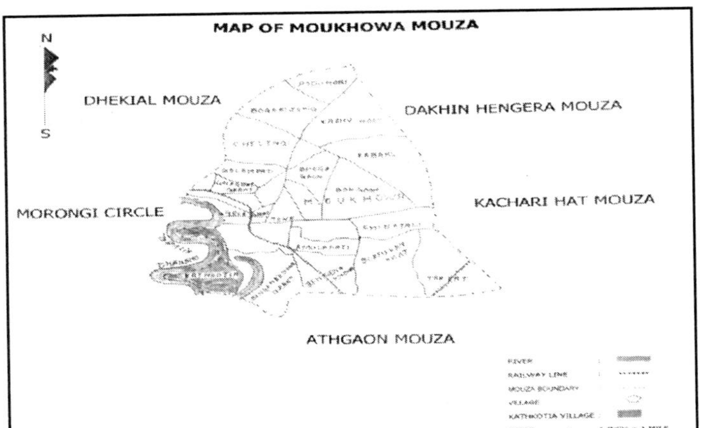

Fig. 5: Moukhowa Mouza

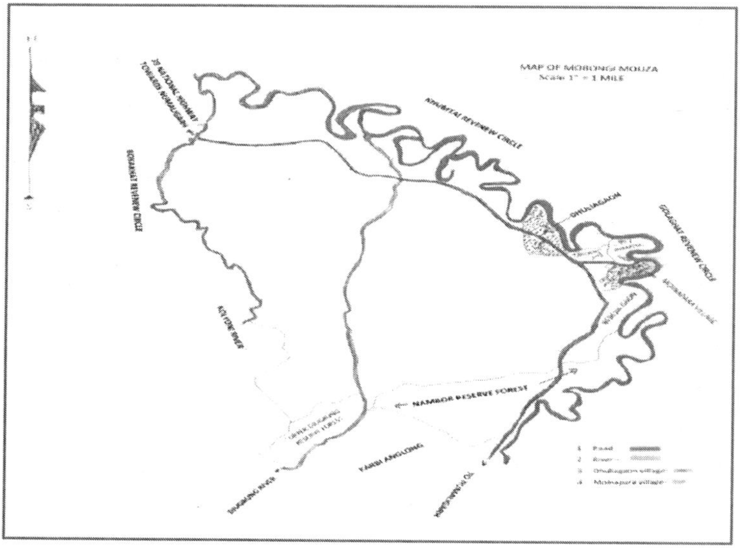

Fig. 6: Morongi Mouza

Moinapara village is also included under Morongi mouza and Golaghat sub-division. It is bounded in the north by Golaghat town and Sonitpur district, to the south by Sarupathar Sadar sub-division, in east Jorhat district and in west by Garampani, Karbi Anglong district. Out of the total population (1250), the village comprises 725 male and 525 female persons and only 35 per cent is literate, where male literacy is 20 per cent and female literacy is 15 per cent.

Puroni Borpathar village comes under Bokajan Sub-division, Borpathar Mouza and Karbi Anglong district. The village is bounded in the north by Golaghat Sadar sub-division and Lakhimpur district, in the south by Sarupathar and Bokajan sub-division, east by the state of Nagaland and Jorhat district and west by Karbi Anglong and Nagaon districts. It has a total population of 818 where 440 are male and 368 female. This village has particularly been selected from Karbi Anglong district, because tremendous flood hits this village every year, though it is surrounded by hilly terrain. The river Dhansiri and one of its tributaries namely, Nambor flows through near the

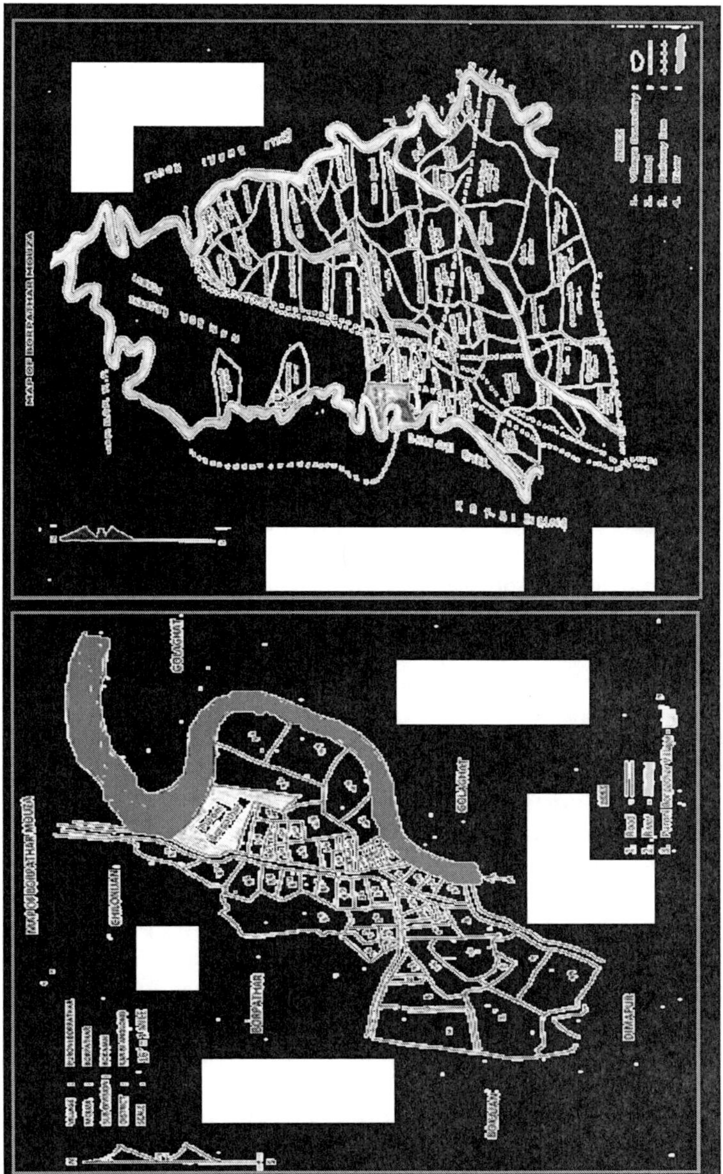

Fig. 7: Borpathar Mouza

village causing heavy floods. Percentage of literates to total population in this village is 37.04 per cent (303 persons) where 16.50 per cent are male and 20.54 per cent female.

The Simoluchapori village falls under Borpathar Mouza, Dhansiri sub-division and Golaghat district. The village is bounded in the north by Golaghat Sadar division, Sonitpur and Lakhimpur districts; we have to the south Sarupathar and Bokajan sub-division, east by the state of Nagaland and west by Karbi Anglong and Nagaon districts. 204 people live in the village comprising of 107 male and 97 female. The village has 72.55 percentage of literate persons to the total population where 39.22 per cent are male and 33.33 per cent female.

No. 1 Dubarani Village, falls under Borpathar Mouza and Dhansiri Sub-division in Golaghat district. The village is bounded by Golaghat Sadar sub-division, Sonitpur and Lakhimpur district in the north, by Sarupathar and Bokajan Sadar sub-division in the south, the state of Nagaland in the east and Karbi Anglong and Nagaon districts in the west. 1823 numbers of populations live in this village comprising 907 male and 916 female. Out of the total population, 1379 persons are literate where 731 are male and 648 female.

V. Assessing the Developmental Skills of the Rural Women for Economic Empowerment

Skills development for economic empowerment of rural women is a key to improving rural productivity, employability and income-earning opportunities, enhancing food security and promoting environmentally sustainable rural growth and livelihoods. In spite of rural women's major role in agriculture and other rural activities, higher barriers in education and training, border their participation in more productive and remunerative work, perform decision-making and management the roles and contribute fully in the development of their communities. Though women are bounded by various societal customs and their own traditional lifestyles, embattled achievement is needed to take apart these barriers from the way of attaining empowerment.

VI. Economic Activities Prevailing in the Study Area and the Role of Women for their Economic Strategies

Agriculture and tea plantation form the backbone of the economy of Assam. In fact, broadly two types of farming have been in practice in the study area; small-scale peasant and large-scale tea plantation farming in the Bokakhat, Numaligarh areas. Cultivation, business, service, daily labor and fishing are the main economic activities prevailing in the study area. Agriculture provides employment of more than 60 per cent of the women in the region. It provides raw materials for many local industries such as tea, sugarcane, rice milling, flour milling, oil processing and canning etc. Moreover, animal husbandry, piggery, poultry keeping, fishing are other related economic activities of the region.

Economic strategy is the process by which a region improves the economic, political, and social wellbeing of its people. Women in the study area perform 66 per cent of the basin's work even if they face various challenges. So, in economic strategies, women in the study area hold a major part of agricultural sector and generating a respectable amount of income for their better livelihood.

VII. Findings and Results

To find out the present economic scenario and literacy rates of the rural women, data have been collected during the survey of the selected villages from five mouzas, and are arranged in tabular form for a comparative study. The numbers of male and female population data and literacy rates have been taken for measuring the sex ratios and percentage of literates to total population (Table 1). A diagram of percentage of literates to total population has been prepared from Table 1 ((Fig. 8) to show the literacy rates which a prime factor for economic empowerment of women because the lack of education especially among women is high owing to hazardous nature of the river which keep the schools disconnected and people are displaced due to floods. Table 1 helped to create a transparent picture of sex ratios from the total numbers of male and female population of the villages which showed in Table 2. It has been furthermore illustrated in Table 2 that nearly half of the total population is

Table 1: Numbers of male - female population and percentage of literates to total population of the selected villages within five mouzas

Sl. No.	Name of the villages	Mouzas	Total population	Male	Female	% of literates to total population	% of male to total literate persons	% of Female to total literate persons
1	2	3	4	5	6	7	8	9
1	Kuruabahi	Bokakhat	1788	915 (51.17%)	873 (48.83%)	70.92 (70.52)	54.99 (55.03)	45.01 (44.97)
2	Rowdoar	Bokakhat	315	163 (51.75%)	152 (48.25%)	77.46	54.09	45.91
3	Hahnara Tup	Dhekial	1540	790 (51.30%)	750 (48.70%)	27.99 (27.92)	58.70 (58.91)	41.30 (41.09)
4	Kathkotia	Moukhowa	478	270 (56.49%)	208 (43.51%)	51.88	54.65	44.35

(Contd.)

(Contd. Table)

Sl. No.	Name of the villages	Mouzas	Total population	Male	Female	% of literates to total population	% of male to total literate persons	% of Female to total literate persons
1	2	3	4	5	6	7	8	9
5	Dhuliagaon	Morongi	2500	1425 (57%)	1075 (43%)	25 (25.07)	68 (68.09)	32 (31.91)
6	Moinapara	Morongi	1250	725 (58%)	525 (42%)	35.04 (35.19)	57.08 (57.14)	42.92 (42.86)
7	Puroni Borpathar	Borpathar	818	450 (55.01%)	368 (44.99%)	37.04 (37)	55.45 (55.37)	44.55 (44.63)
8	Simolu chapori	Borpathar	204	107 (52.45%)	97 (47.55%)	72.55	54.05	45.95
9	No.1 Dubarani	Borpathar	1823	907 (49.75%)	916 (50.25%)	75.64 (75.73)	53.01 (53.01)	46.99 (46.99)

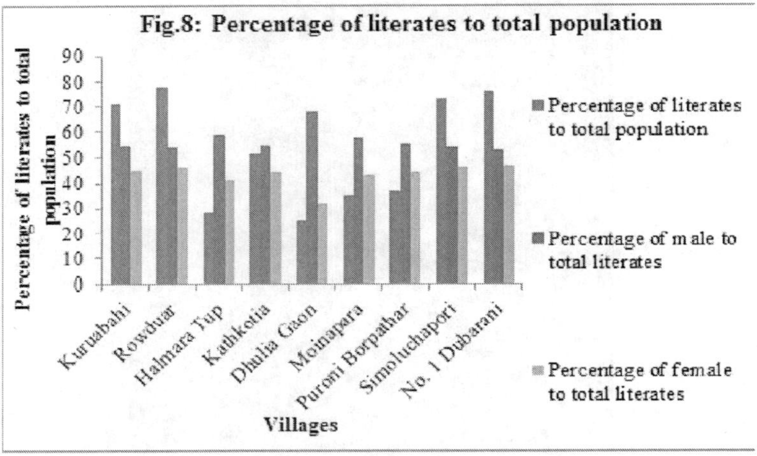

female (46.32 per cent) and 53.67 per cent are male. Hence, female can take a crucial role not only in family but also economic development of the society as a whole. The specific situation and conditions of women in society must be analysed in order to assess the differentiated impacts of stabilisation and adjustment programmes on them in various spheres of activity, such as various occupational patterns of women and percentages of women workers to total workers and production for their community. Such an approach requires to captivating the women participation in economic adjustment policies in different ways for their livelihood.

Table 2
Sex Ratio of the sample male - female population with percentage:

Total No of Persons	*Male*	*Per cent*	*Female*	*Per cent*
10716	**5752**	**53.67**	**4964**	**46.32**

Maximum women in the concerned area are working in different types of agricultural and allied activities (Table 3) which make opportunities in economic development of the society.

Table 3
Occupational patterns and women workers to total workers of the surveyed villages

S. No.	Name of the occupation	Women engaged (in per cent)	Income (in per cent)
1.	Cultivation	66	75
2.	Business	12	10
3.	Service	7	05
4.	Daily labour	10	07
5.	Fishing	5	03
	Total	**100**	**100**

Table 2 indicates that 66 per cent of women, out of the total workers are engaged in agricultural sectors, 12 per cent are in business, 7 per cent are in service sectors, 10 per cent are working as daily labourers and only 5 per cent are engaged in fishing. Table 2 also points out that 75 per cent of income is generated from agriculture, 10 per cent from business, 05 per cent from service, 07 per cent from daily wage labourer and 03 per cent from fishing and make a good quantity of economic support for their better living. Though the income is generated mostly through agricultural activities, is fluctuate and uneven due to flood and bank erosion caused by the river Dhansiri. Interestingly, an analytical study shows that a considerable number of young women are now fascinated towards a business like small scale cottage industries based on locally available natural resources.

VIII. Policy Measures

"Elating as we go up" is a much needed awaken call for forward looking and policy makers.

The following Policy Measures are needed to be implemented by the government in partnership with NGO and other social Community for economic empowerment of women —

(i) The technical and vocational education should be made available for girls and women.

(ii) Different awareness programmes should be held to remove the physical, social and economic disparities.

(iii) Advocate for increase the gratitude and decrease the unpaid care work of women.

(iv) Grown up women's entrepreneurship through training in production skills and techniques, business management and functional literacy.

(v) Supporting efforts to strengthen women's decision-making form and legal rights to property.

Conclusion

Women in the study region are to a large extent wrapped up by various societal traditions that they often cannot or do not want to bring changes in their own conventional lifestyles. Hence, there is a need for creation of socio-economic and political awareness among women. It will be possible when the women empowerment will be realised in its appropriate sense. For materialising this great concept, the approaches of people of the area have to consider genuinely that man and women cannot be differentiated and make the women modernised with all new aspects. The customary law of all the societies desires to be grounded on equality and human rights such that both men and women are given equal rights. To overcome the present crisis from all sides such as education, economic, social, political and legal rights of women in the study area along the Dhansiri riverine belt, there is an urgent need to create awareness.

Government's support for a fruitful result will be incomplete, until the women themselves and men realise the need of the great change. An enormous support to liberate the women, to fight against the social evils, should come from inside. The government along with intended organisations should take up concrete steps to strengthen and stabilise the status of women by providing safe, secured and non-violent life. In the concluding remarks, it has been tried to identify the probable causes from the analysis made, and how the implementation and outcome of policies were influenced by political, economic, social, cultural, environmental and self-related factors. Finally, it can be said that advancement and full participation of women in political, economic, and social territories are key goals of empowerment for economic stabilisation. When women are empowered, educated and prepared to contribute to the society, their families are more likely to prosper, stable and secured.

References

1. Mukut Kr. Sonowal, 'Impact of Education in Women Empowerment: A Case Study of SC and ST Women of Sonitpur District, Assam', *Basic Applied and Social Sciences*, Vol. III, 2013.
2. C. Goswami, 'Female Agricultural Workers in Assam: A Case Study in Darrang District, Assam', *International Journal of Scientific and Research Publications*, Vol. 3, Issue 2, 2013.
3. R. Hensman, 'Globalisation, Women and Work', *Economic and Political Weekly*, 6th March 2004.
4. D. Phukan, 'New Economic Policy and its Impact on Traditional Skills of Women in North-East India', B.J. Dev, K. Sengupta and B.D. Ray (Eds), *Globalisation and North-East India*, Concept Publishing Company, New Delhi, 2008.
5. Ritul Talukdar, 'Women Education and Rural Economic Development of the Bodo Community of Assam; A Case Study in Barpeta and Baksa District of Assam', *International Journal of Science, Environment and Technology*, Vol. 1, No. 1, 2012, pp.41-48.
6. Census Report, 2011, *Provisional Population Total of Assam Series-19*, 2011.
7. Chetan Bhagat, *What Young India Wants,* Rupa Publications, New Delhi, 2012.
8. D. Bora, *Women Empowerment, Present and the Way Forward,* Purvanchal Prakash, Guwahati, 2012.
9. Monica Baneerjee, *Conflicts and Constructive Work: Strengthening Civil Society in the northeast,* Preeti Gill (Ed), *The Peripheral Centre: Voices from India's Northeast,* Zubaan, New Delhi, 2010, pp.177-184.
10. R. Buongpui, *Gender Relations and the Web of Traditions in Northeast India, The NEHU Journal*, Vol. XI, No. 2, July 2013, pp.73-81.

19

Ethnicity and Identity: A Post Modernist Challenge from the Media and the Market

Garima Kalita

Identity and ethnicity are close, mutually respecting phrases but they may not progress forward on the same line at all times. On a hypothetical plane or even imaginary, when the world was not here but subsisting on the basic and primitive norms and values far away from today's landscape, identity was definitely formed around the play of emotive accounts, the surrounding universe and more prominently around land and habitation.

Amartya Sen (2006) in his most thought provoking book, *Identity and Violence* cites a curious case of ethnicity, the contradictory nature of its affect and functioning. It is true that "the sense of identity can make an important contribution to the strength and the warmth of our relations with others ..." but at the same time as he would admit, violence is perpetrated "by imposition of singular and belligerent identities on gullible people, championed by proficient artisans of terror." Of course, this is an altogether different matter that the random and unthinking recognition of competing affiliations would create a problematic for even the best meaning of authors and activists.

Given the fact that the world has grown irreducibly and also shrunk so primarily that, the concepts like identity and ethnicity have become very debatable and very contradictory ideas. In one strong case you tend to forget the relation, which is embedded and integrated between them and join hands in circulating the bias and subjective standpoint. So here you are going for the fundamental and unitary form and matter of things. The identity exhibited here is completely insular, rigid and dogmatic. The Adivasis of Chirang district of Assam who had been victimised to brutal slaughter by the extremists in December 2014 are identified in an insular manner bearing the brand of a particular identity and the Bodo community too are rearing historical stories of grievance in their appropriated present. But the fact is that the history of the geographical locality and the political history of British India need to be probed anew to explain and analyse the contemporary anecdotes of the region. So the vulnerability of the ethnic groups may have to be brought to the surface with compassion for historical reason. The question of ethnicity in some parts of Assam is still a very debatable and thought provoking one. The formation of the Bodoland Autonomous Council has solved some very minor issues but has created more disturbing ones. Thanks to the politics of provocation played by vested political companies and multiculturalism used as a tool for political division.

On the dichotomy of the collective and the individual Frederic Jameson (1983) in his famous *The Political Unconscious* summons individual will and the free choice together and deliberates upon the historicity of cultural artefacts or texts. Contextualising this particular phenomenon on the axes of identity, both political and also cultural, he would presuppose "a genuine philosophy of history" which alone he believes is "capable of respecting the specificity and radical difference of the social and cultural past while disclosing the solidarity of its polemics and passions, its forms, structures, experiences, and struggles with those of the present day."

In this post-industrial, post-modernist age of ours the terms ethnicity and identity have indeed become too fluid and too abstract for us to clearly deal with. In the absence of clear demarcating boundaries issues of this kind at times are evaded on the conscious level, as matters become too tricky and too delicate politically. The history of the society does acknowledge the fact that a people cannot in all circumstances be subservient to the common destiny and fate always. Civilisational progress invariably points to a variety of choices in location, migration and relocation and hence the concept of identity must be something constantly on the move, in the process of becoming.

Race, ethnicity, caste and creed, community, religion, groups, forums, clubs, association etc are community and collective words. The relationship between an individual and the society is vital, vibrant and encouraging and morally and ethically viable. It should never be posted on the level of tantrums and conflict and allegations. But the society in its daily discourse has to involve diverse, at times completely incompatible forces on the collective, community, familial and individual level. So what emerges at the end of every analysis, projection, incidence and coincidence, a thoroughly messed up, convoluted trajectory of social history which needs to be taken care of, read and unfurled in proper perspective. In this modern world this idea is something one needs to look into with seriousness. Here social disruptions and conflict would erupt because of tiny miscalculations and also indifferent apathy. In *Identity and Violence,* Amartya Sen (2006) evolves two catastrophic reductionist ideas that he calls "identity disregard" and "singular affiliation". In the first case he cites the cases of as he says, "wise guy scepticism which makes according to him, huge idiots out of Mahatma Gandhi, Martin Luther King Jr, Mother Teresa and Nelson Mandela". In strong coercive words Sen involves the "single minded self loving human being" who for him no doubt has provided the behavioural foundations of great many economic theories, but who at the same time has been unable to answer critical but significant queries about the society and the collective when confronted on a crossroad. In specific cases even this kind of limited overview also could become valid if only it is in accordance to that specific constant. It could differ from context to context.

The identity superimposed on the mind, sensibility and temperamental trait which works as (I) language (Internalised Language) perhaps is perilous for the notion of identity itself. The religious, advertising oriented trials make man and also mar man. Culture tends to determine the biology, ethics, economics and political will of the individual especially of women. Deliberately I have omitted the identity question of women from the scope of the chapter as this alone demands diverse possible exploration under many headings, political, cultural and otherwise. Nonetheless the subject's acuteness and passion involved demand a distinctive exploration.

Amartya Sen (2007) again in *On Ethics and Economics* charts out the different socio-economic statuses that people consciously involve themselves and achieve what is on individual and collective level called the states of 'well being' and 'agency'. These states that tend to determine the ideas and concepts of identity obtain not only a state of fulfilled desire but also a metaphysical reality. The author propounds these two concepts of well being and agency on the notions that the former concept signifies the "achievements and opportunities in the context of his or her personal advantage", whereas the latter goes further and refers to the wider, social or community aspect of things. The reason why do we consider these two concepts to be extremely relevant for this essay is the fact that in the larger context of society the agency aspect of the individual must correlate fundamentally to the notion of the well being of the person. The norms that tend to work for the fulfilment of the wellbeing must not clash harshly with the notion of the person's role as an agency. To see it from the other point of view, the affective agency of the person must include the basic requirement of the well being. The medial point which also states a state of equilibrium would maintain that identity tends to revolve around these forces, centripetal and centrifugal.

The meaningfulness of the action confers upon man the strength for subsistence and determines the choices that man does undertake. In a society which is regulated by one dimensional thought, positive or negative, as the Frankfurt school theorist Herbert Marcuse observes, the predetermined and repressive action would tend to regulate the identity and existential status of the modern industrial man. He in his famous treatise on the post-Industrial society *One Dimensional Man* cited examples from the identity that is formed by him in the context of one dimensional thinking and dialectical thinking. According to him, in the contemporary society critical and dialectical thinking was "based on rational potentials for human happiness and freedom, which are used to negate existing state of affairs that oppress individuals and restrict human freedom and well being". The question of identity in such a technologically advanced society is bound to be a completely fixed one or a completely fluid one. He perceived in today's juncture that "the achievements of advanced industrial society, critical theory is left in a blank, a void without the rationale for transcending the society".

Without bringing in the reference from the book even it can be authentically and unquestionably affirmed that the industrial society which we inhabit exhibits tendencies and deep structural signs of market centric institutions. The market with its overbearing presence determines the fate of the consumer inside the market. Whatever be the nature of the consumer or the identity of the person in the market the state of the essence is that after all some false needs are going to be created by the market and market is going to be the arbiter of the personality. The absence of valid communication between the man (the consumer) and the society creates situation without overt remedies. In this connection what Frankfurt school social scientist Erich Fromm in his epoch making, *The Sane Society* contends shall not be irrelevant. Taking a close look at this kind of human situation prompted by fateful human behavioural pattern of a consumer, Erich Fromm cites the example of private enterprises for profit that work as the incentive under capitalism. Since in such a society no social laws are explicit and fixed on the basis of political power or tradition the mode of the market bases itself on this that if only everybody strives for himself on the market, the common good would come of it. Along with a description of the nature of the consumer Fromm here also offers an analysis of such tendencies. From this self centric absorption of the individual arises another social malady that he calls alienation and which professes itself between man and man and also man and himself. The relationship between individuals is 'between two abstractions' or 'two living machines'. In summary this social scientist has termed life and living in such an industrial consumerist society in such terms as "profitable investment of capital, my life and my person as capital which is invested." Love is nothing but a "favourable exchange between two people who get the most of what they can expect, considering their value on the personality market. Each person is a 'package' in which several aspects of his exchange value is blended into one ...his personality by which is meant those qualities which make him a good salesman of himself".

This feature of the advanced industrial society also brings forth other dilemmas of a different kind. Rather warnings. Marcuse cites it as follows. The lack of freedom which he refers to as unfreedom' prevails in such a tempo that it is this a comfortable smooth, reasonable, democratic unfreedom prevails in advanced industrial civilisation, a token of technical progress. But this state corrodes the individual from inside, saps him and paralyses and deliberately constraints him. Because of the gradual tendency towards repressive administration begins and the culmination of that tendency happens in an absolutely stable autocratic system.

The closed language does not demonstrate and explain it communicates decision, dictum, and command. As Marcuse observes the functional language is a radically anti-historical language: operational rationality has little room and little use for historical reason. The use of history in this context is somewhat ambivalent though this notion of reversed use of history in this post-modernist scene also redefines the strength of community and archaeology of knowledge. This abuse and corruption of language too tends to over determine or underdetermine identity of persons in cases.

The land and geo specific quest for identity and political affiliation are not without grave questions of humanity and national sovereignty. In today's world this is so problematically winded up with legality and the vulnerability of individual desire and human rights question. The Northeast has become a place of experimentation and laboratory gimmick for statesmen at the cost of the common and little people. They do command ethnicities, and should not be made preys to political ambiguities and deliberately prompted conflicts among themselves. What has emerged after prolonged idiotic mismatching of messages in the communities, a caustic and vile distrust has spread and sapped the spirit of amity. Pitifully all these people are posed in lines like robotic armies, one against the other and they clash ignorantly by night in a blind battle as Mathew Arnold the Eminent Victorian tended to predict in his much read poem "Dover Beach".

And we are here as on a darkling plain
Swept with confused alarms of struggle and flight,
Where ignorant armies clash by night.

On the generic and ethnic terms the question of identity fused with collectively and individual status works in tantrums, most erratically as in the whole complex knotting the historical forces tend to interact most forcefully like evolutionary mechanism. The ideology that is at all levels connected with each other, may work at cross-purposes and manifest itself most unevenly, randomly, even with a chaotic disorder. In this plethora of conjunctures what is working with equanimity is perhaps ethics. This normative principle without so much as defining it could well mean some purpose, peace, a supervising presence of superego.

The question of identity is besotted with complicated tandems of authenticity and problematic questions of ethics. The question of ethnic identity is marred unobtrusively by contradictory and disruptive forces that seek to cause disturbances around some notions of solidarity, sameness, tribe, caste, homogeneity etc. How do these dictionary terms are abused and transgressed in the name of ethnic identity in political economy needs to be observed under close scrutiny.

In a specific instance of the reaffirmation of the Karbis, in the domain of Karbi Anglong as thoroughly described in a very well written narrative by Ajit Singner, *Longri Atamon*, the quest for identity both social and political was reflected in the honest and earnest attempt of Karbi leaders of the forties, Kharsing Terang and Semson Engti in the establishment of a district for the Karbis in Karbi Anglong. After a few decades, the additional movement, which has emerged for a separate state could also be seen from the same perspective of reaffirmation of ethnic identity posed on the same axes of progress, development and self administration. But the problematic is always scrutinised under harsh political light, in the context of the pan Assamese hegemony and overt and covert bias. The contemporary socio-historical scene in Assam and also the Northeast surfaces divisive comments, debates which are corrosive and virulent and which do not in any way help in the respectful determination of the ethnic identities.

The National Register of Citizens (NRC), the policy determinant implement which is being updated now is undergoing through official machinery and that process is bound to confront queries, questions of trust and confidentiality. The process of democracy hence at moments of crises becomes double faced, ambivalent and indeterminate. This becomes a double edged implement, which would be unfit even for a single use in the wake of global tendencies of similarity and uniformity. But the idea of monolithic social or ethnic sameness breeds ennui; diversity rejuvenates. Though it is a different matter whether through this curious mixture of crossed cultural identities, the exhilaration of the carnivalesque surfaces or not, both in the manifest and the latent. But the political identity which would look into too many types of forages is bound to work as a disinfectant that does away with all the bacterial molasses (whether harmful or useful). The problems of welfare economics and consequentialism are very thoroughly explained in the book by Amartya Sen already cited.

Identity after delving deep into the notion and the concept within, it could be read on the axes of real, hyper real, mythic and lucid. The representation of hyper reality is illustrated in his curiously levelled essay, 'Mass Media Culture' by Baudrillard (1990), the cultural critic of post-modernism. He is forthright in his critique of the absence of the real in the individual and the collective plane. He even extends it to the material production of commodities. "When the characteristic hysteria of our time: the hysteria of production and reproduction of the real. The other production, that of goods and commodities ...no longer makes any sense of its own, and has not for some time. What society seeks through production and overproduction is the restoration of the real which escapes it. That is why contemporary "material" production is itself "hyperreal" (The Precession of Simulacra, Simulations). So it is no longer a question of ideology of power but of the scenario of power. Perhaps for him the ideology is constituted in a betrayal of reality by signs and hence this as he sees it, the exhumation of reality in the ideology of banality. The digital media, TV and other mediums constantly make tiresome and tiring exercises of finding the real in various truth experiments like the 1971 TV Verite episodes of Laud family of seven months of uninterrupted shooting, 300 hours of nonstop broadcasting in Big Boss, and other reality shows that only seek truth.

The identity that is mythic perhaps could be illustrated on the plane of ideas and ideology which too actually operates on the illusive. Imagined and even delusional narratives are constructed and a whole community is led to either a dance of death or the artist's creative genius, the exuberate sculpture of new birth. How do we tend to see the ludic, perhaps is best illustrated in the surveillance of media and the world of electronics. The networks of twitter, whatsapp, google and Microsoft, or viber constantly replenishes us and makes us fatigued and exhausted travellers of the Desert of Arabia. The Wordsworth's concept of the song of the Nightingale in that locale would now betray an irritant. Lacan redefining Freud's concepts of ego, Id and superego tends to add the concept of the Gaze to the conscious ego but also reiterates the fact which Freud too admits, that the sense of the self and the other, two most important phases in the formation of the identity are integrally connected to the gaze of the other, that captures you and reflects back at you. In the Mirror stage as the formative Function of the (I) Lacan introduces the concept of the imaginary exemplified in the process of the formation the ego by the subject.

Market has to be redefined in terms of identity and ethnicity and both these terms need to be analysed in absolute and also relational terms. Now what is ethnicity and identity and what do they mean in Anthropology or other social sciences are matters too complex and too convoluted. On one hand, take the world as it is and also as it should or could be. Now no one can deny the fact that the market of arms and ammunitions does control the ethics of identity. This is not a radical statement but it does verify facts and states in the contemporary late capitalist society. Frederic Jameson would perhaps term it as the cultural logic and this term sorts things for further explication and perception. The cultural logic of this late capitalism has been as described in different terms by most of the Frankfurt critical school, e.g. Eric Fromm, Theodor Adorno, Herbert Marcuse, *et al.* completely dependent upon the market and the nature of this market has been all embracing and too overwhelming. About that, much more may be said on a different context.

The topical issue which burns every other issue is the all inclusivity of law and ethics in a society. A modern nation state cannot by any means ignore this all inclusive nature of norm and condition. The general precept of law says that inclusivity is a general imperative and nothing could sideline it. But in pragmatic terms, on occasions when the interests of people clash and tend to conflict the cause of law is subverted or at moments of political decisions redefined. The recent history of Kuki Karbi conflict of 2004 and the pervasive Kuki Dimasa conflict in the October of 2005 does recall moments of bitterness among groups and moments of lawlessness rooted in the concerns for survival and group loyalty.

Details of conflict situations remain in the collective memory and the scars and bruises do disturb the psyche but wisdom of the day would be to forget. The conscious ego would be prevented by layers of repressive tendencies which do support in an oblique manner the Eros, the libido and the Life force, May be the Will of Schopenhauer is a relevant associate. In the evolution of a society the factors that do bind and link as cohesive forces are regulated by time and political unconscious. Otherwise on the social trajectory there would have been pitiful remainders of fateful nemesis of blood and death experienced on the Self and at the same time, indignation and spite focused on the other.

This is not a prediction of socio-cultural crisis but from historical reading of society and community, perhaps it can be surmised that collective call of things and state always becomes obsessive and also irreverent of others.

On a different note, the notion of identity hence has become a saving grace for humanity and also the most perilous weapon that humanity has ever used. Like a double edged weapon it cuts from both the sides. We have to be extremely careful not to overuse it and also not be forgetful to use it at all. The complex contemporary consumerist society that we are inhabiting and enriching with new redefined values and norms could become one like the chimera that shows form of some kind but without cohere aesthetics, a deformed vision or no vision at all.

Various notions and concepts related to the identity are also relevant for ethnicity. Actually in some basic levels the promotion of ethnicity becomes a slogan for identity at least on the collective plane. What is so passionately followed as a norm or principle must contribute towards the idea of individual identity. But collective concerns or group activity too needs to be considered as for an individual, it is always problematic for the correct choice. In the politics of the Northeast the whole umbrella concept supports emotional bonding between innumerable tribes and communities inhabiting the region. Especially it works vehemently against the pan-national agenda of discrimination and unequal social status. But given the microcosmic view of the individual tribes and communities and their aspiration to belong to a bigger conglomerate, the desire to stand alone on a distinct plane of cultural identity, works on a far deeper level than it appears to be. The Bodos, the Karbis or the Koch Rajbonshis, and all other tribes or ethnic groups in Assam are crying for individual political identity. The status of being a distinct cultural group may not fulfil all the desires that seem to present them with a lucrative political future. For them only a state or a six schedule status could save their identity.

But the jinx lies not in the fulfilment or non-fulfilment of the demands or desires. The jinx lies in the competitive market of culture, language and identity. The common people's aspirations that are constructed within a passionate oratory (not on practice, mind it), and politics of egoism and ambition are taken as symbols and metaphors or even icons to which every aware citizen must pay his obeisance. This god of self-determination or identity must be kept perennially on the pedestal. I presume the Lowest Common Culture of Baudrillard would act as the denominator of this ambivalent situation of identity. The LCC prompts us to exhibit something as very sophisticated, very high class and very technically savvy. Baudrillard's notion of Hyperreal and LCC (Lowest Common Culture) is most relevant in the sense that process of identity formation in today's world is based on the constant sliding of the images under layers of images and indeterminacy plays a most crucial role.

Identity becomes a consumer good that one would at any rate love to have. This very highly priced commodity in the political market is sold and bought with exorbitant and impossible prices. This auction house is completely owned by the industrialists and the big media houses that can predict the future of a people. The bloodbath of ethnic conflicts, the irrational stupidity of the mass hysteria that leaves a society sapped, drained are all consequences of fixed unitary norms of identity and rigid catastrophic cultural quotas.

References

1. Theodor W Adorno, *The Culture Industry,* Routledge, London and New York, 2004.
2. Jean Baudrillard, *Revenge of the Crystal Selected Writings on the Modern Object and Its Destiny*, Pluto Press, London, 1990.
3. Erich Fromm, *The Sane Society*, Routledge, London and New York, 2002 (1956).
4. Frederic Jameson, *The Political Unconscious,* Routledge, London and New York, 1983.
5. Jacques Lacan, *Ecrit: A Selection*, Routledge, London and New York, 1989.
6. Herbert Marcuse, *One Dimensional Man,* Routledge, London and New York (1964), 2012.
7. Amartya Sen, *Identity and Violence*: *The Illusion of Destiny Allen Lane*, Penguin Books, London, 2006.
8. Amartya Sen, *On Ethics and Economics,* Oxford University Press, New Delhi 2007.
9. Ajit Singnar, *Longri Atomon*, Aank Baank, Guwahati, 2014.

20

Witch Hunting and the Bodos in Kokrajhar District of Assam

Tamsin Aftab

Bodoland is an autonomous Administrative unit constituted under the Sixth Schedule of the Constitution of India covering an area of 8,795 km. The administrative unit has been created with a mission to accomplish development in the area of economic, education, and preservation of land right, linguistic aspiration, socio-culture and ethnic identity of Bodos and above all to speed up the infrastructure development of communities in the BTC area. But has the fruits of development reached the people in a true sense? If yes then why are people still subjected to such deep-rooted social beliefs as Witch Hunting? Development is not merely economic progress but a progress in all the dimension of social, political, religious and cultural aspects of life. The long drawn movement of the Bodo people for their liberation and Identity was the root cause of them demanding a separate statehood. The basic idea was to set up a state with which the indigenous people can in some sense identify. Now when it is granted, where the tribal identity does follows and where the identity of Bodo community is placed is a significant aspect to be considered.

I. Witch-Hunting

The art of performing charms, spells and rituals to seek to control events or govern certain natural or supernatural forces is generally termed as witchcraft. No satisfactory explanations have ever evolved for the hunting of men and women in the region and the rate of witchcraft killing is alarmingly high among tribal communities and other minor communities in the state.

As the term denotes Witch hunting is killing and torturing of men and women in the name of witches. It is shocking to know that even in the present age witchcraft is a real belief system and one that is very much rooted in the popular mentality of people. This belief in Witches is manifest throughout the world.

They are basically considered to have an evil eye, harmful and threatening to the society as such. Various incidents have been reported so far over ages about the torture and atrocities associated with the victims of such accusations. One thing, which is common on all such incidents, is that such a practice mostly takes place in the tribal belts of the country. The states having reported the highest incidents of witch hunting are Rajasthan, Gujarat, Assam, West Bengal, Bihar, Maharashtra, Andhra Pradesh and Orissa. People from different regions use different names, for instance, dayni, dakan, dayan, banamati, chetabadi, chillangi, hawa or evil eye, dahani, tonhi, etc. The names may be different but the practice seems to take a more or less similar form; witch-hunts remain a persistent scourge in rural parts of India. From the incidences following are the observations to be made:

- It occurs mostly in the Tribal areas.
- It occurs mostly in the rural areas.
- Males and Females both are targeted. It is a gender neutral crime. (In a written reply to a query by BJP MLA Prasanta Phukan, Parliamentary Affairs Minister Rockybul Hussain said a total of 77 persons, including 35 women, were murdered due to the superstition between 2010 and February 2015. Of the injured 60 people, 46 were women)
- Mostly it is prevalent amongst the uneducated and illiterates.

Having taken into consideration the above factors one notice that witch-hunting is a very real phenomenon and such a practice is very prominent in Assam at the present time. Past history and the data referred indicates the following reasons to be instrumental behind the whole practice of witch killing in the district:

(i) Superstition and influence of sorcerers.

(ii) Illiteracy and inequality.

(iii) Lack of economic development in rural areas and poverty.

(iv) Land rights, inheritance and property dispute.

(v) Weak healthcare services.

(vi) Increasing intolerance, jealousy and old enmity.

(vii) Looting money and excessive intake of alcohol

II. Witch-Hunting: A Theoretical Perspective

The various charges that appear during witch-hunts involve accusations of crimes committed against the community or the society. It is the whole of collective existence that is at stake. When a charge is brought of being a witch what is happening is that a ritual contrast is being drawn between images of the corporate order and things, which would oppose it. This can be seen as a construction of the Durkheimian idea of the sacred-profane dichotomy in modern terms. Here the sociology of deviance and the sociology of religion are merged, for the idea of deviant and normal is but another form of the idea of sacred and profane. They both have the same function: a symbolic opposition to collective representations is drawn, and as such representations of the corporate community are redefined (Durkheim, 1912).

In British social anthropology, discussions about witchcraft have tended to take their departure from Evans-Pritchard's classic study of *Witchcraft, oracles and magic among the Azande* (Evans-Pritchard, 1976). Evans Pritchard used the Azande people's own distinction between what he translated as witchcraft and sorcery in his exposition of zande beliefs.

Analytically, his main purpose was to show how for the Azande ideas of witchcraft functioned as a means of explaining misfortunes that were difficult to explain in other ways, these ideas were then, he argues harnessed to a way of settling suspicions between people.

Victor Turner added to the functionalist paradigm his notion of the social drama in which conflicts exposed the weakness of lineage organisation and caused fission in social groups (Turner,1957). In Turners view, witchcraft accusations were seen as the surface indicators of underlying conflicts over land and power. Turner's work on conflict and ritual became widely known and influenced the field of ritual studies in general. He saw witchcraft accusations as "social catalysts" that could precipitate unforeseen results.

Magic for Malinowski is always utilitarian, whereas religion lacks utility. Sorcery implies magic where powers are intentionally used for a harmful purpose, often involving artificial means. Witchcraft implies the possession of a supernatural power through a pact with evil spirits; this power may be exerted involuntarily. Magic, witchcraft, and sorcery generally function at the level of the individual, and often in opposition to organised religions. Magical beliefs deal with the individual crises and acts of fate which religious morality cannot explain. For Malinowski, the many functions of magic included human beings' attempts to increase the probability of success in important activities, and increase confidence to undertake them. Magic opened up possibilities for human action. He did not view magic as a characteristic of particular kinds of societies, but thought that it could be found when human beings were confronted with a lack of knowledge or ability to control something important to their lives. Malinowski also observed that magic had social and moral functions that led to better cooperation among group members. In addition, it gave people access to what he referred to as "miracles," events that were unexpected or unlikely, thus giving them hope.

Soma Chaudhuri in *Witches, Tea plantations and lives of Migrant Labourers in India* says that Witch Craft accusations are not exotic and primitive rituals of a backward *adivasi* community during time of stress but rather a powerful protest organised by a marginalised community against its oppressors. Here she brings the classical Marxian explanation behind the conflict between the two classes: the worker (in this case the tea plantation worker), and the owners (here the planters and the management). The workers are nothing but just a commodity in the eyes of the owners.

The hostility against Witches according to some scholars developed during a period of economic, religious and political transition in *adivasi* communities in central India. Power and order was maintained during this period by legitimising the use of violence against the accused women resulting in myths that provide clues about how the power over land and politics was taken from women by men (Kelkar and Warrier, 1999, 315).

Witchcraft and Witch Hunts cannot be given a one sided explanation. Witch-hunt are a form of violence against women is a one sided explanation. Kiernan (2006) while trying to explain witch craft theories in contemporary Africa said that, sometimes Witch craft emerges as the weapon of the strong, i.e. witchcraft accusations are a form of violence against women. At other times witchcraft emerges as the weapon of the week, i.e. witchcraft accusations are a way for the *adivasi* workers to get control over their lives within the exploitative nature of the plantations. Both of these approaches acknowledge the interplay of local contingencies and global forces in contemporary discourses on witchcraft (Kiernan, 2006, 12-13)

Nathan, Kelkar and Xiaogang discuss how the authority of men is established through witchcraft accusations. Women are viewed as potential source of evil, and such an ideology is conductive to the social process of controlling women. According to this argument, every Santhal women lives under the threat of being declared a witch, and especially during times of crisis (like epidemics), every women of the village could be attacked as a witch.

Witch hunting cannot be only observed in the pretext of age old and traditional practices which are still existent. It is however a modern concept as even in twenty-first century such a dreadful practice is still in existence. This can be noticed in the work of Sundar (2001) who offers a different argument for the accusations in Bastar. She observes that in Bastar both men and women are equal targets of witchcraft accusations (Sundar, 2001, 426). These targets do not fit into any category of gender, age, dependency or kinship. It is obvious and told by many that with the coming of modern education, such practices would disappear but Sundar's argument is that it is difficult to understand witchcraft accusations on the basis of traditional fragments of traditional pasts that disappear with the coming of modern education, instead the accusations happening here should be understood as a modern experience in which people are a part of a nation state from which they get little help in terms of livelihood or health, but which exercises forceful power over them.

As Chaudhuri points out that at the centre of witchcraft accusations within the *adivasi* worker group are the illness and misfortune in the community that are blamed. Lack of healthcare, sanitation and irregularity of payment, health issues and starvation are considered to be major problems in the *adivasi* regions and witchcraft is given as the most common explanation. Similar factors can be attributed to the Bodos in Kokrajhar where people are still relying on Ojhas as there is lack of proper medical facilities. Local politics, personal conflicts and the gendered nature of violence play a huge role. Rumors, gossip and conspiracies play a crucial role during witch-hunts by displacing reality in the mind of the community. There is a power play involved in the displacement and replacement of reality and in its construction. Primarily the men in the community, who manipulate it for a motive that is profitable to some, hold this power; the women are mere passive participants or victims in the hunt.

Scholars like Nathan, Kelkar and Xiaogang's focal point of study is the notion of witchcraft as peripheral, marginal and as non-structured cults. Witch hunting is, in this analysis, not the suppression of a rebellion; it is itself a rebellion, not by women, but by the men in the process of establishing the authority of men. This view supports the ideology that women must be socially controlled. The threat a woman might be declared a witch at anytime will prevent her from deviating from or not conforming to establish patriarchal rules that have been established to benefit men and to preserve their status in society.

Barstow (1994) explains witch-hunts as an outcome of competition between men and women for power during changing economic and political conditions in pre-modern Europe. Karlsen (1998) explains a third factor Religion, in addition to gender and a changing economic climate. In other words, Karlsen links gender (in a way of sexual terrorism) and religion in explaining witch-hunts.

Silviya Federici's rethinks the development of capitalism from a feminist viewpoint. The main questions which she poses are why, after 500 years of capital's rule, at the beginning of the third millennium, are workers on a mass scale still defined as paupers, witches and outlaws? How are land expropriation and mass pauperisation related to the continuing attack on women? And what do we learn from about capitalist development, past and present, once we examine it through the vantage point of a feminist perspective? Why the rise of capitalism was coeval with a war against women? She has placed at the centre of her analysis of primitive accumulation the "witch-hunts of the sixteenth and seventeenth centuries", arguing that the persecution of the witches, in Europe as in the new world was as important as colonisation and the expropriation of the European peasantry from its land for the development of capitalism. The author goes on to show how female sexuality, which was seen as a source of women's potential power over men, became an object of suspicion and came under sharp attack by the authorities. She argues against Marx's claim that primitive accumulation is a necessary precursor for capitalism. Instead, she posits that primitive accumulation is a fundamental characteristic of capitalism itself - that capitalism, in order to perpetuate itself, requires a constant infusion of expropriated capital.

Archana Mishra states that the Indian society is similar to Europe, as it was 600 years ago. She tells that witch-hunting is one the least resisted forms of gender violence today. Joya

Chakraborty and Anjuman Borah in "Witch-hunting in Assam: Strategising alternative media for women empowerment and overcoming superstition", states that between2008-2012 more than 768 women have been murdered for allegedly practicing witchcraft in India. The rate of conviction in cases of crime against women is the lowest in India. Witch-hunting cases are currently registered under sections 302 (murder), 320 (grievous hurt), 351 (assault), 345 (Assault or criminal force to woman with intent to outrage her modesty), 364a (kidnapping for ransom) and 503(criminal intimidation). This practice is most popular amongst the tribal or indigenous communities. They further stress that Assam in the northeastern states has reported the highest cases so far and it is not a coincidence that Assam also has the lowest gender development index among the northeastern states. There have been at least 65 cases of witch hunting reported during 2007-2012 from Assam alone.

III. The Bodo Social Life

K. Brahma has made an observation that due to much simplicity, open heartedness, frankness and due to lack of education the Bodo women become easy victims of the anti-social elements. Witch hunting is one such anti-social element present in today's time. Education is the sharpest weapon of all to protect themselves from the social enemies and to maintain their position in the civilised human society as always high, so that womenfolk also can contribute a lot to the nation. The use of the country made liquor is deep rooted in the Bodo society and this ill habit destroys many Bodo families. Many a times it is noticed that the occurrence of the witch trail take place when the villagers are intoxicated and after a fusion this seems to be kind of a feast and thrill for the villagers. Chaudhuri has also ascribed the role played by *Haria* (local liquor) in her brilliant account of witch hunting in Chandmoni Tea estate in West Bengal. Frustration over the continuing epidemics, anger and under the influence of Alcohol (*haria*) and miscreants are some of the reasons behind the support for the hunts.

Blind superstition and religious faith of high order are intermingled in the Bodo Religion.The role of Deodhani (the possessed women) in Kherai Puja brings out the mystic element in the traditional religious beliefs of the Bodos. The world of the Bodos is crowned with Gods and Goddesses. Disease of men and catastrophes of the world are traced to angry spirits. Spells and incarnations are extensively used. All these require specially qualified persons like *deoris, deodhais* and *deodhanis*. Sacrifice and prayer form the main elements of the culture. So in that case it is evident that false belief or unfounded fear, i.e. superstition plays a pivotal role in the cultural life of the Bodo people. Sorcery and Magic often prevails over the genuine religious spirit.

It is commonly believed among the Bodos that the witch can cause harm to animals, children, men, and women—and even make them fatally ill. The witch can cause illness ranging from diarrhea, malaria, and tuberculosis to the common fever and stomach ailments. Sometimes she may cause barrenness or infertility. The witch's evil eye operates through *ban-mara*. It is through the use of *ban* that the witch causes illness in her victims. The witch was typically seen as responsible for causing illness or death in small children, spouses, infants, or domestic animals. She had the power to interfere with nature. She was capable of causing barrenness, miscarriages, or deformed birth. The witch, thus, symbolises evil and can harm to anyone around her. However, even though the witch's power could bring harm to anyone, her victims tended to be close neighbours, relatives, and people who knew her well enough to anger her. The fear of the witch is deep-rooted in the psyche of the people, and the tribal's blame any event or development that is not-normal on the witch. With such superstition in mind the people of the village get together to discuss the matter and then a calculated attack is planned. Many of the incidents reported are sudden attacks which mainly are because of personal rivalry or property disputes resulting in killing the victim as a witch.

Rev Sidney Endle in his historic book the Kacharis states that the religion of the Kachari race is distinctly of the type commonly known as "animistic" and its underlying principle is characteristically one of fear or dread. Thus, animism and superstitions are in the root of Bodo tribe and thus witchcraft and witch hunting can be associated with such beliefs.

IV. Situation in Assam

Witch hunting is a gender-neutral crime against the society mainly due to property grudge, failure in relationships, village rivalry, and mutual jealousy. It is a killing of mankind, not just men or women. In order to prevent the crime it should be a systematised approach from all cultures and people from all walks of life. The Constitution (Eighty-sixth Amendment) Act, 2002-inserted Article 21-A in the Constitution of India to provide free and compulsory education of all children in the age group of six to fourteen years as a Fundamental Right in such a manner as the State may, by law, determine. Education is a constitutional right given to the citizens of our country but many people even now ignore this right to education.

In a recent report on Witch hunting in Assam brought out by NEN and Assam Mahila Samatha Society, it has been reflected that the victims knew the instigators and perpetrators. They were either physically proximate to the victims or with family ties to the victims. The study shows a high rate of involvement of neighbours as instigators, followed by relatives and co-workers.

Superstition alone does not appear to be a sufficient reason as in most of the cases the victim shares the belief system and has concrete inter-personal reasons that motivate her victimisation. No matter what the belief in the existence of witches and witchcraft is very much prevalent amongst the victims as well as the instigators. Witchcraft as a belief system is very much predominant in the village life.

How does the witchcraft accusation start? Chaudhuri has stated that there are two kinds of attacks: Random attack and calculated attack. In a calculated attack, witch-hunts are preceded by clear motives on the part of the accusers based on what the accusers claim to be instigation from the accused. The motives on the part of the accusers can be almost anything, including maligning the reputation of the accused woman, serving personal motives, seeking revenge to settle disputes over property, or explaining why illnesses or diseases happen. In cases in which witch-hunts serve the purpose of revenge over personal conflicts, disease or ailments play a major role in instigating the hunt? In cases of surprise or random attacks, the women victims and their families were, prior to the attack, were or claimed to be unaware of the accusations against them. The attack happened without any instigation in the form of prior conflict or any history of witchcraft accusation against the accused witch. Even in cases of surprise attacks in which there were no prior warning signals that an accusation was taking place, some immediate cause prompted the attack. In most cases, the cause was an ailment, but in a few cases it was a petty brawl or verbal exchange that preceded the attack.

Verbal taunts and slurs, through local terms denoting 'witch' as well as other abuses aimed at demonising and isolating the victim and her family, often accompanied by minor to grave physical violence and a small fraction of cases resulting in murder.

V. Why Prevalent Mainly Amongst Tribal?

Why is it mainly in the tribal lands that such a practice still has its continued existence? Be it the Bodos of Kokrajhar or the tea plantation workers of Chandmoni Tea estate in West Bengal. One can see that in most of the cases it is the tribal population and not the people belonging to the mainstream. Even after an array of development projects and initiatives undertaken tribals are still under the threat of such atrocities. Who is to be blamed for such underdevelopment of the people? Is it the government or the local authorities or the people themselves?

The struggle over land inheritance, epidemics has been one of the primary causes for witchcraft accusations in the region. The point to be noted here is that such attacks are against the law. Most of the cases involved accusations that the woman attacked had caused illness, disease or death. Scapegoating, village rivalries, inheritance, conflicts and female threats to patriarchy are introduced in explanations of early modern hunts and similar theories are raised to explain attacks on witches in contemporary India.

Age also connected men and women with witchcraft. The elderly were marginal, vulnerable, and overwhelmingly female.

The Elizabethan skeptic Reginald Scot noticed that most people's idea of a witch was a woman who was 'old, lame, blear-eyed, pale, foul, and full of wrinkles, usually a widow dependent on charity'.

As Nathan observe that the indigenous peoples have their own ways of suppressing women, often involving violence. Whether as *dain, tonhi*, or in some other form there is an ongoing violence against women, as part of the process of establishing or strengthening forms of patriarchy. Opposing such culturally-bound forms of oppression and violence is part of the process of further democratising indigenous communities themselves. A remarkable note to be made here is that recent trends and data shows that witch-hunting is not only restricted to women but also significant number of men are targeted.

VI. The Major Reasons behind Such Killings

On being perceived the economic backwardness as to be the vital factor behind this social problem, the government over the years has been launching many developmental schemes for rural areas. But it is slow impact on rural mass still forcing the society to engulf with this perennial adversity.

An important reason instrumental behind the witch killings in the Kokrajhar is illiteracy and inequality. Knowledge is power that saves us from ignominy and exploitation by unscrupulous persons. Literacy dispels the darkness of ignorance, hunger and backwardness. The state has been spending millions to educate the vast army of illiterates, but the goal of achieving 100 per cent literacy still remains elusive, a rosy and distant dream. Education, according to Human Rights Commission, is man's basic right. It is the only courses, which make man self-reliant. No one likes to remain ignorant and illiterate in this electronic age. The literacy rate in the district of Kokrajhar is 65.55 per cent of which female literacy is 58.27 per cent as per 2011 census.

The rural areas of Assam are very much underdeveloped and this results in poverty. Rapid progress in GDP growth and globalisation in the last decade has primarily impacted the urban economy. While software exports, business process outsourcing, etc, have helped urban economic growth, it has done relatively little for the rural economy. Rural India is caught in what is called a development trap. Because of lack of economic opportunities, incomes are low. Therefore, they are unable to pay for goods and services that would enable them to increase their incomes.

Right over property is a very important reason behind such killings. In a substantial number of reported cases, witch-hunting is resorted to, so as to rob the men or women of her property rights. Efforts to exercise those rights are thwarted by the method of declaring the men or women a witch and so rob them of their right to the land. And it is not always the woman's family, which is necessarily involved. Particularly where the woman is unprotected, a widow or a single woman, there is no dearth of others who have an eye on the land, would use the services of the *ojhas*. For example, there are cases where such identification has been made when upper castes want to grab the land distributed to the poor tribal communities.

Bina Agarwal (1994) in her book, *A Field of One's Own: Gender and Land Rights in South Asia* gives a brief elaboration about the pattern she finds in South Asia. Agarwal argues that the single most important economic factor affecting women's situation is the gender gap in command over property. In rural South Asia, the most significant form of property is arable land, a critical determinant of economic well being, social status, and empowerment. But few women own land; fewer control it. "In communities where women never held land, such rights tend to generate hostility - divorces, accusations of witchcraft, threats, attacks, torture, even murder". Thus, witchcraft is also a result of disputes over property and land and it is this gender relation, which plays a detrimental role in such accusations.

Further when the *'jadutona'* of the witch doctor fails to cure the patient, a scapegoat has to be found and mostly it is the poorest and most vulnerable in the society who are sacrificed. The target chosen in such cases usually has little social support. Women in non-stereotypical situations, lacking protection or support, single women, women without children, widows and the disabled, are the most vulnerable. The hunt is usually accompanied by a mob, whipped into hysteria by the *ojha*. Such incidents also reinforce the fear and power of the *ojha*, which suits the vested interests.

Shortage of doctors, nurses and the Primary Health Centre or Public Health Centre (PHC) in remote or rural areas compel the tribal clans to rely or trust on Kabiraj (that is, exorcist or sorcerer, locally called *ojha* or *baiga*) and also the quack, who on failure to cure serious diseases, put the blame on witch-craft and numbers of *Tonhi* or witch. Proper medical facilities should be provided to the remote villages so as to curb such dangerous outcomes.

In few cases it has been seen that victims are killed and attacked only to loot money. In one such incident the accuser killed a victim in the name of witch but he was under the influence of alcohol and in the morning when he was in a normal state he confessed and gave a statement that it was due to alcohol that he committed such a crime.

VII. Steps towards its Eradication by State and Non State Actors

The Assam Police are doing their best by reviving a targeted education campaign called Project Parhari, which aims to disabuse villagers of the notion that malicious sorcery is real. But government representatives can only spend so much time in each settlement, spreading their message of reason. Perhaps the better long-term solution is to provide villagers with better means of dispute resolution and to ensure that justice is swift and certain when killings do occur, even if it means carting off every single participant.

Educating the people and framing laws for the protection of women and people belonging to the 'lower' classes of the society who also constitute another target group of such witch hunts is important. Until then, such beliefs in the existence of black magic and '*dainis*' will prevail along with the prevalence of '*ojhas*' who have a very big influence in village life.

The above facts transpire a very perplexing approach towards the problem. Therefore, all like-minded individuals, social organisations including government shall join hands to form a new mindset with a view to evolve a new mechanism, which will pave the way for a logical and permanent solution to this social problem. However, an analytical study on the past incidences of witch killing in different parts of this district transpires the fact that superstition, lack of economic development and illiteracy cannot merely be the causes of witch-hunt. The argument behind is that the current rate of literacy, per capita income and health care facilities are much more high in comparison to the beginning of this century. Therefore, our focus needs to be concentrated on certain other realities and which perhaps requires serious attention at this moment of time.

Development as a concept is touching every nook and corner of the world, but even then the identity of the tribal is lost? Proper utilisation of the development initiatives and implementation is required. We need well planned more effective schemes to contribute to the welfare of the people. Tribal communities traditionally brew liquor from rice or other food grains for their consumption and this has started impoverishing of the tribal population leading them to suffer from indebtedness and exploitation.

With special reference to the Bodo Community, it will develop only when the women empower themselves to fight for their rights and lives. Men and women should not be differentiated and everyone should be treated equally in society. Only then can such a practice be eliminated with initiatives from the government.

The belief in witches among the indigenous communities of Assam gets perpetuated through a vicious combination of government apathy and ignorance of the people. The communities, which are otherwise deprived of resources probably, express their frustration through the acts of witch-hunting. The women within these communities become vulnerable owing to a lack of support system within the family or community; for not being economically self-reliant and for lack of information about better opportunities.

Gender violence is a multifunctional phenomenon containing political, social, cultural and interpersonal conflicts. It is partly a result of gender relations that assume men to be superior to women. But as per the latest records we see that men and women are equal targets and hence power inequalities or gender violence cannot be a appropriate reason behind such killings.

Chaudhuri says violence is often used as a mean to disrupt order (riots, genocides) and it is often the beginning of Anomie. Anomie is the state of normlessness in society. Here the Durkhiemian notion of Anomie comes into existence. In a state of Anomie no development can ever take place in a true sense. Law alone cannot diminish the problem. Rigid and severe laws are essential part to deal with the problem but society must be more gender sensitive and discard prejudice based on irrational beliefs. Social biases or any kind of dogma should be done away with. Justice is something, which is granted by law, and it cannot be taken in one's own hands, which is illegal. The villagers should be educated so as to not take laws in their own hands. Focus should be on shifting attitudes of the general people and initiatives should be taken to broaden their outlook towards the society. This is important because violence against women is related to development outcomes. Sustained focus from government, donors, international organisations, civil society and research community are essential.

Despite the fact that many social organisations as well as NGO's are making continuous campaigns for generating awareness against witch-hunting, this phenomenon has still persisted in the tribal societies, causing innumerable loss of lives of innocent villagers. So, it is assumed that such kind of awareness campaign has not reached the minds of those, who indulge into such evil acts. Now, it is a high time for all of us to evolve a new mechanism having more realistic and sensible approach, which can possibly help the society in getting rid of this modern scourge.

Conclusion

It is the interplay of religion, power relations, social and cultural life, economic backwardness and lack of medical facilities, which are in existence for such a continued practice of Witch hunting in the region. Development of the Bodos and the identity of the tribe can only be retained if a new mechanism is evolved with a gender sensitive approach, stringent laws, tribal empowerment and good quality education. Very recently the state government has assured the Guwahati High Court that the draft Bill on witch hunting would be placed in the next Assam Assembly session. The significance of the Bill is that Section 438 of the Code of Criminal Procedure will not apply and no person can seek anticipatory bail in relation to any case involving the arrest of any person on accusation of having committed an offence under the said law. Every offence under the new law will be cognisable, non-bailable and non-compoundable, which proposes punishment from three years to life imprisonment and is the strictest bill in the country so far.

Apart from stricter punishment for terming someone a witch and for physical, sexual or mental torture leading to suicide and displacement, the Prevention of and Protection from Witch Hunting Bill, 2015, Assam, aims to check illegal practices by quacks. It also proposes action against negligence in investigation, formation of special courts for trial of witch-hunting cases and free legal aid to victims, among other provisions. If such a bill is passed at least there is a hope that acts like Witch hunting can be eradicated from the society and one would witness less number of such occurrences.

Witches are humans. They belong to the society- a disguised enemy within. They are the other and yet they are also us i.e. the self. To quote Gail Omvedt (2015) in her keynote speech, "the end of identities of self and other playing the role of obstacles in the road to liberated humanity, could be removed only by creating a healthy democratic space for a non-domineering identities of various 'self' and 'others'".

References

1. A. Chakravarty and S. Chaudhuri, 'Strategic Framing Work(s): How Micro-Credit Loans Facilitate Anti- Witch Hunt Movements', *Mobilisation*, Vol.17 (2), 2012, pp.175-194.

2. A.B. Choudhari, *Witch Killings amongst Santals,* Ashish Publishing House, New Delhi, 1984.
3. Ajay Skaria, 'Women, Witchcraft and Gratuitous Violence in Colonial Western India', *Past and Present*, 15, 1997, pp.109-141.
4. Albert James Bergesen, 'A Durkheimian Theory of 'Witch-hunts' with the Chinese Cultural Revolution of 1966-1969 as an Example', *Journal for the scientific Study of religion,* 17 (1), 1978, pp.19-29.
5. Atta Mallick, 'Witch Hunting in 1857', *Economic and Political Weekly*, Vol. 43, No 39, Sept 27- Oct 3, 2008, pp. 118-119.
6. Bina Agarwal, *A Field of One's Own: Gender and Land Rights in South Asia,* Cambridge University Press, Cambridge, 1994.
7. Bronislaw Malinowski, *Magic, Science and Religion and Other Essays,* Free Press Publishers, New York, 1954 (1925).
8. Christina Larner, *Enemies of God: Witch Hunt in Scotland*, John Hopkins University Press, Maryland, 1981.
9. Christina Larner, *Witchcraft and Religion: The Politics of Popular Belief,* Basil Blackwell, New York, 1984.
10. D. Nathan and G. Kelkar and X. Xiaogang, 'Women as Witches and Keepers of Demons: Cross-Cultural Analysis of Struggles to Change Gender Relations', *Economic and Political Weekly,* Vol.33, 1998, pp. 58-69.
11. Darren Oldridge, *The Witchcraft Reader* (Routledge Readers in History), Routledge, London, 2008.
12. De Simone Beauvoir, *The Second Sex,* Vintage, (Reprint) 1997.
13. Diane Purkiss, *The Witch in History: Early Modern and Twentieth-Century Representations*, Routledge, London, 1996.
14. E.E. Evans Pritchard, 'Witchcraft', *Africa: Journal of International African Institute,* 8(4), 1935. pp. 417-422.
15. E.E. Evans Pritchard,*Witchcraft, Oracles and Magic among the Azande*, Oxford University Press, London, 1976 [1937].
16. Edward Miguel, 'Poverty and Witch Killing', *The Review of Economic Studies,* 72(4), Oct 2005, pp.1152-1172.
17. Emile Durkheim, *The Elementary Forms of Religious Life*, Oxford University Press, London, 2001 (1912).
18. F.G. Bailey, *A Witch-Hunt in an Indian Village or a Triumph of Morality,* Oxford University Press, Delhi, 1997.
19. G.M. Carstairs, *Death of a Witch: A Village in North India, 1950-81*, New York, 1983.
20. Geschiere, Peter. 'Witchcraft as the Dark Side of Kinship: Dilemmas of Social Security in New Contexts', *Ethnofloor,* 16 (1), 2003, pp. 43-61.

21. Govind Kelkar, 'Women and Structural Violence in India', *Women's Studies Quarterly*, 13(¾), 1985, pp.16-18.
22. H.S.Versnel 'Some Reflections on the Relationship Magic-Religion', *Numen*, 38, 1991, pp.177-197.
23. Hilary Rose, *Love, Power, and Knowledge: Towards a Feminist Transformation of the Sciences*, Indiana University Press, 1994.
24. Hiren Gohain, 'Bodo Stir in Perspective', *Economic and Political Weekly*, 24(25), 1989, pp.1377-1379.
25. Ipsita Roy Chakraveti, *Beloved Witchan Autobiography*. Harper, India, 2003.
26. J. Chakraborty and A. Borah, *Journal of North East Indian Studies*, Vol. 3 (2), Jul-Dec, 2013, pp.15-24.
27. Jennifer M.Wilson, *Witch,* Author House, Bloomington, 2005.
28. Jeuti Barooah, *Single Women in Assamese Hindu Society*, Gyan Publishing House, New Delhi, 1993.
29. Jogesh Das, *Folklore of Assam*, National Book Trust, New Delhi, 2012.
30. Judith Butler, *Gender Trouble*, Routledge, 1999.
31. Jyotsna Chatterji, 'Challenging Witchcraft and Cultural and Customary Practices', V. Mohini Giri (Ed), *Living Death, Trauma of Widowhood in India'* Gyan Publishing House, New Delhi, 2002.
32. K. Brahma, *A Study of Socio-Religious Beliefs Practices and Ceremonies of the Bodos*. Punthi Pustak, Calcutta, 1992.
33. Keith A Roberts and David Yamane (Ed), *Religion in Sociological Perspective*, Sage, London, 2011.
34. M. Chatterjee, *Violence, Silence and Memory of Witches in Violence against Women,* Avnishkar Publishers, Jaipur, 2006.
35. M. Tineshowri Devi, 'Women Status in Assam', *Journal of Business Management and Social Sciences Research*, Vol. 2, No.1, January 2013.
36. M.L. Bose, *Social History of Assam*, Concept Publishing Company, New Delhi, 1989.
37. Malcolm Gaskill, *Witchcraft a Very Short Introduction*, Oxford University Press, Oxford, 2010.
38. Mary Douglas, *Purity and Danger,* Routledge, London, 1966.
39. Mary Nelson, 'Why Witches Were Women', *Women: A Feminist Perspective,* CA Mayfield, 1975, pp. 335–50.
40. Maya Majumdar, *Protecting our Women, Victimised Women: Repression and Social Response,* Dominant Publishers, New Delhi, 2001.
41. Micheal D. Bailey, 'The Meaning of Magic', *Magic, Ritual and Witchcraft*, 1-2, 2006.

42. Pamela J. Stewart and Andrew Strathern, *Witchcraft, Sorcery, Rumors and Gossip*. Cambridge University Press, Cambridge, 2004.
43. Paul R. Turner, 'Witchcraft as Negative Charisma', *Ethnology,* 9 (4), 1970, pp. 366-372.
44. Perry Anderson, 'Witchcraft', *London Review of Books*, Vol. 12, No. 21, 1990, pp. 6 -11.
45. Premalata Devi, *Social and Religious institutions of the Bodos*, Geophil Publishing House, Guwahati. 1998.
46. Radha Kumar, *The History of Doing: An Illustrated Account of Movements for Women's Rights and Feminism in India,* Zubaan Books, 2000.
47. Raisa Maria Toivo, 'Women's History Revisited'. *Historiographical Reflections on Women and Gender in a Global Context* (The 20th International Congress of Historical Sciences, University of New South Wales), Sydney, Australia, 2005.
48. Rakesh K. Singh, *Witch-Hunting: Alive and Kicking. Crime against Women*, Vol. 17 No 1. January-March, 2011.
49. Rev Sidney Endle, *The Kacharis (Bodo)*, Low Price Publications, Delhi, 2010 (1911).
50. Samar Bosu Mullick, 'Gender Relations and Witches among the Indigenous Communities of Jharkhand, India', Govind Kelkar, Dev Nathan and Pierre Walter (Ed), *Gender Relations in Forest Societies in Asia: Patriarchy,* New Delhi, Sage, 2003, pp. 119-146.
51. Shashank Sinha, 'Witch-Hunts: Adivasi and the Uprising in Chota Nagpur', *Economic and Political Weekly*, Vol. 42, No. 19, May 12, 2007, pp. 1672-1676.
52. Silvia Federici, *Caliban and the Witch: Women, the Body and Primitive Accumulation*, Phoneme Publishers, New Delhi, 2013.
53. Siv Kumar Tiwari, *Encyclopedia of Indian Tribals, Vol. I*, Rahul Publishing House, New Delhi, 1994.
54. Soma Chaudhuri, 'Extending the Logic of Functional Explanations: A theoretical model to explain the Victimisation Process during an Indian Witch Hunt', K. Jaishankar and Natti Ronel, *Global Criminology: Crime and Victimisation in a Globalised Era,* CRC Press, March, 2013.
55. Soma Chaudhuri, 'Women as Easy Scapegoats: Witchcraft Accusations and women as Targets in Tea Plantations of India', *Violence against Women,* 18, no. 10 October, 2012, pp.1213-1234.
56. Soma Chaudhuri, *Women, Tea Plantations and Lives of Migrant Laborers in India*. Cambridge University Press, New Delhi, 2014.
57. Sucheta Sen Chaudhuri, *The Bodo Movement and Women Participation,* Mittal Publications, New Delhi, 2004.

58. *Support Services to Counter Violence against Women in Assam: A Resource Directory*, North East Network, Assam, 2003.
59. Thomas J. Schoeneman, 'The witch hunts as a cultural change phenomenon source', *Ethos,* 3(4), 1975, pp. 529-554.
60. W.A Breyfogle, 'The Witch-Women', *The North American Review*, 235 (1), 1933, 77-86.
61. W.Turner Victor, 'Social Dramas and Stories about Them', *Critical Inquiry,* 7(4), 1980, pp. 141-168.
62. W.Turner Victor, 'Witchcraft and Sorcery: Taxonomy versus Dynamics', *Africa*, 3(4), 1964, pp. 314-324.
63. Wolf Bleek, 'Witchcraft, Gossip and Death: A Social Drama', *Man*, 11(4), 1976. pp. 26-541.

Internet Sources:

1. http://www.sociologydiscussion.com/society/types-of-society-tribal-agrarian-and-industrial-society/2190.
2. http://www.telegraphindia.com/1150409/jsp/northeast/story_13497.jsp#.VS4sgKYxGRY.
3. http://zeenews.india.com/news/assam/77-killed-in-witch-hunting-incidents-since-2010-in-assam_1566297.html.

Index

C

D

O

P

Rupnath Brahma, 36, 246